DEVELOPING YOUNG WRITERS IN THE CLASSROOM

Educators want young people to grow up knowing that writing is an important and deeply satisfying life skill, one that helps them make more sense of themselves and their world, and one that helps them to communicate effectively. Sadly, too often writing becomes merely an exercise in 'getting words right', or writing to teacher-prescribed tasks.

Developing Young Writers in the Classroom explores the principles of developing literacy through authorship, allowing children to describe, question and celebrate their own experiences and personal creativity. The book offers detailed guidance, supported by planning documents, poetry and prose, examples of children's work and stimulating visuals.

Inspiring topics explored include:

- creating a classroom environment which supports an independent writer

- students' lives brought into the classroom

- finding significance in our experiences

- the use of memoir for recording experiences

- description in all kinds of writing

- choosing and writing about a character

- writing in all curriculum areas

- linking reading and writing

- using other authors as mentors and teachers

- collaborative learning.

Illustrated throughout with accessible activities and ideas from literature and poetry, *Developing Young Writers in the Classroom* is an essential resource for all teachers wishing to inspire writing in the classroom.

Gail Loane is an Educational Consultant based in New Zealand, where she is well known for tutoring and coaching school leaders and teachers in the development of literacy. Gail has previously worked as a teacher, associate principal, principal and school adviser, as well as on a range of national projects for the Ministry of Education, New Zealand.

Sally Muir has been a successful teacher of writing and now writes for other teachers. She has worked alongside Gail on national projects and as a teacher educator for the past fifteen years, developing ideas and resources for their work in schools.

DEVELOPING YOUNG WRITERS IN THE CLASSROOM

I've got something to say

Gail Loane with Sally Muir

 Routledge
Taylor & Francis Group

LONDON AND NEW YORK

Revised Edition published 2017
by Routledge
2 Park Square, Milton Park, Abingdon, Oxon OX14 4RN

and by Routledge
711 Third Avenue, New York, NY 10017

Routledge is an imprint of the Taylor & Francis Group, an informa business

© 2017 G. Loane and S. Muir

First Edition published 2010
by Aries Publishing Ltd., Whitianga, New Zealand
© Gail Loane 2010
Gail Loane asserts her moral right to be identified as the author of the work.

First edition ISBN 9780473142605

British Library Cataloguing in Publication Data
A catalogue record for this book is available from the British Library.

Library of Congress Cataloging in Publication Data
Names: Loane, Gail, 1946- author. | Muir, Sally Anne, 1953- author.
Title: Developing young writers in the classroom: I've got something to say / Gail Loane with Sally Muir.
Other titles: I've got something to say
Description: Revised edition. | New York, NY: Routledge, 2017.
Identifiers: LCCN 2016003991| ISBN 9781138653887 (hardback) | ISBN 9781138653900 (pbk.) | ISBN 9781315623528 (ebook)
Subjects: LCSH: English language-Composition and exercises-Study and teaching. | Creative writing-Study and teaching.
Classification: LCC LB1576.L585 2017 | DDC 372.62/3-dc23
LC record available at https://lccn.loc.gov/2016003991

ISBN: 978-1-138-65388-7 (hbk)
ISBN: 978-1-138-65390-0 (pbk)
ISBN: 978-1-315-62352-8 (ebk)

Typeset in Interstate
by Cenveo Publisher Services

Printed and bound by CPI Group (UK) Ltd, Croydon, CRO 4YY

Developing Young Writers in the Classroom

Education is not the filling of a pail,
but the lighting of the fire.

Attributed to William Butler Yeats

CONTENTS

1   The Teacher of Writing: Becoming joyfully literate   1

The joyfully literate teacher – living a readerly/writerly life • Teacher beliefs •
Every student has something to say – it is our job to believe it and have our
students believe it too • We begin with the awareness of the potential for
a love affair with language: for ourselves and for our students • We read
and write to make sense of ourselves and our world, and to communicate •
Children's lives need to be brought into the classroom • We trigger memories
of life experiences through personal stories and literature • We lead children
to become closely observant in their environment, raising their awareness,
sensitivity and response • We explore with students how authors put their
work together • We demonstrate how reader-writers think and behave

2   The Writing Classroom: Conditions for writers to flourish   10

Writing happens daily • Opportunities for independent writing must be
provided • Daily mini-lessons develop authorship • Explicit teaching •
Classroom environment – arranging furniture and displays for maximum
learning, emotional safety, intellectual stimulus and independence •
Quality literature – linking reading and writing • Developing oral language •
Responding to the writing of others • The Helping Circle and Peer Response
Groups • Teacher-student partnership

3   From the Head to the Page: Getting it down   27

A notebook develops independent writers • Notebooks are seedbeds for
writing – with a variety of seed ideas • Notebooks lead us to become authors
• Teachers model, alongside students, the use of the notebook •
Younger writers need to be supported to own and use notebooks • Authors
record noticings, observations, wonderings, opinions, ideas, responses to life
events and to literature • The use of Quick-Writes for drafting • Moving from
jottings to a crafted piece • Draft books: through daily writing, a place to
grow and craft ideas; it is a record of progress

I've got something to say

You cannot kindle a fire in any other heart until it is burning in your own.

Attributed to
Ben Sweetland

FOREWORD

By Stan Boyle

Something wonderful happened to me when I was a young, bored twelve year old. It changed the course of my life. Miss Salmon, an elderly middle school teacher opened my eyes and ears to the world about me, and engendered a love of life, a passion for learning, and an interest in people, that have never left me. Eventually and unsurprisingly, I became a teacher.

Among the many literary learning doors she opened for me, was her introduction to Latin. She brought Rome alive. I walked down the streets with Romans, ate their food, drank their wine in sleazy taverns, slept through bacchanalian banquets, listened to their scandalous stories, lived their everyday life and even became involved in their plots and assignations. She engendered a love for those ancient people that whispers still. She was an exceptional teacher.

Gail Loane is one of these rare exceptional teachers. They have in common an unshakeable belief that every child has a potential for excellence in some aspect of learning and life. This belief permeates her philosophy of teaching, and central to this belief is the determination to provide a learning environment where such potential might be realised. Throughout all the years I have known her, in classroom teaching, in auditoriums giving keynote addresses, in courses for teachers, in work as an educational adviser, and in personal contact, I have seen how she has developed a sense of self-worth and a love of learning in those she has influenced, and in so doing, Gail has enriched their lives.

That belief is there in the writing of the children she taught. It is there in the renewed passion for teaching, sense of vocation, and ongoing endorsement of the principles and approaches embodied in this book, which have been embraced by the teachers she has influenced. These are teachers who have gone away from Gail's courses and implemented the approaches in which they themselves were immersed as emerging writers.

Practising teachers were convinced that this philosophy is a way to ensure the highest level of literacy in their students, and of its importance, not only in the education of young writer-readers, but also in the overall education of the young.

This is a book to inspire teachers and lead them to the keys which open doors to explore and evaluate experience, both past and present. It will enrich the lives of teachers and those they teach who share an impelling urge to communicate feelings and ideas. By working side by side with children as fellow learners, and sharing with them the complexities and problems that face all aspiring writers, a sense of security and self-worth will develop in the leader and the led. *Developing Young Writers in the Classroom* is more than just another book on the teaching of writing and reading. It embodies a vibrant philosophy of education. It is about a shared journey: teachers and students working together, listening, looking and sharing experiences of life. There arises the realisation that all have thoughts and ideas that help towards an understanding of self, of others, of place, and of their social and physical environments.

It is the ability to look, listen, think and see things in new exciting ways that spurs on the emerging writer to communicate and give permanency to discovery. It is in these roots that the skill of the writer-reader is developed along with a growing sense that they have something worthwhile to write, and a belief in their growing capacity to handle the difficulties they encounter. It is then that learning becomes an absorbing joy and lifelong challenge. As a reader-writer, the joyfully literate student can look forward to an enriched lifetime of learning.

As the author emphasises throughout, much of the quality writing of young children lies in their everyday life experiences. It is the ability of a good writer to interpret common experience with understanding, and communicate ideas and vision, in a fresh personal way that speaks to the reader and stimulates a positive personal response.

Throughout this book, carefully selected literary examples enable the learner to see the world through others' eyes, listen through others' ears, share the thoughts and feelings of others, and to understand that the familiar is often unfamiliar, that beauty can be found amid ugliness, kindness amid cruelty, and that love can coexist with hatred. As they listen, read and discuss, students realise that they too have experiences, thoughts, ideas like the poets and authors to whom they are being introduced, and that they, too, feel an urgency, a need to communicate and share exciting new ways of seeing and hearing. It is in this sharing and appreciation of their fellow authors that the important sense of self-worth develops.

I have mentioned the valuable literary examples in the process of stimulating children's interest and recollection of memory and personal occurrences. As the book progresses and the range of writing expression is considered, there is a continued illumination of how these and similar exemplars can be used and serve as the beginning of extended thinking and purposeful discussion, leading to writing being read.

Indeed there is a practicality about this book. Questions that teachers of writing continually ask themselves are foreseen and answered in a way that reinforces sound practice, supporting the overall philosophy. How, when, and where the teacher of writing intervenes, when a pupil is gaining confidence and is moving towards an expected level of competence, is made clear. Faced with the raw material promising excellence, the teacher needs to know how to lead the writer to the next level of competence. Where exactly do the questions of spelling, grammar, legibility, and such basic elements of good writing, fit in this overall approach to writing? As the reader moves through this book, these and similar questions are addressed and answered. Of particular help when re-reading, or looking for reference to some particular aspect of writing, the chapter summaries in the table of contents are invaluable pointers. Of even more importance are the recapitulations at the end of each chapter which encourage the reader to reflect on the key elements involved in the material read, and to consider their response in terms of their own ideas and classroom practice.

Does this approach to the teaching of writing really work across learners from different backgrounds and cultures? Yes, it certainly does in my experience. Some years ago, I was teaching writing to third-year English majors in a university in China. Over the course of a year, I followed this approach without any concession to the fact that my students were from quite a different culture. I was warned that since cultural differences are important, and because the approaches I followed relied heavily on the inner life of the learner, this would not work. It did. I still have some of the wonderful, sensitive writing these young Chinese students produced.

I, with others, have long awaited the publication of this book. Now the author's years of practical classroom experience, endless hours of discussion with fellow teachers and leading educationalists, both here and overseas, are available to the widest possible audience. Gail deserves the widest audience.

Stan Boyle

INTRODUCTION

The most perfect oak tree stood in the grounds of my last school. With each seasonal change, it brought its own differing delights to those branches and the activities that went on around and beneath it. It seemed to be the heartbeat of this small, rural school. As we observed, sketched and studied the tree, we often wondered at the ability of a tiny acorn to become such a magnificent specimen. Clearly, given optimum conditions a seed will grow and transform into splendid maturity and in poor conditions it may never reach its prime, but it has the potential to be perfect. So it is with the children in our care. When nurtured, they too will grow and reach out, taking advantage of the fertile environment to become fully functioning and fulfilled human beings. Everything we do as teachers needs to contribute to the healthy growth and development of these young citizens as they step forward in their lives. Helping them to express themselves in writing is an important part of this growth.

As a young teacher I was fortunate to cross paths with educators who helped me find my own authorship, a gift that has helped me be a better teacher of writing, and to keep searching for knowledge and inspiration from others. In 1990 I committed myself to a five-week writing project in North Carolina (Capital Area Writing Project) – a real challenge and one that was to shape my future teaching. With my increased understanding of the positive effect we can have on our students when we teachers become co-learners and discoverers, I returned to New Zealand and designed a weeklong residential course for teachers. The teachers who attended this course were asked to participate in a team of learners, writing and sharing their work with me as their coach, their fellow learner. Of the twenty participants in each intake, no more than three teachers would ever have described themselves as writers at the beginning of the course. My aim was for each teacher to say at the end of the week,

'I am a writer', or at the very least 'I am a learner-writer', as a result of having had new insights into the process of writing from the learner's point of view.

In the next twelve years, forty of those residential courses were run, with around eight hundred teachers committing themselves to learning about writing by being part of a team of learner-writers. This book was originally written at the request of those New Zealand teachers as a summary of the course, in the hope that it would ignite some enthusiasm and provide fresh inspiration to teachers in their support of our young authors.

I became instead a teller of stories, a listener to stories, a writer and a reader of stories, an enactor, a collector and a maker of stories. But I only shared in this. What really happened was that we all became all of these things – tellers, listeners, readers, writers and learners together.

Patricia Grace (1986)

My recent experience involves working alongside teachers, both in their classrooms as they practise their craft of teaching and develop their own knowledge, and with school leaders of literacy so they can carry the learning forward. The more teachers understand language and the way it works (in parts and as a whole) and the more knowledge they gain on how to teach it, the less complicated and more meaningful the writing programme becomes.

When we go beyond the isolated teacher-prescribed topics and tasks so often seen in classrooms, to a community of developing writers, then we see students using writing as a means of describing, pondering on, clarifying, questioning and celebrating aspects of their lives. As writers, and as teachers of writing, we learn to be more aware of the world around us, noticing things that other people 'just walk by'. We become more conscious of our own lives, finding significance in our experiences. We also wonder about a whole lot of things outside our own existence and we find ways to write about all of them.

Gail Loane 2015

LESSON PLANS

We made a decision to include some lesson plans in the appendices of some chapters. Every lesson we provide should help our students develop as writers. There will be something that they can make connections with what they already know about writing, whether it is around the content, the purpose, the structure or shape, or the features of a particular piece. The students will make connections with their own lives, what they know of the world, and what they know about language and writing.

When I am using a model of writing with students, I provide a copy for each of them. Having established the expected routines, my student writers arrive in the Helping Circle armed with their pen, their writing book, a highlighter – and the expectation of being handed a copy of a piece we are about to explore. These explorations of a selected text involve much reading, thinking and talking. They do not have to be explored immediately before writing. If you think the reading and discussion will take time, it is better to plan to lead this part of the learning at a separate time – perhaps the day before, just before the students go home. At writing time, it will be easy to refer back to the model and the valuable discussion that has already been had: 'Remember that piece we looked at yesterday … let's have another quick look. Today we're going to have a go …'

Every time I prepare a lesson, it will be different from the time before, even when using the same piece of text, or when the learning need is one I have addressed before. The 'Lesson Plans' included in the appendices to some chapters are what we have come up with at various times, for various reasons. They may help with prompting you, as a teacher of writing, in how to lead the learning with your own students. They are not 'recipes', to be adhered to strictly, but will need to be read and understood in the context of your own understanding of the selected text and the literary devices offered, and in the context of your own class and the learning needs of your students. Make the plans your own.

ACKNOWLEDGEMENTS

This book has been in the pipeline for many years. It has had long periods on the shelf but with continual urging and support from friends and colleagues, it is now ready to go.

My sincere thanks to...

All the young authors whose work is at the heart of these pages. They have been my touchstone and my inspiration throughout, letting me learn and grow with them. They have also generously allowed me to use their work to inspire others.

Sally Muir, exemplary teacher and my valued work partner, who is the breath behind this book. She has been the person at the computer through all of the drafts and redrafts. She has fronted up in classrooms to trial ideas and approaches, and she has sat in my lounge for hours on end as we sifted ideas and made decisions for writing.

Pennie Brownlee, teacher, author, longtime friend and mentor, who took on the job as designer of this manuscript and has brought it to life with the most gorgeous photos and with her artist's eye for layout. She has been generous with her time and expertise since we were Playcentre parents together in the 1970s, when we chewed the fat together and set about changing the world ... I am grateful for her ongoing friendship, challenge and advice.

Dr Ruie Pritchard, the guest tutor as a Fullbright scholar on 'The NZ Writing Project', a week-long course for teachers, run throughout the country in 1988. I was invited as one of the participants and, as preparation for our learning, Ruie asked us to write a personal piece to bring to the course. For me, being asked to write and to share, was the turning point of my career. She led me to a new occupation as a fledgling writer, teaching me that I had something to say. Not only did she lead me to my own authorship, she also led me to a body of knowledge about writing that excited me; it connected what I knew intuitively to be effective practice with the research and theory about the teaching of writing. I followed Ruie back to the University of North Carolina in Raleigh, for a further five weeks of writing, learning and challenge. This experience set me up for the next step – designing and tutoring a week-long course for New Zealand teachers.

Sue Douglas, a Curriculum Manager for the Ministry of Education in the 1990s who accepted my proposal for a 'Teachers as Writers' course and supported me with funding for two years until the course could run itself. Around eight hundred teachers completed the week's course over the next ten years. Sue continued to involve me in Ministry literacy projects: membership on 'The Literacy Taskforce' (2000) and as a developer of 'The New Zealand English Exemplars' (Ministry of Education 2003), giving me an added dimension and responsibility to my work.

Pam Lord, in her role as an adviser to schools, who encouraged and supported me to set up an academically rigorous developmental programme in my senior classroom. It was accepted that junior classrooms were oriented this way, but not a common practice once students reached the seniors. As an Inspector of Schools and later as an Education Review Office evaluator, and friend, Pam continued to take an interest in my work. She invited me to share my practice with other teachers, launching me into a new direction in my career as a teacher educator. It must be said that Pam saw more in me than I saw in myself and for that I am grateful. She nudged me to write this book, and more.

Stan Boyle, a school principal and lover of language, who, with one of his teachers, Carolyn Smith, helped me to see what was possible to achieve with young writers.

Stan showed me how to turn theory into vibrant practice and have a whole class of enthusiastic young learner-writers. Right into his eighties, Stan was still keenly interested in my work and encouraged me for years to get this manuscript to the publisher.

Lynne Fothergill and **Sheryl May**, exemplary teachers, who attended my week-long residential course. They translated all that they learned in the workshops into vibrant practice back in their classrooms. They were my teacher touchstones – if ideas were going to work, they would make them work and they were an inspiration to other teachers.

Mentor authors
Lucy Calkins, **Shelley Harwayne** and **Nancie Atwell**, who have confirmed and strengthened my beliefs in the teaching of writing over many years and continue to inspire me in my work through their ongoing publications. I have read them until their words have become my words. Shelley welcomed me to her school in Manhattan where I could experience firsthand the effect of twelve 'joyfully notebooking teachers' on their young learners.

Writers
For permission to print and reprint their material. Every effort has been made to ensure that writers, including teachers and children, have given permission to reprint their material. Regretfully, some pieces of student writing were unable to be connected with a particular author. I am happy to be contacted so that I can rectify this omission in future editions of this book.

"Holiday Memory" By Dylan Thomas, from THE COLLECTED STORIES OF DYLAN THOMAS, copyright © 1954 by New Directions Publishing Corp. Reprinted by permission of New Directions Publishing Corp.

With thanks to The James K. Baxter Trust for kind permission to allow the reproduction of lines from 'The Town Under the Sea'.

Photographers

Thank you to the generous friends and to the photographers on Flickr who have given their images for these pages: Emily Bell - USA p 243. Mel Buckley - NZ p 179. Kirsty Griffin - NZ pp 203, 257. Gail Loane - NZ p 11. Gary Healey - NZ p 144. Gavin Woolnough - UK p 30. Harry Powers - Boston, MA, USA p 245, Jennifer Glenn - NZ p 107. John Caro - UK p 100. Kim Artus - NZ pp 62. Liz Henwood - UK pp 233, 235. Nick Caro - UK p 220. Patricia Grieg - UK p 43. Pennie Brownlee - NZ front cover, pp iv, x, xv, xvi, xx, 4, 6, 28, 38, 68, 75, 80, 91, 109, 119, 124, 130, 135, 138, 147, 155, 187, 193, 202, 210, 217, 229, 238, 262, 269, 270, 279. Rebecca Dufty - NZ pp 26, 282. Tracey Richardson - NZ p 260.

I am still learning.

Michaelangelo

1　The Teacher of Writing
Becoming joyfully literate

*We tell children how to be
and they keep mirroring back what we are.*

Joseph Chilton Pearce (1977)

Every child has something to say

I am a teacher of writing. And probably, if you are reading this book, you are too. I know that every child will have something to say about a whole lot of things. I see my job as helping each student find what it is that he or she has to say, and how best to say it.

Children arrive at school with at least five years of life's experiences to draw on. There will be a range of experiences, from a range of cultural backgrounds, and it is not our job to judge and dismiss those we deem to be lacking in experience. However, it is our job to accept each child as a unique human being, and to begin a learning partnership from day one that will tap into the richness and potential that is there.

There can be no significant innovation in education that does not have at its centre the attitudes of the teachers ... The beliefs, feelings and assumptions of teachers are the air of the learning environment; they determine the quality of life within it.

N. Postman and
C. Weingartner (1969)

Teacher beliefs: we teach who we are

Teaching may be a multi-faceted profession but there are some basic beliefs that have proved fundamental to my teaching practice. I believe that to be an effective teacher of writing, I have three things to consider:

- something about the young people in front of me;

- something about the art of teaching;

- something about writing itself.

My beliefs have evolved over time as I researched and learned through reading, writing, musing and talking with colleagues – but mostly through teaching, noticing the results, and inquiring into 'what works?'

One of my author mentors, New York educator Shelley Harwayne, talks about the need for learner-readers and learner-writers to be surrounded by joyfully literate adults: significant adults who demonstrate the joy, satisfaction and necessity that the written word brings to their daily lives. I attended a presentation once where I remember Shelley producing a bulging leather-bound journal: her personal poetry collection. She shared the poems she had attached beside photos of her family members. For her husband, she had pasted in Marge Piercy's 'Sentimental poem' –

> *You are such a good cook.*
> *I am such a good cook.*
> *If we get involved*
> *We'll both get fat.*
> *Then nobody else will have us.*
> *We'll be stuck, two*
> *Mounds of wet dough*
> *Baking high and fine*
> *In the bed's slow oven.*
> (Piercy 1978)

I subsequently visited Shelley's school in Manhattan and saw the vibrant way she connected literature to the lives of her students, and to everyone else in the school, including the caretaker and receptionist – literature was at the heart of school business.

Part of my self-styled job description was to become a joyfully literate adult in the lives of my students. I knew that I needed to magnify the role, to make overt and explicit how functioning readers and writers behave and respond. I needed to be 'larger than life' in my efforts to demonstrate and teach how to be a lifelong reader and writer – to be visibly passionate about life, people, ideas, language and my immediate environment, and to show how these affect us in our daily lives. So, as teachers, we need to give ourselves permission to be practising readers and writers so that we are, indeed, joyfully literate adults in the lives of our students.

We can teach only who we are, and we are guided in our actions by our personal philosophy and beliefs, whether or not they are conscious. In this text I will share some of my personal beliefs about the teaching of writing that I have found useful in developing young, and not so young, writers.

The teacher of writing will first and foremost take a deep interest in the students in their care as precious human beings

A teacher of writing values the lives of children, knowing that they talk, read and write to communicate and make sense of themselves and their world.

An early inspiration in my teaching career was the work of New Zealand educator Elwyn Richardson. Reading and re-reading his book *In the Early World* (Richardson 1964), where he describes his work in a two-teacher school in Northland in the 1950s and 1960s, I came to understand that children, all children, could write about issues close to their lives and hearts. Their lives mattered, and aspects of those lives were worth recording.

Taking this philosophy into my own class, I started by talking with my students to prompt the recall of a common experience. One of our first examples was recalling the first time we crossed a swing bridge near our school, working out what we had to say about that experience, writing and sharing what we had written. Without exception, the writing showed voice and substance, and the students learned not only that writers must choose the words to say what they mean, but that others, including me, were actually interested in what they had to say. Writing was not an exercise; it was about recording 'a bit of my life' that others wanted to hear. My next challenge was to have students finding their own topics for writing.

As humans we all have a need to make sense of the world and our place in it. Reading and writing helps us fulfil that need. Over time, my students began to realise that they had much in their lives worth writing about and that they could craft their experiences into cohesive pieces of writing.

The teacher of writing brings the children's lives into the classroom and helps them tap into their experiences, finding the significance. Bringing their lives into the classroom implies that we must know, acknowledge, and value the child totally: the cultures and cultural perspectives of home and school working in partnership. We will help children tap into their own lives and experiences by telling our own stories. Shared stories, wonderings, observations, opinions and responses need to be at the heart of writing times. We will be developing trust and sincerity as we exchange stories orally and will also be modelling how these stories can be crafted into writing.

A sensitive teacher will know that Monday's writing will not necessarily spring out of 'What I did at the weekend'. We must look for the significance within the experience – the personal response to it – not a bland recalling of events past. Just as I prompted common experiences of my students, I recognised that writers need to write about what is important and relevant to them, not always topics of my choosing. My experiences were not the same as those of my students, but I was able to tell my life stories and prompt a response in each child.

We respond to children's experiences with excerpts from literature so that they are exposed to rich and varied ways of describing similar experiences. It is not uncommon for any of us to feel

The teacher of writing triggers memories of life experiences through literature so that the child feels the blood rush to his cheeks because he has become so filled with his own life story.

Shelley Harwayne (1992)

that we have nothing in our lives worth writing about, but through immersion in stories, real and imagined, we see and hear the multitude of universal experiences being recorded. Children are able to empathise with characters and events in stories from a very early age; telling or reading traditional tales to infants evokes a response as the young listener recognises the common emotions and reactions, and the descriptions portrayed. We need not limit young children to nursery tales, however. A group of five year olds visited the surrounding rural area and spent time looking closely at the ferny streams and describing what they saw.

On their return to school, their teacher shared a paragraph from Katherine Mansfield's *At the Bay* (1921):

> *Ah – Aah! sounded the sleepy sea. And from the bush there came the sound of little streams flowing quickly, lightly, slipping between the smooth stones, gushing into ferny basins and out again; and there was the splashing of big drops on large leaves, and something else – what was it? – a faint stirring and*

shaking, the snapping of a twig, and then such silence that it seemed some-
one was listening.

'That lady's been up the same creek as us!' exclaimed one child.

And by that very act – taking children to explore their environment, not just to look, but to look with seeing eyes – we fulfil another task.

The teacher of writing will lead the children to become closely observant in their environment, becoming more aware of their own existence, helping them to look and see things that they might not have seen before, thus raising their levels of sensitivity and response.

We need not leave the school grounds to become observers, but some of us may need directing to notice the things around us, whether it be the leaves falling off the trees, the wet concrete or the patterns of the raindrops. Our students need to

know that a personal response, and recognition of significance, is not limited to events or people: we respond when we notice what is around us. Much has been written about William Carlos Williams' poem:

> *so much depends upon*
> *a red wheel barrow*
> *glazed with rain water*
> *beside the white chickens*
> (Williams 1923)

Students may enjoy exploring the history and meaning behind it. I find this poem to be a useful model to explain our job as writers: to notice, and, in noticing, allow ourselves to respond and see some significance in the text. Useful models are everywhere; we need to notice them, savour them, collect them, share them.

The teacher of writing is constantly aware of the way words are put together and, with students, will explore what authors do

Reading, making meaning from the written word, and writing, creating meaning with the written word, are intrinsically linked: much of what we learn as writers comes from reading and responding to the texts of other writers. As we investigate published authors' work, we will discover what writers do when writing for a particular purpose. If we are attentive ourselves about the way words are put together, then we will model how a reader-writer thinks and behaves. I am always struck by how quickly students can identify the meaning, the effect and the significance of a writer's carefully selected words – and how quickly and ably they will imitate a writer's style.

If we are fortunate enough in our school lives to have even one teacher with a passion for the way words are put together, that teacher will make all the difference to how we come to love literature and poetry. I have learned that an emotional, passionate response is not enough, though; the passion is strengthened when the teacher can model and name the techniques that the author uses for a particular effect. In this way, the learner-writer has the author's power revealed as a power they too can learn to wield. We can all build up a repertoire of literary tools that will be useful to us as writers, through exploring, identifying and learning about the way words have been selected and ordered. The teacher prompts or shares in conversations with students daily – about what a writer may have meant, or about what a writer has done to convey an idea successfully.

The teacher of writing reads and writes

For some children, their teacher will be the only (or the most significant) model they see who demonstrates how a competent reader and writer behaves and responds. If the teacher does not model this behaviour effectively, then reading and writing can become mere school exercises, rather than a joyful life activity. Just as teachers need to demonstrate keen interest in response to reading published authors, they also need to demonstrate that, as co-learners in the writing process, they write themselves. They write, as their students do, in response to observations, wonderings, experiences, and enjoyed passages from literature – and they share their jottings with their students. The teacher who writes will have a notebook (see Chapter 3 – *From the Head to the Page*) which becomes a basis for future writings, a sounding board and a reference point.

The teacher who writes will know and demonstrate how writing begins as a seed and grows, thereby helping students to develop strategies and habits of life which allow their own writings to branch out and develop. I was well into my teaching career before I understood the value of actually writing myself, and sharing this with my students. The response I got then, and continue to get, showed me that to be a truly effective teacher of writing, I must know how it is to be a writer. We can learn much about writing through reading about it, but we can learn to write well only by practising the art of writing ourselves.

I have found that bringing about success in writing impacts on every other aspect of school life. In my experience, when I get that bit right, my students are anxious to perform as well as they are able in all aspects of their lives. They feel valued and supported, and are more likely to be eager learners and contributors in every subject. For me, being a joyfully literate adult in the lives of my students is a prerequisite for the job as coach of a team of writers.

Summary - *The Teacher of Writing*

- Every student has something to say - it is our job to believe it and have our students believe it too.

- We begin with the awareness of the potential for a love affair with language, for ourselves and for our students.

- We read and write to make sense of ourselves and our world, and to communicate.

- Children's lives need to be brought into the classroom.

- We trigger memories of life experiences through personal stories and literature.

- We lead children to become closely observant in their environment, raising their levels of awareness, sensitivity and response.

- We explore with students how authors put their work together.

- We demonstrate how reader-writers think and behave.

2 The Writing Classroom
Conditions for writers to flourish

One of my great pleasures before the start of a new school year, the start of a new week, or indeed, the start of each day, was to prepare myself, and my classroom, in readiness for my students. It has been my experience that time spent on careful preparation - of lesson content, resources needed and the physical surroundings - is time well spent. Having taken claim to be a joyfully literate adult in the lives of my students, I wanted them to know that they were part of 'the team', a joyfully literate community, where we all learn more about reading, writing and talking.

Writing time

Schools are, by necessity, governed by time constraints. Every teacher must have experienced at some time the frustrations of not having enough hours in the day to fit everything in. In schools where one teacher has their own class for most of the day, a timetable will need to be managed effectively to satisfy requirements as well as student learning needs.

Teachers will be well versed in filling in daily, weekly and long-term plans. I have often been heard to say, 'Don't get your plans laminated!' It is inevitable that they will change. It is important to know where you are heading with your team of independent writers, but the details of what you will need to include will emerge as you notice where your learner-writers are performing.

On topics for writing, we are limited only by our own thoughts. Our lives are full of fodder for writing. When we really understand and believe that ourselves, we can lead our students into their own realisation that they can make sense of the 'stuff of their lives' as they respond, talk, wonder, muse - and write it down.

Conversations with many teachers over time have included such questions as: How do I plan for writing? What should I include in my writing lessons this term? What will I get my kids to write about? How do I organise my class so that I can attend to everyone's needs? I do not believe that there is a one-size-fits-all plan, but the following principles have enabled me to provide students with the lessons they need to become better writers.

Provide time for reading, talking, listening and writing daily

Apart from those predictable sports days and class trips, every school day will have time for writing, and talking about writing, just as we expect to provide time for reading and responding to the texts we read. The further up the school they progress, the more writing I would expect students to produce, sometimes writing more than once in a day in response to curriculum needs – certainly beginning to juggle more than one piece of writing at a time. I also expect students to enjoy their authorship, and I want them to know that in this class we are all interested in what they have to say about a variety of topics.

Small children will also need the time to gain skills in forming letters as well as learning about creating meaning through the marks they make on paper. The determination and perseverance they require for the variety of necessary language tasks we design for them as they practise will stand them in good stead as they mature. I expect students of any age to have the stamina for writing independently every day, as well as being actively engaged in reading, talking and learning about writing.

Plan daily teaching sessions that build on the knowledge and skills that students have already acquired

Notice what students are able to do in their writing, and make decisions about specific instructional sessions that address what they need to learn. Sometimes these lessons will be around the mechanics of writing, sometimes around a literary device that will enhance writing. Whatever the focus of the lesson, it must be seen within the context of a whole text. We might draw out and put a magnifying glass on a particular use of punctuation, or a well-crafted simile, but we must ensure that the device explored is then returned to the whole text for the effect to be realised. It is important for students to have the meaning of the whole piece under their belts before deconstructing it. We start with the whole and its meaning, draw the teaching point out for exploration, and then return it to the whole, and be able to articulate the effect.

We must always alert students to make meaning from texts as readers, as well as create meaning as writers; every part of this process is about making or creating meaning. Instruction will focus on strategies for writing that will be useful in any piece of writing, whether it be at school or in the wider world, whether it be a personal memoir or a factual assignment. There will be times, of course, when we need to show our students the structure and features of a particular writing purpose or form. We need to 'walk them through' a process which may take days. A way to approach these types of lessons is described in subsequent chapters.

Mini lessons

In large classes, it would be difficult to provide instruction for, or conference with, each child every day, but when each day's writing session begins with a mini lesson, this becomes the forum for sharing what we know about writing. We are building our skills and knowledge as writers in what could be described as a 'writers' club'. This regular gathering of writers may serve the function of a writing conference by focusing on problems that young authors are experiencing, with the solutions coming from collaborative problem-solving, or from a carefully planned modelling session. It may also serve to highlight the successes that students are demonstrating in their writing, the excellences and the adaptation of skills and strategies already learned. It becomes a place where the 'club language' of a community of writers builds and flourishes.

The mini lesson, usually focused on one strategy, skill or concept, can be taught to a whole class, a selected small group or individual students.

> *Mini-lessons grow from teachers' observations of what students don't know or will need to know to produce excellent, literary writing in a range of genres. Teachers research mini-lessons. They learn about different genres and their features, poets' and authors' inspirations and processes, poetic and literary features and techniques, kinds of writing for kids to try, writing-as-process, pieces of writing that demonstrate different techniques, how different punctuation marks cue readers, format conventions, usage conventions, techniques for organising information and argument, elements of fiction, character development, theme, purpose, and so on.* (Atwell 2002)

It needs to be said that a mini lesson should not take up the entire writing session – the word 'mini' is used deliberately. The mini lesson may precede or conclude a writing session where students are engaged in a specific writing task.

Guided writing

When we plan to 'walk students through' a process of writing, as perhaps in the introduction of a new genre, or the collaborative composition of a poem, we may use the whole session, or a series of lessons, directed and guided by the teacher with a particular goal in mind (for example, a character portrait or a persuasive essay). Such lessons are described in the following chapters. Mini-lessons can become part of those longer guided teaching sessions on the way to achieving the desired written outcome.

Teachers explicitly teach reading and writing, leading to independence

While acknowledging that we are co-learners within our classrooms, we know that our role is an active, authoritative one. We need to demonstrate, explain, direct and prompt, as we guide and teach, noticing how our students are responding. Children may be intuitive about a whole lot of things in expressing and communicating ideas, but we can't expect them to demonstrate knowledge of structure and syntax, literary devices and punctuation, entirely by intuition.

> *So, these days I directly teach my students during our writing conferences. As an experienced adult, I sit down with less experienced children and make*

suggestions, give advice, demonstrate solutions, and collaborate with them on pieces of their writing when I think they need to see how something could work ... I teach with a capital T. I don't leave things to chance. (Atwell 2002)

Students will know that, even as a skill is practised through guided instruction, they will be expected to have a go at applying what they have learned in their own independent writing efforts. So if we are working towards developing independent writers, that will also have implications for how we organise our learning environment and writing time.

Physical environment

If a classroom is to be a shared place of learning, then I see it as the teacher's job to ensure that learning is optimised through the way it is set up. We may not have unlimited funds for replacing essential furniture or moving walls, but we can manage what we have in such a way that it is conducive to students feeling comfortable - comfortable physically and comfortable emotionally - to allow learning to take place. All students in the room must be allowed, and indeed encouraged, to feel part of the group within, that they have a right of place, and that they will be heard.

Tables or desks can be placed in such a way that each student is part of a small group within the larger class group. It will also be useful to arrange the group tables to allow room for the entire class to gather in a sharing circle. King Arthur knew a thing or two about group dynamics when it came to calling his knights to a round table ... being part of a circle enables us all to feel an equal member of that group. Indeed, our goal is for each student to be a responsible, contributing member of the group, where they are 'party to contract'. Junior classrooms have traditionally had a 'mat space' for the children to gather, but it is equally important for senior rooms to have that space for the whole class to become one learning unit. A sharing circle, where students are physically and emotionally included, is the ideal forum for sharing student writing, discussing specific teaching points, sharing models of effective writing, sharing stories, and so on. The teacher is part of that circle, and, while maintaining the role of guide, is able to model effectively what it is to be a participating learner within the group.

In large classes you may need to be creative about the formation of the circle so that everyone can participate fully; one solution is to form a double circle, one half of the class on chairs in a semi-circle and the others forming an inner circle on the floor. Whatever arrangement you choose, it is important that students are able to be one hundred per cent involved in the activity. Ken Macrorie (1984) refers to this circle as 'The Helping Circle', and it is central to a community of writers.

As well as the arrangement of furniture, there are opportunities to arrange displays, books and other classroom resources in an attractive way. When our students see the importance of books – the way they are stored, displayed and handled – and that writing is afforded as much value as a work of art, whether it be professionally published or published in the classroom, and displayed appropriately, their enthusiasm for having ensured that they have chosen exactly the right words in their own writing, and presented them in a pleasing way, will be obvious.

> *The bulletin board*
> *looks like it's*
> *blooming words*
> *with everybody's poems*
> *up there*
> *on all those*
> *coloured sheets of paper*
> *yellow blue pink red green.*
> *And the bookcase*
> *looks like it's*
> *sprouting books ...*
> (from *Love That Dog*, Sharon Creech 2001)

As we are constantly at pains to encourage close observation and a personal response to not only books and words, but just about everything (see Chapter 7 – *Observing and Noticing*), it is also useful to remember the value of ensuring that displays in the classroom are attractive as well as meaningful. Whether it is a collection of pine cones or sea shells or artefacts relating to a unit of study, how we present them to our students will make a difference. It will say to your students: 'In this classroom we care about your work and the work of others: how we present matters'.

Immersing the students in quality literature

The writing classroom will be saturated in print - print which is appropriate to the needs of the students and print which will be a source of a variety of literacy strategies and resources. Every classroom, regardless of the age of the students, should be a place where quality literature is on hand for students to explore, albeit through the teacher when students are emerging as readers.

We can draw from rich texts that are available for children, but also our own adult reading will provide excerpts that can be useful and enriching models for all students, as demonstrated by a five year old's response to Katherine Mansfield (see Chapter 1 - *The Teacher of Writing*). Not only does the writing serve a purpose, but when the teacher brings this to the notice of her students she models the role of someone who reads - reads and takes note of the language used. Students will soon begin to acknowledge, and even expect, the literature we share with them and will start bringing offerings of their own. How heartening it is when we have students sharing their personal reading: 'Listen to this Ms B - this author talks about feeling cold. That's just how I felt when I was up Mt Ruapehu! It was *sooo* cold.'

> *The mountain air, misty and edged with snow, cut across my face and crept into my bones.* (*Winter of Fire*, by Sherryl Jordan 1993)

This comment, from a Year 8 student, prompted much searching through novels by classmates for alternative ways that different authors described the sensation of being cold.

> *... but that was at four in the morning when the temperature always dropped and his thin blanket failed to keep him warm.* (*The Fire Raiser*, by Maurice Gee 1987)

Immersing students in quality literature is a starting point for students to begin a serious appreciation of literature and of an author's style, as well as developing ideas of how to express themselves as writers, by identifying what the author has done.

Although it is essential to acknowledge the clarity and richness to be found within transactional texts, it is often in fiction that we find satisfaction, pleasure, enjoyment of words and a wealth of literary devices that we can identify and discuss as learner-writers. Students learn to transfer their knowledge of language across genre and purposes.

Children may put up with, and sometimes desire, a diet of words that are not necessarily put together in a particularly literary way: if we use the analogy of a bodily diet, children may desire cakes and sweets to satisfy their hunger, but we know that they will not thrive on these things alone. So it is with words. While reading a comic or a selection of silly limericks may provide some enjoyment, and some appreciation of the specific skills required to compose such texts, these things alone will not suffice as fodder for young writers to flourish. We need to provide a smorgasbord of rich and varied texts for our learner-writers, and all will become accustomed to responding to the way the author has put the words together.

Opportunities for developing oral language

We have come a long way since a silent classroom was thought to be a good classroom. Just as immersing our students in quality literature is important, so is providing the opportunity for them to talk about the stories they hear and read. By providing rich texts, we can expect our students to go beneath the surface in their appreciation and understanding of the author's message. We can formalise this discussion with a prescribed format which encourages students to make inferences from the text, such as a Three Level Guide (for example, see Chapter 5 – *Tapping into Universal Experiences*), but there must be an expectation that we think critically in unprescribed discussion too, with open-ended questions posed for the students to ponder on: '*I wonder what the author meant ...?*' There will also be questions requiring specific answers: '*How has this author given us clues to the way this character was feeling?*'

Students can be guided to search for clues and respond to them in visual text as well as the written word: '*How do we know that the giant was feeling*

Fiction matters, ultimately, because it expands imaginative experience, connects us to others and deepens our response to living.

Students need a language to understand and talk about the fiction they read and the feeling it engenders. There need be no division between formal understanding and living response.

Peter Abbs and John Richardson (1990a)

Writing is a rehearsal in meaning-making. What we like to call 'mind texts'. The teacher's role in all this is to support those rehearsals, to help kids bring those mind texts to the page as powerful writings. It is the head-to-page trip that is so frightening and difficult for writers.

D. Kirby and T. Liner with R. Vinz (1988)

cross?' might come from a junior shared book, while there are countless sophisticated picture books for senior students to respond to, searching for subtle clues and visual links to meaning within the illustrations. Whatever the objective of sharing a selected text with our students, it is essential that they fully understand what the author is trying to say. As readers we must expect to gain meaning from a text and respond to its effect. Only then would we pull it apart in order to learn more about the craft of writing.

Learner-writers will need to talk about their own stories too; the opportunity for the oral telling of a story is often a prerequisite to writing it down. A simple *'Turn to the person next to you ...'* as a way of saying what is inside their heads will support the beginnings of that 'trip' – from inside the head on to the page.

We rarely hear the words 'I don't know what to write ...' when students have had the opportunity to find the words to express themselves, and share those words orally before endeavouring to get them onto a page. There is an absolute expectation that all students store experiences, and it is the teacher's job to draw the stories and opinions out.

Responding to the writing of others

Readers, listeners and viewers respond to texts on at least two levels. Unless our mind is 'elsewhere', we first respond to the message within a text on an emotional level. The emotion can vary, from simple pleasure or satisfaction to that of feeling disturbed or stirred. Much of our reading can be left at that response, but when in the role of learner-writers, we need to acknowledge the intellectual response which is one that needs practice. As teachers of writing we need to notice our own intellectual response to text, building our own expertise and mentally 'tucking away' models that we may be able to share with our students to illustrate a specific literary device.

Discussion opportunities need to be set up with our students, with the purpose for discussion made clear to them. They may have a piece of published text to read and respond to, with specific expectations of the sorts of things to be discussed. If we structure this process effectively for our students, we will have moved a long way past such responses as 'It's a cool poem', or 'It's got interesting words'. Being able to respond to reading not only helps, but is also an essential part of making meaning, and will enhance that understanding of the inextricable connections between reading and writing.

In his social development theory, Lev Vygotsky (1978) describes language learning as a 'socially mediated' process, one where interaction with others plays a fundamental role in language development. Taking this theory into our classrooms, we can see that dialogue between writers about their writing can be called a mediating process, one where the collaboration between two or more young writers takes them towards greater understanding and a way forward. Research tells us that where students respond to the writing of others, and seek response to their own efforts, the progress of those writers is more evident. In a classroom, at a practical level, we can do this in several ways.

Writing in isolation without lively response is like other solitary activities: singing in the shower or dancing in a coal mine. They may be pleasurable diversions, but without some response from an audience, they do not get much better. Most writers, and particularly your students, need the reactions of other human beings both during and after they write.

D. Kirby and T. Liner with R. Vinz (1988)

Partner conference

Habits of responding to the writing of others need to be established from the beginning. For younger students, this may be initiated in pairs for short, directed tasks. For example, *'Listen to your friend's writing and notice the action words.'* For older students, you can use a variety of response arrangements, depending on the purpose and situation.

The helping circle

As described above, the whole class team assembles in a 'helping circle', usually at the beginning or end of a writing session, so that writers can share their work and consider the effect of the writing and what might improve it. After receiving an initial response, the writer will expect some specific feedback about the effect of the writing and the choices made.

Over time, as students gain confidence and success in the helping circle, they will also expect to be helped, questioned, nudged and challenged to improve. Initially the teacher takes the lead, modelling the expectations of the helping circle and establishing protocols around language that builds confidence and skills in developing writers. As students are guided to respond competently and confidently, the responsibility shifts more to the students themselves for response and help. They become less dependent on the teacher and more confident in using the community of writers within the classroom.

Peer response group

A peer response group is a positive and constructive activity that can be part of the writing process, and can be set up to enable students to comment on each other's writing.

Peer group responses allow:

- immediate feedback;

- the opportunity to amend while writing;

- a wider range of opinions, not just the teacher's;

- a greater awareness of what works;

- a less threatening small group audience;

- the chance to take risks, not just to please the teacher;

- the opportunity for everyone's work to be heard.

The best time to organise for the peer groups to operate is after the first draft writing session has taken place. This may be only a part of the writing, such as the introduction or just the first sentence. There may be times during the writing process for further consultation within the group while writers are preparing their final draft. After further work, the peer group may become a forum to 'showcase' the final version.

Peers have the potential to be effective teachers and collaborative learners.

Dyson and Freedman

(2003)

For older students, a more formal and sustained procedure can be set up. The exact structure and rules would be devised to suit the age level, the needs of the students, and the content. In order to establish the more formal peer response groups, create groups of four children who work together regularly for the length of the writing activity or longer – the more trust the group develops, the better. Once the philosophy of peer responding has been introduced and accepted, it can be used in a variety of ways: from the formal group session to the informal 'get a friend to comment on ...'. It is important that teachers and students recognise that this process is an aspect of writing that enables learner-writers to get beyond the superficial, and not just another meaningless ritual. At the same time as they respond to the writing of others, both published authors and their peers, they are sensitising to their own writing; they link aspects of the discussion to their own writing efforts and become more sensitive to possible improvements. This sensitivity and skill builds up over time, developing in writers the habit of revision and re-crafting.

Example

Teacher direction: *Listen to Molly's character sketch. Listen for details that she has included and let her know if she has given you a good picture of her grandma. You might hear things about what she looks like ... or the things she does.*

Writer: *I wrote: 'My grandma takes me to the shops. She wears a dress. Her hair is black and some bits white. Her hair is tied up. Sometimes she lets me brush her hair.'*

Listener 1: *Why does she take you to the shops?*

Writer: *She goes shopping and I can go with her.*

Listener 1: *Does she buy you things?*

Writer: *Sometimes.*

Listener 1: *She's a nice grandma!*

Listener 2: *She's nice letting you brush her hair. It was good how you told us about that.*

Listener 3: *And you told us what she looked like.*

Writer: *Which bit?*

Listener 3: *About her hair.*

Listener 2: *And her dress.*

Listener 3: *I can see what her hair looks like now – the colour and everything.*

Listener 2: *What kind of dress does she wear?*

In this junior room, the discussion in response to one child's attempt at a character sketch proved useful for both this writer and the listeners in the peer response group; all the children engaged in the discussion were able to see how certain details were appreciated by an audience, and what further details might be useful. The responses include some acknowledgement of skills demonstrated, some acceptance of the clues to character provided by the writer, and some questions seeking clarification – demanding more detail. Even at the most informal level it is important to have some structure so that:

- the listener-reader is trained to notice specific detail;

- the writer receives thoughtful, specific feedback and carefully worded suggestions;

- each writer is treated fairly;

- the group runs smoothly and effectively.

Responding to others - the protocol

There are protocols around how we respond to the writing of others, and the less experienced or tentative writers need a more structured framework to begin with. I have used the following ground rules with adults (adapted from the protocols practised at the North Carolina Capital Area Writing Project) as they share their writing:

- Everyone in the group should be able to see a copy of the writing - to make notes for reference.

- The author reads the writing without explanation or apology - developing confidence as a writer.

- Listeners make notes as they listen, without comment - to keep the focus.

- There is a pause after the reading - time to reflect on the writing.

- Beginning with the person on the author's right, everyone in the group makes one positive comment about the writing - in specific terms.

- On the second round, everyone has a chance to note a suggestion for some improvement or clarification - the language of this feedback is of utmost importance and needs to be taught.

- A leader keeps the group moving and does not let anyone dominate the flow of ideas.

- The author does not speak until everyone has finished. The author may then respond, answering questions or presenting explanations or points of view.

- No arguments or debates. There is nothing to argue about - no right or wrong answers - only honest reactions.

These rules keep the group engaged and focused on the job at hand and ensure a safe learning environment. With students, a modification of the above process is essential to begin with, according to the age group of the children, to ensure full participation and a gradual building of confidence in the process of giving and receiving feedback.

For students, this process might follow these guidelines:

- Ensure students are clear about the reason for the response they are about to offer their fellow writers. They may be prepared with a framed sentence. As with adult writers the language of the feedback will need to be taught – this teaching will happen as teachers lead discussions in response to shared texts, drawing attention to the specifics. For example:

    You have included_____senses

    You have drawn the reader into your writing through the use of _____

    You have convinced me of your point of view by_____

    You have shown me that it is autumn by_____

    You have added extra information by using_____

This will link with the current learning and ensures a tight meaningful feedback. They may be asked to jot the responses for fellow writers, allowing full engagement and learning for all members of the group. It is important to note that while they are responding to the writing of others, they will be making connections with their own writing.

- Four group members are arranged in a circle – physical arrangement is important for maximum engagement – on the same level, all on chairs or all on the floor, knees nearly touching, no table in the middle. Students have paper and pencils for taking notes, or they may have a copy of the writing being read (optimum but not always practical).

- The first writer reads their writing.

- There is a pause for reflection.

- Beginning with the person on the reader's right, everyone offers a comment about the writing according to the agreed process. The reader listens without comment until everyone is finished.

- The author then responds, answering questions or presenting explanations and points of view.

Ground rules that you decide upon can be modelled as a whole-class teaching point, using a group to demonstrate the process. Time spent on modelling this process will be time well spent. It is essential that the teacher is clear about the process, in order to make each step crystal clear to each student. No student should be left wondering what is expected of them.

The teacher-student partnership

Providing specific feedback for our students helps them to grow; sometimes this is written in draft writing books and sometimes it is what we say. If we are considering the interests of each student, we nurture them with carefully chosen words, words that confirm a student's authorship: for example, 'You have listed the attributes of fog, using present participles – just as Charles Dickens did', or 'You've used a listing sentence just like Bill Naughton's … and if you …', or 'As authors, we need to …'. It is important to remember that every word uttered in a classroom has an effect on students and their learning. We need to be aware of that effect in order to develop student partners who expect to be heard, who expect to respond to texts and ideas, who expect to question and critique, who expect to contribute.

How we talk to each other – about anything – will undoubtedly impact on the climate of the classroom. Peter Johnston (2004) makes the analogy between the protagonist in a narrative (a character who encounters a problem and solves it, through acting strategically) and a student who is given the opportunity to be the successful protagonist in their learning journey. A child who is in the habit of telling himself he doesn't have stories to tell, or can't spell, will need his teacher to be a conversation partner – the partner who initiates conversations where the child is invited to be proactive in describing what he has achieved and how he got there. By thoughtful choice of words, the teacher then positions the student as a learner or author, with the expectation that the student will consciously recognise that he has some control over his learning decisions. Not only are we able to confirm a student's authorship – 'You've done 'a Maurice Gee' with your use of metaphor…' – and draw attention to what they have done well, but we can set students up with the motivation to develop their authorship further: '… and if you include direct speech, it will give me an even clearer picture …'.

A partnership between teacher and student, where there is mutual and sincere respect, and a valuing of each child's life experiences - no matter how different from the teacher's world - will be the essential ingredient in the writing classroom.

Summary - *The Writing Classroom*

- Writing happens daily.

- Opportunities need to be provided for independent writing.

- Daily mini-lessons develop authorship.

- Classroom environment - arranging furniture and displays for maximum learning, emotional safety, intellectual stimulus and independence.

- Quality literature - linking reading and writing.

- Developing oral language.

- Responding to the writing of others.

- Teacher-student partnership.

3 From the Head to the Page
Getting it down

The notebook

It seems to me that if we are developing independent writers, then we need to look to the behaviour and habits of successful authors for clues to living an 'authorly' life. It has often been said that a writer (or artist) is someone who is struck by things that others just walk by. I have to admit that I was one of those people who just walked by, not noticing the magnificence and potential that the world is charged with, nor taking the time to do so.

I was first alerted to this shortcoming while watching my artist friend as she noticed and described the magic and beauty of a spider's web one winter's morning. She shared her noticings and wonderings with our children who became entranced and absorbed in the activity of the spider. They watched as the vibration of the web alerted the spider; the eight spider legs elongated as it darted across the delicate strands, only to be disappointed.

I began to realise that this was education in the true sense of the word, not only for knowledge of the living world, but for the opportunities for recording it as well. As a fledgling adult writer, I was led by my mentors to notice and to record my noticings. I am now a more conscious noticer, realising that I have to do the same deliberate leading for my student writers - they may not just 'catch' it. I also know the power of supporting teachers and students to make connections between their own world experiences and school learning experiences. This connection brings relevance and authenticity to their learning and to their subsequent writing efforts. Authors I have met always carry a pad, journal

or notebook for jotting their thoughts and noticings. They find inspiration in the world about them and notebooks become a place to save their words, observations, memories, reflections, thoughts, wonderings, quotations, captured conversations, writings of others, interviews ... and any of these entries can become what a writer wants it to be. It is about seeing the world through the lens of a writer and finding possibilities. So it seems logical to me that if we are seeking independence in our young writers, we need to develop in them the habit of using a notebook, a habit that helps them realise that their lives are filled with the material for writing.

Teacher as model

Over the years, I have seen teachers become very enthusiastic about providing students with a notebook and then reporting back some time later that it didn't really work. Unfortunately, it takes more than the provision of a bound book to establish the writer's notebook as a habit of life. Without a real understanding of the role of the notebook in the big picture of true authorship, and without the necessary explicit teaching to lead the students to that same deep understanding, they most often fizzle. Students need to be taught how to make meaningful entries. We need to consciously demonstrate authorly behaviour: how the notebook is reached for at any time of the day, according to the possibilities that arise. The teacher needs to plan time to teach strategies for writing meaningful entries – until the behaviour is learned and becomes habitual.

As the teacher, I understand that I am the model of a writer for the students. I use my notebook on a regular basis; it is central to who I am as a person, a writer and a teacher. I talk with my students about my entries and what prompted them, I also prompt and guide students to make entries of their own. By sharing myself as a learner-writer I build our community of writers, taking the same risks I am asking my students to take.

We want the students to view the writer's notebook in the realm of possibility, relevant to their own lives, rather than another school chore, so how we 'sell' it and model its use will be crucial to its success. A teacher needs to take time to establish the habit of jotting in a notebook. It needs to be out on the desk throughout the day so that students can see and experience how possibilities present themselves and how they can be recorded. Recently I watched one teacher listen to what a student was telling her and then turn to her table and visibly jot in her notebook. 'Rangi, your story reminded me of something very similar when I was at school. I had forgotten that. Thank you. I may use that in my writing later.' This teacher is actively demonstrating how an author works. As well as responding to a student's discourse, there are numerous other occasions on any given day that could lead to jottings.

In a junior classroom, where children are still emerging as writers with their energies on the technical aspects of recording what they want to say, the teacher's notebook is an essential model for what they might grow into. The teacher is making explicit what she does as a writer through regular demonstration of making

entries in her notebook, and talking about what she's doing. In her modelling sessions, she may demonstrate how her jotted ideas can become a piece of writing. Some teachers have made their notebook large poster size, so its use becomes more shared, visible and deliberate. Some junior children will appear at school with a new notebook, having 'caught the bug' of living as an author from their teacher's modelling. They have quickly grown into being independent authors, beginning to embrace the use of a Writer's Notebook.

Responding to literature and the writing of peers

Making note of an author's excellences, sentence structures, and descriptions help students link to their own experiences:

Gavin Bishop: *Piano Rock* – show don't tell:

> *Among the matagouri, briar roses were speckled with scarlet hips and at our back door the lilac leaves sat poised to fall.* (Shows it was autumn.)
>
> *The water struck my skin like ice …* (Shows the water was cold.)

Jottings of a 6 year old girl during and after zoo visit

Auckland Zoo

✓feeding Giraffe (celery,
gentle, wrap tongne)
✓Serval cat (small head
spotted, big pointed sharp
ears)
✓Tiger (striped, fed meat,
one pregnant)
✓Alligater (Doris, bumpy,
hiding, not eat for
two months, Question
for a zoo keeper)
✓Meer kat (stand up,
look for danger, went
threw tunnels to see
closer)
✓Ringed tailed lemur
(black ringed tail, fed
high in tree, Gold
fish pond)   ✓

- Great day!

Maurice Gee: *The Fire Raiser* – using similes:

> *Darkness spread like water ...*
> *... the telescope, up on its back legs like a praying mantis ...*
> *A window was open like a mouth ...*
> *His arms, as long as rakes ...*

Students can initially be directed to find and record excerpts that interest or 'speak to' them. Teachers need to make regular time to share and note when these excellences appear in student writing: 'I can see the influence of Bryce Courtney in your writing.' Responding to a text might be even more directed by the teacher, such as: 'Our main character makes an important decision in this chapter and I am asking you to jot your response to that decision in your notebook. We will share our thoughts at the end and see where they might connect with our own lives.'

World events

We can share our own entries around world events and use them for discussion, and we can direct students to make note of an event that moves them during the week.

> *The election of Barack Obama as President of the United States brings new hope to millions of people all over the world.*

> *I watched Jesse Jackson at the announcement of Obama's victory and could feel ...*

> *A plane landed on the Hudson River... first responses from New Yorkers on hearing news that another plane had gone down.*

> *Five hurricanes in five weeks – is this the effect of climate change?*

Wonderings

We need to wonder and share our wonderings. Some wonderings are satisfied by simply being recorded in the notebook. Others may be taken through to the draft book and crafted into a variety of forms.

Emma: *Why is it so cold today when we've got global warming?*

Rose: *Grandad's died. Who will Nana talk to now?*

Teacher: *Why do we get fog in some places and not in others?*

In one classroom, this last jotting turned into a class research project: Where does fog come from? The research was supported by the teacher immersing students in a variety of texts which included rich descriptions of foggy scenes from literature: novels and poetry (see Chapter 8 – *Inside or Outside*) and also included the scientific response to the initial wondering. The learning from the science research provided an opportunity to craft an explanatory piece together:

> *In autumn, the weather is cooler and the nights longer. The land and water surfaces that have warmed up during the summer are still evaporating a lot of water into the atmosphere. This makes the air humid. The longer nights allow the ground to grow cold enough to condense water vapour in the air above it, which is seen as fog ...*

This in turn prompted a comparison between the language used for scientific explanation with the poetic language of legend – legends being the earliest of explanations.

> *'The warmth that I provide the earth,'* continued Sun, *'must be given back to me. And as the earth gives back my warmth, so I receive it. But as Summer ends, and before Winter begins, the people must be warned most strongly to take heed of the change of seasons. As I reduce my rays, and the air cools, the earth's warmth will form a mist – a cloud over the ground – which will fill them with wonder, and hasten them to prepare for Winter ...'* (See the appendix of Chapter 8 for full texts and lesson plans.)

In this example we see how the use of a notebook can lead to:

- satisfying curiosity as we make sense of the world;

- close reading of texts, scientific and poetic;

- exploring language;

- crafted pieces of writing.

Observations - capturing moments

We need to lead our writers to observe and record. This will require very careful questioning from the teacher to lead them to look closely and to record exactly what they see, hear, feel, smell. Eventually young writers will do this independently.

This time of year everyone's a smoker. (Sam)

The naked branches bend into the wind. (Levi)

The leaves are showing the way in the wind. (Nikki)

Oyster, clinging onto the rock for life. (Joe)

Interviews

Interviewing can be a powerful tool for writing, bringing relevance and a directness to learning and recording. In a Year 7 and 8 class, students were exploring the controversy that surrounded the 1981 tour of New Zealand by the South African Rugby Union team (known as the Springboks). The tour had caused division in the New Zealand public, and even in families, as the opposing sides argued about the place of politics in sport. The following comes from an interview that the students conducted with a policeman who had been on duty during the Springbok tour of 1981.

Child interviewer: *How would you describe your involvement with the Springbok tour of 1981?*

Policeman: *Didn't enjoy it at all. Every time I put the riot gear on I knew there would be trouble and I didn't want to have to hurt anyone.*

Oral and written interviews were studied by this Year 7 and 8 class before inviting the policeman to the classroom. This interview supported the current curriculum learning (Social Sciences) as well as the learning around writing for this particular purpose.

Reviews

There are often opportunities for students at school to enjoy a live performance. At times these performances can be enjoyed for what they are, but usually there is an expectation that students will respond on an intellectual level, and be able to make connections to wider learning opportunities. I have observed students prepare for live performances (from puppet theatre to opera) through research and notebook jottings. The initial jottings are often framed as questions, as students think critically about what they expect to see. The notebooks can be taken to the actual performance and used, if appropriate, to bring jottings, noticings or further questions back to the classroom, for optimum learning from the experience. Children who have been exposed to this 'authorly' behaviour will inevitably bring the skill to aspects of their wider lives.

Response to events

A recent warehouse explosion in Hamilton provided a nearby school with the opportunity for meaningful interviewing of first-hand witnesses.

> *My mum was sitting on the deck having her first sip of wine when she heard a huge explosion. She looked up and saw the roof of the store rise into the air and smash down in a million pieces.*

Students wrote from their own responses to the explosion. They had all been close by and for many days the rancid smell of burnt cheese hung in the air. Jottings were made throughout the following days as students came to realise the full effects of the local tragedy.

Capturing memories

This will happen often in a classroom while students are telling their stories. Others will link to the story and make a jotting for future use.

> *I remember getting a shock off a fence and liking it so much I went back for another. I remember falling out of a tree and putting toilet paper up my nose to stop the bleeding.*

The teacher may direct a jotting for homework. Note that this is a jotting, not a finished piece. Students will need to be taught how to craft their jotting into a completed piece.

> *Ask your family to tell you any stories about you when you were very young. This could be a time when they thought you were lost, or about your special cuddly toy or blanket or as this teacher did:*

Ideas to jot down tonight ...

*Think for yourself, and talk with your parents and family about a **favourite** item that you **outgrew**. For example, a favourite piece of clothing, pair of shoes, toy, blanket, etc. that you eventually had to throw out, give away, or that just wore out! Jot down some words to:*

- *describe the item*
- *explain why it was so special*
- *describe how you felt/what you did when the day came that you outgrew it.*

*Choose something that you had until recently; it is really important that **you** remember it clearly so that you can write about it.*

Maddison made the jottings that follow and, from these, crafted her memories of her red dress, while on page 38 Yasmin recalls her doll, Jemma.

My ~~X~~ Red Dress
- Short puffy sleeved.
- red velvet.
- came down below my knee
- red satin went around waist
with tiny red and white flowers
- round neck
- ~~it made~~ felt like princess
special when wearing it.
- ~~wa~~ wore on special occasions
~~and~~ discos, and cristmas.
- anoyed and sad cause didn't
I wanted to still fit it.

My Red Dress

I remember wearing, for the first time ever, my dark red velvet puffy-sleeved dress. The red satin that went around my waist with tiny red and white flowers on it gathered it in.

Every party, Christmas, disco or special occasion I went to, you'd see me wearing it. Dancing around, it swung below my knees, swish, swish. Wearing it around the house made me feel like a princess.

I remember the day my Mum pulled it out of my drawer and said I couldn't fit it any more. I couldn't believe it. I felt annoyed and sad. That dress had felt wonderful. I loved how it was just like Dorothy's ruby red slippers. I just couldn't believe that this was the end of the memories that lived in my red velvet dress.

Maddison
Year 5

Jemma

I remember those plastic soft blue eyes turned purple by age, I remember her two small feet with tiny faint tooth marks well embedded in the plastic. I remember five thin fingers nearly chewed to bits. I remember the times when I used to take her in the bath with me, then have her hanging up for days.

I remember the day that she retired to the corner of my bedroom because I was throwing her up and around in the air, then I stumbled and lost my grip on her arms. She flew up and then she crashed in the corner of the room. A large black empty hole appeared in the side of her neck.

I ran to my room and laid her gently in the corner of my bedroom, then ran away, too sad to look at her.

Yasmin
Year 5

> **Ideas to jot down tonight ...**
>
> *Tomorrow we will be writing our explanation. Tonight, take some time and look at a can opener to see how it works. In your notebook:*
>
> - *sketch it*
> - *make a note of each part*
> - *how each part works in with the other parts*
>
> *I look forward to seeing your discoveries tomorrow.*

Homework jottings can also include students being asked to record their observations from their bedroom, from the kitchen window, of a sunset on a clear winter's evening, or of a common household appliance, which can then lead to factual description or explanation.

Another teacher directed her students to talk with their parents about the character they were writing about and to record an anecdote about the behaviour of that chosen person.

> *Aunty Jane hated sitting on the grass so when we went on picnics she would always bring her tartan rug. She would hold it by two corners, flick it into the air and lay it carefully down on the grass. She would then sit with her legs outstretched and hold her hand out for a sandwich* ... Year 7 student

Bits of writing you like

Until this becomes a habit in your classroom, you can ask students to have their notebooks on hand when you, or they, are reading. 'Jot down one snippet of text that appeals to you. Be prepared to share these later.'

> *She sat there majestic in her armchair, filling every inch of it.* – from *The Witches* by Roald Dahl

> *Her voice was full of money* – from *The Great Gatsby* by F. Scott Fitzgerald

> *A man in white gumboots fished with his rod set vertical in a holder, a single finger crooked over the line as if taking the ocean's pulse.* – from *A Land of Two Halves* by Joe Bennett

Gathering bits of your life

You may use photographs or other artefacts. For example, you might ask students to bring something 'old' from home, which would lead to rich talk and possibilities for writing in a variety of ways.

> *On Mum's wedding day, Granny wore different shoes. She was in a hurry.*

What people say

'Listening in' to the conversations of others or snippets of what we hear from others can be an inspiration for writing, even if it is tucked away for future use.

The words of a public figure could fire up a young writer to write an opinion, for example:

A politician: *America is ready for a woman president.*

or

A sports personality: *Get off the couch and kick a ball.*

Including the way a particular character speaks can enhance a character portrayal. The following reported speech jottings came directly from the teacher asking students to close their eyes and imagine their chosen character speaking:

'Nip downstairs and get us a beer from the downstairs fridge would you son?'

'Love you Courtney.'

She then invited them to add the quotation to their character portrait if they felt it would enhance their writing. Students can be directed to take their notebooks home to 'listen and record' snippets of speech, ready for sharing the following day.

Quick-write

A notebook is a place to put small scraps of time away where I can take them out and look at them whenever I need to remember.

Jean Little (1987)

A technique that Sally has found successful with older 'reluctant' writers is what we have called the quick-write. She shared with them an example text 'The street where I live', led some discussion about what the description provided, and then gave them six minutes to write non-stop about their own street. The results astounded the teachers and the writers themselves. Previously they had not had pleasure or success from writing and in less than ten minutes they had drafts of substance and satisfaction, if somewhat raw and revealing. The 'stuff of their lives' was the fodder for their writing and many had not known that before.

The example text Sally used is from Keith Waterhouse's *There is a Happy Land* (1964):

> *Just remembered, suppose I ought to tell you something about where we used to live. Well you know these big housing estates, well it was one of them. They were right wide streets with like big grass verges and that. We'd only lived there since just before I was born. It was all new, and even now they were still building bits on it all over the shop ... we used to go down there on Saturday afternoons. There were splashes all over the walls where we'd been throwing mud balls, and all the fences had footmarks where all the kids from the catholic school had been seeing how high up they could kick.*

And from a twelve year old student:

> *The street where I live it's full of graffiti all over the fences. The graffiti was put there from the street people. All the tyre marks on the ground are from the people who do donuts all over my street. There are people going around kicking your rubbish bins over.*

The description from Keith Waterhouse was deliberately chosen as one that showed 'kids being kids'. It may have been set in a different time, in a different place, but it is the empathy with the narrator that strikes a chord with students.

Moving from jottings to a crafted piece – from the notebook to the draft book

We need to guide students in how to take their jottings into prose or poetry. What the child wants to say will be the first priority, followed by the form that will best suit the idea. This process needs to be modelled, articulated and scaffolded by teachers until the student can work the process independently.

The child's notes from observing the spider's web became a simple description, a factual account of what was observed with some very deliberate use of literary devices, such as repetition to enhance the telling. It was not merely a repeat or a tweaking of the notes, but a considered crafting into a piece which says exactly what she wants it to say. This young writer demonstrates a developing control of her writing as she shapes her descriptive piece.

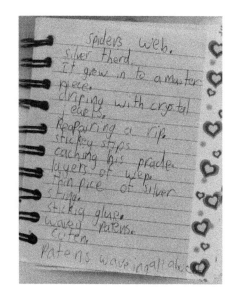

Often in schools I see students being assigned writing topics around a focus genre as the only approach to writing. 'This term we will be *doing* explanations.' It is hardly an invitation into the wondrous world of the writer ... everything is determined by the teacher with no purpose or reasons given. This single approach most often puts the genre, or form, ahead of the content and purpose. With the writer's notebook, however, the content usually determines the form the writing will take. Students start with an idea in their notebooks and then decide what form they might use to express or develop that idea into a polished piece of writing. This then gives the teacher a lead about what form needs to be taught.

Shiny sticky.
Waving about.
Invisible.
The spider hangs on
waiting
waiting for his prey.
Pieces of cotton
hang around.
Legs spring out as he
slides along.

I was in Sheryl May's classroom one morning when a student came rushing up to Sheryl.

> Student: *Ms May, Ms May, I want to write an obituary.*
> Sheryl: *So?*
> Student: *Oh! I need to find a model don't I?*

This exchange told me a lot about what was happening in this classroom of students, who were well down the track of independence. This student had recorded in his notebook about the death of the class budgie that: 'Bluey was lying on the bottom of his cage this morning'. In deciding how he would develop this seed of an idea into a developed piece of writing, he had decided that an obituary would suit best. Unsure of the form of an obituary, he knew that he needed to find out how an obituary is put together. That was the cue for Sheryl to do her exploratory work into obituaries. Where do we find them? What is their purpose? What are the features of an obituary?

This became a class focus into the genre of obituaries and Sheryl used the notebooks to explore the genre. Examples were found in the local newspaper and together the class explored the texts. Having annotated an obituary about a rather controversial celebrity, students noted that this form of writing, besides the facts, actually brings in a large amount of opinion, and also the descriptive elements of character writing. These students were learning that real-life writing is often a combination of forms and that the purpose is of utmost importance.

Later that year a student was tragically killed outside the school gates and the obituaries were transformed into eulogies for their classmate. The real and urgent need for writing in the obituary form had heartfelt significance for those students.

We will not have notebook entries behind all of our writing. Reasons to write and possible topics emerge constantly, especially when a teacher is providing a language-rich classroom for students, raising issues and 'scratching the itch', as Nancie Atwell (2002) describes a teacher's deliberate act of creating interest in a topic. Sometimes the purpose for writing, such as an assigned task, a class focus, or a special event, dictates the content and form. However, when learning about a particular genre, the notebook can be searched for seeds of ideas alongside new entries being created for the purpose. What is gathered in the notebooks will reflect the genre being studied at the time. If persuasive essays are a focus, the entries will be around topics that we feel strongly about and might include quick-writes, personal responses, interviews, questions, and wonderings, as raw material for writing persuasively.

Finding significance

Lucy Calkins, in her latest edition of *The Art of Teaching Writing* (1994) shares her development as a teacher of writing:

> *This is how I write. I take a moment – an image, a memory, a phrase, an idea – and I hold it in my hands and declare it a treasure. I begin by writing about my son's frayed blanket and end up realizing I'm suffering from empty nest syndrome. I once saw writing as a process of choosing a topic, turning the topic into the best possible draft, sharing the draft with friends, then revising it. But I've come to think that it's very important that writing*

is not only a process of recording, but also of developing a story or an idea. I now describe writing episodes that begin with something noticed or something wondered about. When writing begins with something that has not yet found its significance, it is more apt to become a process of growing meaning.

In my classroom, I helped students to understand that they were surrounded by hundreds of potential topics by sharing my own potential writing topics. Some as ordinary as having a pillow fight with my brother or describing the first buds appearing on the forest pansy in my courtyard. But what makes one topic stand out from another? What draws me to this topic? What is its significance for me? These are the questions I need to ask myself as a writer, and of my younger learner-writers. We can all see the difference between students simply telling something that happened to them and actually revealing something of themselves in expressing what it means for them. We have to support our students in finding that meaning, within any chosen moment or experience.

Teachers need to take the time to teach different strategies for finding entries to write in the notebook. We guide its use, lead students through processes for topic generation, present strategies that help them look at their world in a way that seeks out writing possibilities and we direct particular entries. But in the end, it is about developing independent writers.

Sometimes we write things of significance, sometimes we don't - it's the act of writing and the practice of generating text and building fluency that leads writers to significance. The act of writing in a notebook leads you from one thought to another until you too experience the writer's joy of discovering something you didn't know you knew.

Aimee Buckner (2005)

When we transfer our thoughts to written text, our writing is expressive - we are expressing ourselves in written form. Whether our subject matter is personal, fictional or factual, we often begin our written articulation as a personal response. It is the preparatory, or expressive, function of writing.

There will be opportunities for all students to write each day - and very often there will be more than one occasion where writing is required, particularly as children progress through their schooling. Preparation for composition may include one or more such activities, as talking, visualising, brainstorming, mind-mapping, listing, non-stop writing, and jottings. From their jottings, students will eventually become adept at choosing an appropriate form for whatever purpose the writing task presents. Until this level of independence is reached, the teacher will need to scaffold the learning experiences very deliberately. Gradually, we would expect to give more choice and decision-making to our students around their writing.

Draft writing

Sometimes in the learning process the draft writing will be structured with the framework or scaffolding provided by the teacher, or co-constructed between teacher and students (see Chapter 10 - *Writing across the Curriculum*). We need to be mindful that writing involves exploring a subject, gathering and linking ideas, noticing things and making discoveries. Just as a personal memory can be recalled in expressive writing, so too can the responses, observations and investigations from a social studies or science lesson.

Our job is to ask questions of children so they internalise those questions and ask them of themselves and their emerging drafts.

Lucy Calkins (1994)

When used daily, for a multitude of written tasks, it is draft writing books that provide us with a continuing source of data, as we check what is written, and provide specific feedback to support our learner-writers. In each student's draft writing book, we should be able to see evidence of the following:

• Regular entries: we need practice to improve.

• A variety of purposes for writing with a variety of forms to suit the purpose.

- Student editing, crafting and self-correction:

  Students will need to be aware of the expectations, for example:

  - *Underline the words in green pen that you think may need to be checked for spelling, and work on three*
  - *Read through your work to see if you have used the words that say exactly what you mean – do you want to change any?*
  - *Does it say what you want it to say?*

- Specific feedback, for example: the teacher writes in margin: 'I see you have thought about <u>imagery</u> here – using a <u>simile</u>. It works well. Let's talk about using <u>strong verbs</u> in your <u>descriptive writing</u>, to see how they can help with the <u>image</u> you are providing the reader.' Or 'I got a good picture of Nana wearing her spotted shirt from your description.' This feedback concentrates on the *deeper features* of the writing.

  Or: 'You have used capital letters and full stops in all the right places today – we'll talk about speech marks tomorrow.' This feedback is concerned with the *surface features*.

- Examples of studied texts (models) for frequent reference, for example: 'Glue this piece into your draft book – we will be exploring how the writer has structured this piece …

  Turn back to the model we looked at last week when we were talking about structure. This writer has used a variety of descriptors. We will be identifying what she has used …'

Summary – *From the Head to the Page*

- A notebook helps students to become independent writers.

- Notebooks are seedbeds for writing – with a variety of seed ideas.

- Notebooks lead us to behave like authors.

- Teachers model the use of the notebook alongside students.

- Authors record noticings, observations, wonderings, opinions, ideas, responses to life events, and to literature.

- Younger writers need to be supported to own and use notebooks.

- Draft books. Daily writing: a place to grow and craft our ideas, and a record of our progress.

4 Personal Expressive Writing
I've got something to say

Experience is the only thing we share equally.

Martin Amis, *Experience* (2000)

We all have stories to tell

One of the requirements for all teachers who enrol on my writing courses is to complete a pre-course task of writing a childhood memoir. Teachers arrive armed with their personal stories, ready to share. Probably there have been many of those teachers who felt, as I did once, inadequate and unsure of their own abilities as a writer. But by the end of the week, those same teachers leave feeling rightfully proud with a collection of their own writings, and those of their peers, bound in a precious anthology of memories, observations, descriptions and viewpoints. They return to their classrooms determined to lead their students into discovering their own authorship, and with a greater understanding of the process that learner-writers, of any age, go through. The reasoning I use in deciding what we will write about as a pre-course task, and the subsequent writings we do during the week, is simple. We write best about what we know - and we all have stories to tell.

The stuff of our lives is a great cargo and sometimes it is heavy. Teachers and children need to bring those cargoes to school because it is by reading and writing and storytelling, musing, painting and sharing that we human beings find meaning.

Richard Wilbur (1988)

As we greet a new class at the beginning of a new school year, we begin our relationship as coach of a team of writers. From the start we want to instil in our youngsters an expectation that we are all writers, or learner-writers, and that we all have a wealth of things to write about. We all have personal stories: pieces of our lives that are worthy of recording.

One young teacher, who knew a thing or two about the power of suggestion, was voicing similar sentiments to her class at the beginning of the year, 'We are going to love writing this year. We will be writing a lot about our own experiences and what is important to us. We've all got so much to write about ... only trouble is that we have only got two hundred days!' She wanted them to know from Day One that the only prohibitive aspect to their developing into credible, independent writers was a lack of time in which to record the myriad of stories they had to tell. She certainly set the scene by clearly expressing her beliefs and expectations; writing began in earnest on the first day.

What we do with our experiences may differ: novelists may draw on their experience to write about imagined lives and places, conversationalists may draw on their experience to entertain; friends may catch up on each other's lives, exchanging news of remembered events. By asking our students to draw on personal experience, we infer that they have lives worth recording. The life of each and every one of our students is valuable, and so are the incidents, thoughts and feelings within them. When children write simply and honestly from their own experience or concerns, they develop a personal voice and sincerity. Our children need to have

We can't give children rich lives, but we can give them the lens to appreciate the richness that is already there.

Lucy Calkins (1991)

It all begins inside; inside the heads of our kids. There are ideas in there and language and lots of possibilities. Writing is a pulling together of that inside stuff. Writing is a rehearsal in meaning making.

D. Kirby and T. Liner with R. Vinz (1988)

awareness that they all have a wealth of personal experience to record. Not only do they need to develop a consciousness about the number of writing topics available to them from their own lives, they need to be aware that by reflecting on their experiences, they can find significances within those experiences: making more sense of themselves and the world they are part of.

Territories for writing

Nancie Atwell, in her book *Lessons that Change Writers* (2002), talks of 'territories for writing'. These territories can be our prompts for having something to say about a particular topic, and are the things we would expect to see jotted down in a notebook. They may include vignettes (otherwise known as snapshots, moments in time, or slices of life) that can be developed into memoirs – remembered moments of our lives or people we have in our lives; or everyday aspects of life – the sort of things that we might have on our mind on any chosen day; specific issues that we have been thinking about, and so on. A list of writing prompts will change over time – what is pressing to us one day will seem insignificant on another. A personal memory that is triggered by something today may lie undisturbed for another year or two. If we examine the sorts of things that pop into our minds, we see that they can be categorised: some of the things we think about are deeply personal and seem relevant only to ourselves (Grandma, my new shoes, when my cat died); some involve our immediate surrounds and our place in them (a recent parent interview, the local garden centre); others entail details of a geographically wider sphere (a newspaper report, the town where I grew up); and yet others take our thinking to global terms (the country I would love to visit, the plight of refugees). These territories can be paralleled with our own development; our world gets bigger as we go along. As we mature, we can relate to a number of things in the wider world – and beyond – but that doesn't mean that the stuff of our personal lives becomes any less significant. We simply encompass more.

Leading students to topics worthy of writing

If we accept that the number of 'territories', or prompts for writing that we hold in our heads are numerous and inevitable for every one of us, then we need never be in that place of dreaming up topics to get our young writers started.

When we assign topics we create a welfare system, putting our students on to writers' welfare.

Donald Graves (1982)

What we do need to do to ensure that children aren't left wondering which piece of their life to record, is to lead them in *selecting a topic*, and then support them in *tapping into the significance* within their selected topic. If we are to be responsible for leading our students to recall a particular aspect of their lives, then we must also accept responsibility for leading their thinking towards what is meaningful.

A simple illustration of this guidance comes from my experience of sharing a favourite picture book: *John Brown, Rose and the Midnight Cat*, by Jenny Wagner (1980). This book can be enjoyed on a number of levels, the simplest being that of relating to the companionship that can be enjoyed by owning and caring for a pet. After reading the story, teachers can prompt personal connections for small children through their questioning, to elicit what the children know about animals kept as pets. Even if they have never had one of their own, there would be few, if any, small children who have not experienced a dog or a cat up close.

Teachers can relate their own personal experience of a pet they have had, or have known, voicing specific details of what it looked like, how it behaved, or an anecdote about the creature. There is no recipe for telling stories, questioning, or simply talking with small children – we must rely on our desire to relate to them in a warm, affable way on an emotional level, as well as being mindful of the opportunities for challenging their thinking and extending them in their intellectual development. I have found that the more we practise conversations with children in a classroom setting, and notice the effect of the words we choose, not only does it become easier and more natural, it becomes second nature for us to frame our questions and thoughts in such a way that we connect those children with their own questions and wonderings – about whatever topic we wish to discuss.

It is essential to notice when the conversations we may have (about a pet or anything else) is one that is an end in itself, or one where we need to seize learning opportunities. In the case of *John Brown, Rose and the Midnight Cat*, if I am intending to use the story as a springboard for writing, my personal stories that follow become consciously detailed, to prompt what the children know about, for example, the feel of a cat's fur, the shape a cat makes as it settles on a chair, and so on. In other words, I see my job as supporting those children to notice the details of their own experience by my own voicing of the sorts of things I notice. If I am successful, the children before me will all be able to recall their own 'cat story' or details of a pet they have had contact with. They, in turn, can then talk about the details with one of their peers. This oral storytelling will be their pre-writing preparation as they choose the words they need to tell their story.

This is what I remember of one such conversation:

Teacher: *Sometimes my neighbour's cat comes into my kitchen. I'm sure he knows he's not supposed to be there. But he strolls in as if he owns the place, with his tail pointing high, and his soft cat paws padding across the slate. He sometimes even dares to leap up onto the bench.*
Student: *My cat does that! Mum shouts at her and the cat takes a giant leap to the floor and gets out!*
Teacher: *Cats can leap a long way, can't they? Does your cat make a noise as she dashes out?*
Student: *No – she just disappears. She's noisy if she sits on you though.*
Teacher: *What sort of noise does she make?*
Student: *She starts to purr.*

Teacher: *She must be happy. Tell me about the purr.*
Student: *It starts off small, but gets louder and louder. It's like an engine.*
Teacher: *Oh, I know what you mean … that rumbling in the throat.*
Student: *Yeah - it's like a rumbling engine and I can feel it too. It's like I've got something vibrating on me.*

The student who had become so engaged with recalling the behaviour of her own cat was able to describe sounds and movements with some precision. This led to a wider discussion as other students recalled their experiences with animals. They questioned each other, in the way I had questioned this student, to get more details, and by the time they went to write, they were clear about the words that would convey what they meant to say.

There is an underlying theme of jealousy in the story of John Brown, and it is this theme that may be explored with older children. I demonstrate how a reader responds to the message of the story by sharing my own thoughts and responses. I demonstrate how a story might prompt my own thoughts or wonderings, or trigger a personal connection as I empathise with the characters from the story. My students will be encouraged to share their own thoughts, as they will be expected to have a response of some sort. Again, these thoughts, once voiced, will be preparation for writing down what they have to say about the topic. I use this illustration as just that, an isolated example. What we find as prompts for writing, and how we might help our students to tap into their own list of writing territories will have many possible starting points - a picture book may well be one of them.

Finding significance in our experiences

Once we have raised a topic, or prompted some connections for students, it then becomes our job to explore the significance. Nancie Atwell (2002), who describes so well the 'So what?' aspect of any piece of writing, talks of 'scratching the itch'. Sometimes we have to provide that itch, the topic for thinking, talking and writing that will capture their interest and involvement. But if we simply raise a topic, and expect children to write about it, we will undoubtedly leave those learner-writers in hollows, with no real connection to the topic and unsure of what their readers will want to hear. The itch needs to be scratched, and we need to guide our young writers to actually care about the topic they have been led to. If we believe that we write best about what we know, then it will follow that we will be keen to write about what we care about.

A young friend of mine was working on a writing assignment, developing a persuasive argument around a local issue: open cast mining. It was clear that she was struggling to get started. I asked her if she needed some help with structuring a persuasive piece, or if she wanted to talk about the language features we would expect to find in written argument. She neither needed nor wanted any help - it appeared that she was fully aware of the structure of a persuasive essay, and the features that would be effective. The sticking point for her was simply the topic - open cast mining was not a concern she had any strong feelings about.

Yes, we do need to have students write around the same topic for common learning needs, but we also need to spend the time hooking the students into the topic until they feel something for it. In her eyes, this student had been provided with a subject that had failed to prompt an itch worth scratching. Further exploration of the subject from a variety of angles may well have led her to care deeply about this very same issue. Not only would that include research of facts and opinions, but it would also include a personal emotional response as local writer, Jan Bradley, demonstrates in her poem - in this case an adult response for an adult audience.

Waitekauri Mine

These tall hills,

green clad, bush masked,

stand in silent attention.

as mid-wives, old in lore,

steeped in experience,

watchfully they monitor.

A private theatre

for this hillside

wracked

by contractions.

Now stripped and shaved,

obscenely exposed,

she lies contorted;

outstretched,

as the men

with lights and equipment

penetrate and probe,

excavate and extract;

inducing her to produce.

(Jan Bradley 1992)

I can recall my own memories of required essays from secondary school. If we are to write about the relationship between Hamlet and his mother, we must be guided to the position where we care about these characters. So, at all levels, whether talking with five year olds or leading discussions with secondary students, we teachers need to be attentive to the kind of talk that engages students in seeing some relevance to their own lives as they ponder and examine the words and thoughts of others. It is unrealistic to expect that all human beings are interested in the same sorts of topics, but we all know of teachers who have a passion for a particular subject and are successful in conveying the passion they feel, to bring their subject alive for their students. As teachers of writing, we need to bring a passion to our subject.

Sally showed me some pieces of descriptive writing that her Year 8 students had produced. The pieces described peeling an orange, hardly a gripping topic for adolescents. The success of the pieces could be attributed to the way 'the itch was scratched' for those students. They had been introduced to a deliciously sensory piece of writing from a local magazine, which used a description of removing the skin from an avocado to seduce the readers into thinking that an avocado was the most desirable fruit imaginable. The teacher shared the piece with her students and conveyed her own interest in the way the piece had been put together to achieve the effect it had. Unsurprisingly, her students were equally impressed, and managed to identify many features that the writer had employed for deliberate effect. They had a clear learning focus within the exercise, and were, without exception, keen to try the strategies that the published writer had used to describe a simple and familiar action – peeling an orange.

> *An avocado is held in both hands. Fingertips press gently around the eye of the stalk to check that the flesh yields. A small sharp knife splits the avocado from end to end. A firm twist eases one half of the fruit from its large glossy pit. The pit is reluctant to leave its buttery cradle. A sharp-pronged fork insists. The halved fruits are laid on a plate and their alligator skin carefully peeled back, exposing soft, green velvet.*
> Food by Lois Daish (in *The Listener*, 1996)

... and from Tracey, a Year 8 student:

The orange sits lonely on the glassy white plate, its only company its shadow. Picked up and stabbed with the sharp blade of a knife and sliced into quarters, it reveals a deep scar in no time flat. The thick skin is like leather being peeled off. As soft as velvet, the white flossy pith is left frayed and free to dangle. Orange flesh is exposed. Pressing down gently, fingers rip the orange into separate segments; little juice cells break and juice dribbles out, leaving a small, shrivelled piece of skin. Each segment drops helplessly, bruising the divine fruit.

Many children have been labelled as 'reluctant' writers, and many teachers have recalled dilemmas when a student grumbles, 'I don't know what to write about'. When children are asked, repeatedly, on Monday mornings, to write about what they did at the weekend, there may be those who have been to a family wedding, or played a game of rugby, but it is inevitable that there will be cries of 'But I didn't do anything!' leading to 'I don't know what to write about'. Even for those students who do have a starting point, I have found that unless we support them in finding the significance within the past experience, we run the risk of getting a bland recalling of events, lacking in sincerity and voice.

It is generally well-meaning teachers who counter the dilemma by *providing* a starting point: a 'story starter'. But this well-meant intent often leads to unsatisfactory results, as shown in the accompanying piece. This young writer quite possibly has never experienced sweat pouring down his face but has made an attempt to imagine what might have been happening to have caused it. And he was in quite a hurry to get to the end of the task. The resulting piece does not have the credibility of personal experience. When

The sweat was pouring down my face because I was raning in a race I was caming first and the girl that was behind me was about two steps behind me. There was about two cups of sweat that was puring down my face. When I got home I had a nice hot Shower and when I got out I falt nice and fresh again. Hay Ha I have got no Sweat runing down my face Ha Ha Ha That is the end of my story!

Boy, Year 6

talking with the teacher about the results of the 'story-starter' lesson that gener-ated this piece, we agreed that to have sweat pouring down our faces may be exag-geration – and there are ways that would provide a more relevant starting point for the young writers.

I introduced this class to Patricia Grace's story 'Beans' (1980). In this short story, we get to know the young boy narrating his experience of getting himself to rugby on Saturday mornings in winter. Being written in the first person, with a conversational, credibly childlike voice, we get to know him as a person, not just learn about him. Here we have another example of the importance of fiction in which we can immerse our students, providing that 'connection with others'. (See Chapter 2 – *The Writing Classroom*.)

The way the narrator in 'Beans' describes playing hard provides a short piece of text that students can empathise with, whether they are boys or girls, rugby players or not. To 'really go for it' is a common experience, one that we can all recall from some point of our lives.

Readers (and listeners) comprehend the meaning of the text being read through a variety of strategies: visualising and making connections are obvious strategies that we draw on as we read this depiction of a boy 'really going for it'.

> *I can't wait to get on the field and get stuck into the game; I really go for it. I watch that ball and chase it all over the place. Where the ball goes, I go.*
> *I tackle, handle, kick, run, everything. I do everything I can think of and I feel good. Sometimes it's cold and muddy and when I get thrown down into the mud and come up all mucky I feel great, because all the mud shows that I've really made a game of it. The dirtier I get the better I like it because I don't want to miss out on anything.*
> (from 'Beans' by Patricia Grace, 1980)

In other words, we respond as a reader and as a human being, with the common-ality which that implies. Not only do we engage with the text on an emotional, responsive level, we can delve deeper, exploring how the writer has given her readers such a vivid, sensory image. Student writers can identify where the writer has included specific detail, where she has appealed to our senses, how the pace of the listing enhances the depiction of the pace of the activity. Through the opportunity to explore how other writers describe activity – which may or may not lead to 'sweat pouring down my face' – the writers who were initially provided with a story starter were then able to draw from their own experience, understand the significance within their own story, and write expressively to record how it was for them.

The results, which show the influence of Patricia Grace's writing, also display a sincerity that was lacking in their first attempts. The difference for them was to do with relevance and personal connections, alongside criteria to work to. They needed an opportunity to make a connection to something they had experienced, and then the opportunity to pull up the details from that experience, including how the experience made them feel.

A possible checklist for writers:

Checklist for authors ...
I have

- *a paragraph about playing hard*

- ~~*playing hard*~~ *I have not used these words*

- *included actions that show I am really 'going for it'*

- *included a listing sentence*

- *included how I feel about the experience (reflections)*

Even when it's cold and foggy I still love going to netball in winter. I put my team uniform on and have a hot milo before I go. When we get to the netball courts I start to warm up to make sure my body is going to work properly. Our coach makes us run around the courts and jump up and down flapping our arms. Then we go onto the court. I reach, stretch, dodge, mark, everything. I make sure I get the ball as often as I can. I love it the most when we win.
(Inspired by Patricia Grace)

Another common cry from teachers has been that the students who find the processes of reading and writing to be challenging will also develop reluctance to teacher-directed writing tasks. It is my belief that as teachers we can turn our students off the very thing that we are trying to foster and develop, quite unwittingly. Our first response is so often to comment on the lack of the writing's surface features of spelling and punctuation, thus being seen as the judge and critic, not as someone who is being communicated with. It is worth remembering that the essential feature of a piece of writing based on personal experience is the impact it has on us, the reader. Not the impact of misspelled words, which is a separate issue, but the impact of its sincerity, its sense of wholeness, the impact of the language chosen and the impact of its appeal to our senses. Just as we respond to personal experience, we respond to the experiences of others as they are recorded. It is human to respond to experience, however simple, and these responses are unique and personal. In our teaching practice, when we are successful in conveying a genuine interest in what our students have to say, they respond by discovering a renewed enthusiasm for finding their voices and a willingness to record what they have to say in writing. I find that many students who have not previously felt interest or success in their writing can respond immediately to such an approach and certainly do not deserve or need the title of 'reluctant writer'. Of course there are other factors why students are reluctant to write, but too often that term is handed out when the problem is with the teaching approach.

In a sense, all of our writing comes from personal experience – experience of relationships, events or actions, sensory perceptions, discovery of self, problems experienced or observation of things, places or characters. We may draw from reflections, responses, memories, wonderings and thinking critically. By expressing ourselves in writing, whether it is to describe an experience, state an opinion, explain how something works or state historical facts, we are helped to order our thoughts and clarify information about the topic. We become personally involved with the topic, making it mean something to us.

Sometimes expressive writing is eloquent, poetic or factually accurate immediately, as it is written. Sometimes it is in note-form: a list or a collection of ideas or key points. Sometimes thoughts are half-uttered, attitudes half-expressed. Writers can craft their expressive writing, shaping and re-working it to become a finished piece.

Sometimes the crafting will head towards a sensory, poetic text; sometimes a factual piece with a transactional purpose; sometimes including both – factual information expressed in a poetic, literary style.

The writing we find all around us includes a huge variety of purpose and form – very few examples of published writing, whether in books, magazines, bill-boards or brochures, bear much resemblance to the kind of writing that teachers often are at great pains to lead students to generate in a classroom. Calkins (1991) suggests that 'writers live their lives differently; in adopting the behaviour of a writer, using a notebook to jot down thoughts and responses, we will lead more wide-awake lives' (see Chapter 3 – *From the Head to the Page – The notebook*). If we truly believe that our students will become richer beings through being able to express their thoughts and their ideas, and record what they have to say in writing, we need to go beyond the traditional 'school writing' to writing that will have the most relevance in our daily lives. We need to help our students to understand that we write for a purpose, and we write for an audience – even if that audience is ourselves. The purpose of the writing, and the intended audience, will dictate the form that the writing will take. Whether we are describing the process of a scientific experiment or attemptng to capture the mood of a landscape through description, we explore ideas that suit the purpose of the piece.

Ultimately, we are working towards having a class of independent, strategic writers, or learner-writers, who know that they have a voice to be heard, know that they have something to say (on any number of topics) and know that they have the strategies a writer needs to draw on when communicating their message.

Independent writers will not only show independence in recording what they have to say on a teacher-selected topic, but they will be constantly and independently on the alert for topics worth

Personal expressive writing can be the seedbed from which more specialised and differentiated kinds of writing can grow - towards greater explicitness of the factual (transactional) or the more conscious shaping of the sensory (poetic).

James Britton *et al.* (1975)

writing about. They will know that they have something to say and they will set about finding the most appropriate way to say it. All of our teaching needs to lead to this point.

Summary - *Personal Expressive Writing*

- Teachers learn about writing by writing.

- We all have stories to tell - our lives are worth recording.

- We all have writing territories.

- Prompts for personal writing topics.

- Finding the significance in our experiences.

- Making connections for students.

- Working towards independent writers.

Appendix - *Personal Expressive Writing*

Guided Writing Plan

Model text: 'Beans' by Patricia Grace

Purpose for the lesson: Why are we writing today?	• We are focusing on ideas for writing, finding out what makes a connection for us. • We are writing to record a moment in our own lives as a 'vignette'. • Some of us have been dependent on others for topic ideas and selection and so our writing lacks 'voice'. We need to tap into the wealth of experiences that we all have, find the significances in them and bring our stories to life for our readers.
Resources	'Beans' by Patricia Grace. The 'bare bones' of the story.
What are we learning today? Long term learning focus: helping students extend ideas through including specific detail.	We are learning to look closely at the choices an author has made in order to involve us in her story. We are learning to *show* rather than *tell* in our writing in order to make it more effective.

Leading the learning
Lesson design

- Read the 'bare bones' (main ideas) of the story.
- Elicit response.
- Read the full story 'Beans' by Patricia Grace and students follow the text.
- Discuss - pull out the main ideas.
- Introduce the concept of effective writing by identifying what the writer has done:
  - How has she made it sound like a child talking?
  - How does she make it seem as if she is talking to you directly? (sense of audience)

- Which part stays with you?
- Do you get a picture of the character and the scene? What do we know about the boy?
- What tells us how he is feeling?
- What senses does the writer include?

- Discuss – identifying specific details.
- Look at the simplified sequence of events or the 'bare bones' (summary statements at the side).
- Direct students to the paragraph around 'playing hard'.
- Locate, identify and highlight in the text what tells us more about 'playing hard', for example, *I really go for it. I watch the ball* …
- Discuss why it is more effective than the 'bare bones'.
- Draw attention to the listing sentence – *I handle, tackle, kick, run, everything*.
- Ask students to remember participating in a game where they 'played hard'.
- Share their stories.
- Practise forming a listing sentence with their own 'playing hard' experience.
- Lead a visualisation to pull up the details.
- Share with a partner.
- Prepare for writing by co-construction of criteria for success (what needs to be included).
- Write.
- Peer response for effectiveness, checking with success criteria.

Success criteria How will we know that we have been successful? Co-construct with the students	The description of my playing hard in my game would include: <ul><li>at least three sentences to *show* I have played hard;</li><li>sensory words/images;</li><li>evidence that I have 'shown' rather than told;</li><li>a listing sentence.</li></ul>
Challenges for writers	<ul><li>to make decisions about what to include and what to leave out</li><li>to think about the cohesion of the piece: linking ideas effectively with appropriate sentence structure</li></ul>
Transfer to other writing	Link listing sentence to other genre, for example, explanatory writing where there may be a list of requirements, or report writing where species are listed. (Note some lists are nouns, some verbs and some are groups of words.)

Beans *by Patricia Grace*

I play rugby
I ride my bike
I play hard
I have a shower
I get a drink
The ride home is easier
I go past a pig farm
When I get home I eat lemons

Bare Bones

Every Saturday morning in the winter term I bike into town to play rugby. Winter's a great time. We live three miles out of town and the way in is mostly uphill, so I need to get a good early start to be in town by nine. On the way in I don't get a chance to look around me or notice things very much because the going is fairly hard.

I play rugby

I ride my bike

Now and again where it gets a bit steep I have to stand on the pedals and really tread hard.

But it's great getting off to rugby on a Saturday morning with my towel and change on the carrier, and pushing hard to get there by nine. It's great.

By the time I get to the grounds I'm really puffing and I know my face is about the colour of the clubhouse roof. But I'm ready to go on though. I can't wait to get on the field and get stuck into the game; I really go for it. I watch that ball and chase it all over the place. Where the ball goes, I go. I tackle, handle, kick, run, everything. I do everything I can think of and I feel good.

I play hard

Sometimes it's cold and muddy and when I get thrown down into the mud and come up all mucky I feel great, because all the mud shows that I've really made a game of it. The dirtier I get the better I like it because I don't want to miss out on anything.

Then after the game I strip off and get under the shower in the club-room, and sometimes the water is boiling hot and sometimes cold as any-thing. And whatever it is, you're hopping up and down and getting clean, and yelling out to your mates about the game and saying is it hot or cold in your one.

I have a shower

I need a drink then. I get a drink from the dairy across the road and the dairy's always jammed full of us boys getting drinks. You should hear the noise, you should really hear it.

I get a drink

The going home is one of the best parts of all. I hop on my bike and away I go, hardly any pushing at all. Gee it's good. I can look about me and see everything growing. Cabbages and caulis, potatoes and all sorts of vegetables. And some of the paddocks are all ploughed up and have rows of green just showing through. All neat and tidy, and not much different to look at from the coloured squares of knitting my sister does for Girl Guides. You see all sorts of people out in the gardens working on big machines or walking along the rows weeding and hoeing: that's the sort of place it is around here. Everything grows and big trucks take all the stuff away, then it starts all over again.

The ride home is easier

But, I must tell you. Past all the gardens, about a mile and a half from where I live, there's a fairly steep rise. It's about the steepest part on the way home and I really have to puff up that bit. Then I get to the top and there's a long steep slope going down. It's so steep and straight it makes you want to yell, and I usually do. That's not all though. Just as you start picking up speed on the down slope you get this great whiff of pigs. Poo. Pigs. It makes you want to laugh and shout it's such a stink. And as I go whizzing down the stretch on my bike I do a big sniff up, a great big sniff, and get a full load of the smell of pigs. It's such a horrible great stink that I don't know how to describe it. We've got a book in our library at school and in it there's a poem about bells and the poem says 'joyous'. 'The joyous ringing of bells' or 'bells ringing joyously', something like that. Well 'joyous' is the word I think of when I smell the pigs. Joyous. A joyous big stink of pigs. It's really great.

I go past a pig farm

It's not far to my place after I've taken the straight. When I get home I lean my bike up against the shed and I feel really hot and done for. I don't go straight inside though. Instead I flop myself down on the grass underneath the lemon tree and I pick a lemon and take a huge bite of it. The lemons on our tree are as sour as sour, but I take a big bite because I feel so good. It makes me pull awful faces and roll over and over in the grass, but I keep on taking big bites until the lemon is all gone, skin and everything. Then I pick another lemon and eat that all up too because I don't want to miss a thing in all my life.

When I get home I eat lemons

We have an old lady living next to us. She's pretty old and she doesn't do much except walk round her garden. One day I heard her say to Mum, 'He's full of beans that boy of yours. Full of beans.'

5 Tapping into Universal Experiences
Nurturing awareness

We have established that our students initially need our support while learning to tap into their experiences and to find significance in their memories. And through this focused support we expect that they will soon develop independent strategies for topic selection. Children need to know that they don't have to have been to Disneyland at the weekend to give them something to write about. All of our waking hours give us raw experience, often repeated in routines, but, nonetheless, a valuable part of our valuable lives. As we need to give them that support, it is useful to be able to draw on common experiences, and these are times when specific teaching can be put to a whole class.

Scientists assure us that retrieving memories is a normal function of normal brains. And with that retrieval comes a very personal perception of the moment recalled. Brain research has shown that normal memory retrieval involves not only facts but also all of the sensory perceptions that accompanied that moment in time. So we are able to recall sounds, smells and emotions along with the 'picture'.

For those of us attuned to 'noticing' things around us, it might not be difficult to recall a waking sequence with great clarity, but there are some of us who need that ability finely tuned. We need to remind ourselves to notice things – to take notice with all our senses – and to be able to draw the attention of our students to these. A friend of mine, who often shared the same route as me, would say, 'Gail – have you been to Hamilton this week? Aren't the alders through Matangi beautiful right now?' On occasions like these, I would sometimes have to confess that yes, I had been to Hamilton - twice - and no, I hadn't seen the alders; I would make a special point of noticing them next time.

Mornings

Exploring a model - retrieving a memory - using our senses - walking writers through a common experience.

Regardless of where we rest our heads at night, an experience common to us all is getting up in the morning. The diversity within that experience might be enormous, but the getting up is an essential part of being human. So whatever the surroundings, whatever the circumstances, whatever our mood and whatever the time - after sleeping, we wake.

With this assumption for all of our students, within the diversity that makes up our class, we can draw children into discussion about this common experience. This may take the form of sharing stories and anecdotes, getting the children to share with one another, or with the whole class. The teacher may invite the students to close their eyes and 'put themselves into their waking place'. Teachers who know their students will be aware that this isn't always a comfortable bedroom - and the surroundings should not detract from the value of the experience. As the children are encouraged to form the image of this place in their minds, the teacher can begin a 'walking through' process, confident that each student will be forming individual sights and sounds in their recollections.

Visualisation

Not all recollections are precise. Sometimes it will be specific colours and patterns of the wallpaper, at other times it may be an overall impression, but, with prompts, students will be able to focus on the various aspects of their mental image. This can lead to a description of the immediate surroundings, which can stand alone as a piece (see Chapter 8 - *Inside or Outside - describing the place*), or may be given a time frame: for example, the routine between waking and getting to school. Teachers may support their students to focus by talking them through a sequence.

The teacher introduces the process:

> *Think about waking up on a school morning. I am going to ask you to take*
> *yourself to the moment of waking up, entering the world again after a night's*
> *sleep, ready to start a new school day.*
>
> *I will talk while you form a picture in your head about waking; your picture*
> *will be different from everyone else's, so close your eyes - it will make it easier.*

After checking that everyone is ready, the teacher leads the actual visualisation, asking questions and allowing silent time between, for students to form their own images.

> *You have just woken up - and it is a school morning. Go back into that place,*
> *and just spend a moment feeling what it is like there.*
>
> *Be aware of your body - its position, how it feels. What covers you and how?*
>
> *As you look around, what do you see?*
>
> *Is there a window you can see out of? Maybe it's covered?*
>
> *How do you move? What do you do with the bedclothes?*
>
> *How do you feel about getting up?*
>
> *What are you saying to yourself? Or to someone else?*
>
> *What can you hear?*

... or similar. When you lead a visualisation like this it is important to keep the questions to a minimum, just enough to lead students to all aspects of their image without the clutter of teacher talk. It is also important that we do not give suggestions of what might be in the image. If the questions are carefully prepared and delivered with silence in between, then each student will have optimum opportunity to 'plug into' their own mind text.

As the students return to the present, I usually take one of two courses of action.

I might invite one or two students to share their mind pictures with us all, using similar prompts that were used in the visualisation. This supports other team members to clarify their own memories and to add details to the picture. The purpose of teacher questioning at this point is specifically to draw out the details while taking a genuine interest in the description that unfolds:

> *Tell us about your waking up Tom.*
>
> *Where are you waking up?*
>
> *What is the first thought that pops into your head?*
>
> *I know exactly how you feel Tom ...*
>
> *What is the first sound that you hear?*

Sometimes students surprise themselves with the information they are able to draw on and articulate. Students enjoy hearing what others have to say and the descriptions of a peer most often triggers new responses and memories in themselves. All students will be prepared and confident to write.

Alternatively, we sometimes move directly from the visualisation to the writing. As students return to the present from their waking place, they are given the opportunity to write down all they can recall, uninterrupted. I usually allow around ten minutes. This expressive writing may take the shape of jottings, phrases, a stream of consciousness, or it may come out in fully grammatical sentences. After this initial writing, the students are given time to share what they have written, in whatever form works for them. I call this a zero draft, a rehearsal for writing. We can provide specific feedback at this stage, as we conference with students.

> Teacher: *I see you've written 'dad yelling' here. What sort of things might you hear him yell?*
>
> Student: *Oh, things like 'C'mon! You're going to be late!'*
>
> Teacher: *Would you include the actual words you hear?*
>
> Student: *I could do.*
>
> Teacher: *How would that help your reader get an idea of what your morning is like?*
>
> Student: *It could help them picture it if they could hear the sort of things people were saying.*
>
> Teacher: *It could also spark off similar memories for the reader.*

As we learn to become writers, we are learning that the events of our lives can be drawn from memory and that we can create meaning in written text. Students need to realise the intrinsic links between reading and writing, and that as we can create meaning in writing, so too can we gain meaning from reading and understanding the writing of others. Both processes, of reading and writing, involve an interaction with text. Readers must engage with a written text, and interact with it in order to comprehend. Writers must know that they have something to say, and work through the process of deciding how best to say it, so that it is understood by the reader. When we support our students to see these links, we are helping them to 'read as writers' and 'write as readers'.

How other authors do it: exploring models

As well as 'walking students through' a visualisation process, where they retrieve a personal memory of such a common experience as waking in the morning, we can also introduce models of text that describe a morning sequence, drawing attention to some of the language features.

Monday Morning

This morning at what seemed about 3.00 a.m.,
Mum came into my bedroom and woke me up.
'Remember, school today.'
I didn't want to get out of bed,
so I lay there for a few more minutes,
staring at the misty fog that was wrapped
around the tall poplar tree outside my window,
looking like a great blanket of candyfloss,
hiding the towering hills,
blocking out the sun.

Everything was quiet,
except for Dad, who was making breakfast,
banging pots and pans around in the kitchen.
No birds singing,

no cattle lowing,

no sheep bleating.

Just an eerie silence.

Having kissed both my parents goodbye,

my sister and I stumbled down the rutted driveway,

on our way to the old corrugated iron bus shelter.

I looked around me.

Everything was sparkling with dew,

from the pale green grass crunching underfoot

to the delicate cobwebs hanging on the fences.

Everything still, beautifully still.

Finally, my sister and I arrived at the tiny bus shelter.

The fog was lifting, leaving a trail of clouds.

The sun came up from its hiding place behind the clouds,

showing itself to the world.

Birds started singing,

cattle mooing and softly communicating with one another,

sheep bleating.

Everything alive,

everything moving.

The fog had lifted.

The bus had arrived.

(Rachael Tombleson 1999)

This model has numerous language features, and one way to recognise what the writer is doing is to 'unpack' the text as written. This takes practice: learning to recognise how a writer has achieved a particular effect takes us beyond the initial response to the text. We have to become actively engaged in exploring the ideas and messages that the author intends. Sometimes this can be done in small chunks – as

we explored how Patricia Grace provided an impression of a small boy 'really going for it' in 'Beans' (see Chapter 4 – *Personal Expressive Writing*).

There will be times when it is useful to explore a whole text – a short story, a poem, a memoir. When we want to lead our students into a text, we need to ensure that they understand it. If we have provided them with a text that they can read themselves, this will involve a close reading and a search of the text for specific words and phrases, used for a particular purpose. If the text is too demanding for some students to read independently, we can support them by reading aloud and involving them in discussions around the meaning of the text. In either case, it is important that students have a copy of the text in front of them, to be able to interact with it.

For students who are able to read the piece, one way to effectively unpack what the writer has included is to introduce a 'Three Level Guide'. While this is a useful tool for comprehension, the resulting discussion from using a Three Level Guide with a whole class will enhance not only the understanding of what the writer meant, but also help the students to focus on the specific language features to be found. This could also be a starting point for teachers as they develop habits for eliciting deeper level thinking in response to texts.

The students read the text, and then go through the series of statements.

Three Level Guide:

Monday Morning by Rachael Tombleson

Literal meaning (we find the evidence in the text)

> The writer wanted to stay in bed longer.

> Mum was making breakfast.

> The writer had to catch a bus to school.

Inferential meaning (we read between the lines to infer what the writer has implied)

> The writer lived in the country.

> Everything seems quiet when it's foggy.

> The writer had a good relationship with her parents.

Applied meaning (we decide what the author might think from what has been said)

> The countryside is beautiful.

> Corrugated iron is useful for building bus shelters.

> The weather affects how we feel.

The Three Level Guide is designed to be a non-threatening comprehension tool, hence the use of statements rather than questions (see Appendix to this chapter). Students are expected to say whether the statement is true or false, and to be able to justify their response. This can be done orally as a whole-class activity, or with a group. For example, at the inferential level:

Teacher: *The writer lived in the country – is this true?*

Student: *Yes – it's true.*

Teacher: *How do we know that?*

Student: *It says there were trees and animals.*

Teacher: *Can you find a place in the text that mentions either?*

Student: *… the tall poplar tree outside my window …*

Teacher: *Mmm – anything else?*

Student: *There's the hills, then she talks about birds, cattle and sheep.*

Teacher: *Okay – so does the writer use the word 'country'?*

Student: *No.*

Teacher: *So she's giving us clues, using specific details in her description. She is showing not telling, creating images in the reader's mind.*

With the inferential and applied level statements, there is opportunity for deeper thinking as the students study the text and apply their own knowledge in interpreting the writer's meaning. Using this tool, or the levels of discussion we find in the framework of a tool like this, we are helping our students with the close reading and comprehension of the text.

We want them to see the links between their reading and their writing of course, so our objective will include supporting them to identify what one writer has done, and then having a go themselves, 'borrowing' the devices identified as they craft their own writing. In this instance, in an attempt to make things as clear as possible, students have been presented with a simplified version of Rachael's 'Monday Morning', including the key ideas, but not the details we find in the published piece:

> Mum woke me really early and I didn't want to get up. It was foggy. It was quiet except for Dad. He was making a noise in the kitchen. After we said goodbye, we walked to the bus shelter. When we got there, the fog was going away. The bus came.

We were keen to see if students could identify what the differences were, and acknowledge that there is the same sequence of events described, that it could be the same writer, writing about the same morning. They got it. One student, reading the simplified piece responded: 'I think this must be Rachael's draft.' The class discussion very quickly developed into an agreement that we were unable, as readers, to get an image in our minds from the basic detail provided in the simple version. We tried comparing one of the ideas:

> *It was foggy* becomes … *staring at the misty fog that was wrapped around the tall poplar tree outside my window, looking like a great blanket of candyfloss, hiding the towering hills, blocking out the sun.*

Students were able to see very quickly that the published piece includes many devices that help us to visualise the scene, as intended. The basic *It was foggy* may provide us with an image, if we make connections to what we have experienced ourselves regarding fog, but there is no clear image to be found.

The language features the writer uses, to describe the fog, include:

- personal response (the piece is written in the first person, and the writer is the one staring);

- use of imagery, appealing to the senses (the fog is wrapped around ...);

- strong verbs (staring, wrapped);

- use of simile (like a great blanket of candyfloss);

- use of present participles (-ing words: staring, looking, hiding, blocking);

- personification (fog ... hiding the towering hills);

- specific nouns (the tall poplar);

- selective use of adjectives (the misty fog ... tall poplar tree ... great blanket ... towering hills);

- variety of sentence structure - some phrases and some full sentences.

The result is a much more vivid, precise description than 'It was foggy.'

When we lead our students, deliberately, through a piece of text, helping them to notice what has been achieved, and how, it is not surprising that they will become more critical readers. They will be on their way to independence – independently selecting texts to read, independently drawing their own impressions and, as writers, independently selecting the best words and putting them in the best order, to say what they want to say.

Many other writers have written to describe a morning routine or scene, and some of these models of text can be shared with the class. Students will be encouraged to share extracts from their own reading that they discover. How does Patricia Grace describe mornings in her writing?

> *The houses sit on their handkerchiefs, and early in the morning begin to*
> *sneeze. They do not sneeze in unison but one at a time, or sometimes in pairs*
> *or threes, sometimes in tens or dozens. The footpaths and roads beyond the*
> *borders of the handkerchiefs quicken with the aftermath of sneezing.*
> (from 'The Dream Sleeper' by Patricia Grace 1980)

> *I walked out of the house this morning and stretched my arms out wide. Look,*
> *I said to myself. Because I was alone except for you. I don't think you heard me.*
> *Look at the sky, I said. Look at the green earth.*
> *How could it be that I felt so good? So free? So full of the sort of day it was? How?*
> *And at that moment, when I stepped from my house, there was no sound. No*
> *sound at all. No birdcall, or tractor grind. No fire crackle or twig snap. As though*
> *the moment had been held quiet, for me only, as I stepped out into the morning.*
> (from 'Between Earth and Sky' by Patricia Grace 1980)

> *How we hated Wednesdays. We always tried to be sick on Wednesdays, or to*
> *miss the bus. But Mum would be up early yelling at us to get out of bed. If we*
> *didn't get up when we were told she'd drag us out and pull down our pyjama*
> *pants and set our bums on the cold lino. Mum was cruel to us.*
> *Whoever was helping with the milking had to be back quickly from the shed*
> *for breakfast, and we'd all have to rush through our kai (food) and get to*
> *school. Wednesday was Mum's day for shopping.*
> (from 'It Used to be Green Once' by Patricia Grace 1980)

> *Woke early this morning into shouldered silence with light just signing in, and*
> *thought how it was, how it could be, to sit silent in a silent house, in a warm*
> *corner drinking tea. Just me.*
> (from 'Mirrors' by Patricia Grace 1980)

Student writing examples:

> *Sunshine sneaks into my bedroom. My eye lids flutter open. They don't want*
> *to be awake. I snuggle into my duvet. I want to stay there forever.*
> Boy, 6 years

'Love you Courtney,' whispers Dad at the door.

Agghh! Torture day. I hide under my duvet. Bang! The door slams behind my dad as he leaves for work. Next Mum gets up to make the lunches and breakfast. Here comes Jack dragging Mum's red and green sweatshirts that he goes to sleep with. 'Ching!' goes the TV button. That means Gregory is up. 'Courtney!' yells Mum.

Oh dear, here comes Mum. I jump out of bed and change out of my PJs and into my uniform. I walk into the kitchen like a zombie. I wish it was Saturday I say to myself, and then I wouldn't have to go to school. I hate school. I eat my cheese sandwich, pull on my black school shoes, open the door and step out-side into the freezing winter wind.

Girl, 11 years

Your students will appreciate some time to absorb the language power of the litera-ture shared, and can be encouraged to crib ideas to try in their own writing. They will begin to shape their ideas, crafting their expressive writing into completed, poetic pieces.

A Hiding Place

Exploring a model – retrieving a memory – using our senses – walking writers through a common experience

Hide and Seek

Call out. Call loud: 'I'm ready! Come and find me!'
The sacks in the toolshed smell like the seaside.
They'll never find you in this salty dark,
But be careful that your feet aren't sticking out.
Wiser not to risk another shout.
The floor is cold. They'll probably be searching
The bushes near the swing. Whatever happens
You mustn't sneeze when they come prowling in.
And here they are, whispering at the door;
You've never heard them sound so hushed before.
Don't breathe. Don't move. Stay dumb. Hide in your blindness.
They're moving closer, someone stumbles, mutters;
Their words and laughter scuffle, and they're gone.
But don't come out just yet; they'll try the lane
And then the greenhouse and back here again.
They must be thinking that you're very clever,
Getting more puzzled as they search all over.
It seems a long time since they went away.
Your legs are stiff, the cold bites through your coat;
The dark damp smell of sand moves in your throat.
It's time to let them know that you're the winner.
Push off the sacks. Uncurl and stretch. That's better!
Out of the shed and call to them: 'I've won!
Here I am! Come and own up I've caught you!'
The darkening garden watches. Nothing stirs.
The bushes hold their breath; the sun is gone.
Yes, here you are. But where are they who sought you?
(Vernon Scannell 1996)

In much the same way as we help children recall their waking moments, we can prompt students to retrieve a memory of the common experience of hiding. This Vernon Scannell poem has been used successfully with students from age five to fifteen, as a model of effective writing to evoke a personal experience. There are times when I have used the poem as just that – a prompt for a personal connection. In these instances, I share the poem with my students, and elicit an initial response, as I would with any text. My wonderings, or 'thinking aloud', would include reference to how I feel towards the person hiding, how my senses were stirred, not only with emotion, but with the sights, smells, textures and sounds, and as I share my own responses, I will be certain to invite students to turn to the person next to them and talk about how it made them feel.

At this point, I often tell of a personal experience – a memory that has been stirred by the poem. I share my personal story – and we must surely all have one – of a well-remembered childhood hiding place, the linen cupboard in our home. I relate the story of the game of hide and seek with my brother, with as much drama as I can muster, for it was indeed dramatic. Hiding in a linen cupboard can hardly be described as a life-changing event in one's childhood, yet if we are to be consistent with our resolve to support our students in seeking significances within very ordinary experiences, we can recall the drama of such an event by focusing on the senses that were stirred: the physical discomfort of being cramped in a small space, the feel of the wooden slatted shelves digging into my back, those same shelves scraping my tummy as I squeezed myself upright, the smell of freshly laundered linen, the sounds of the outside world as I held my breath, the darkness and the feeling of absolute panic as I realised that I had been locked in! As I relate my story, I include specific details – for I know, just as with written text, that the more clues I give to my audience, the easier it will be for them to create the scene in their mind.

After sharing a story of my own, I can walk my students through a memory that belongs to them. In my experience, there has never been a child yet who has not remembered what it feels like to be hidden. As with the morning memory, the students can be encouraged to recall the sensations that they experienced by carefully worded question prompts. It is not helpful to suggest sensations, smells or sounds that students may have heard; asking if they can hear someone calling 'Coming, ready or not!' will only serve to distort their personal image. Far better to ask if they can hear any sounds … any voices … What words do they hear? Students gradually learn to access their memories through visualising independently.

Students will be able to turn to the person next to them and tell them about their hiding experience. Partners may question the speaker, seeking more information to clarify the image provided. The speaker will be encouraged to divulge more clues as to how it was for them. By the time the students are expected to record their experience in writing, they will be clear about the content that they want to include.

There will be times when I want to use the Scannell poem as a model to learn about some of the deliberate techniques we can use, for effect. We can explore the text as a whole piece – *What images does the poem give us? What do we find out? What senses does it appeal to? How does it make us feel about the narrator?* and so on. We can also put the lens onto portions of the poem – to sharpen our skills of being able to identify just what the writer has done to create the image he did. For example, there will be agreement that the writer is successful in depicting that the hiding child is feeling uncomfortable in his hiding place, even though the word uncomfortable has not been used. Students can search the text, to find the words and phrases that the author has used to describe the discomfort:

> *Your legs are stiff, the cold bites through your coat;*
> *The dark damp smell of sand moves in your throat …*
> *Uncurl and stretch.*
> *That's better!*

Teachers can lead discussions where students practise being able to articulate how the selected words affect our senses. *Your legs are stiff …* is a simple statement, which provides us with the essential information. Our comprehension skills will lead us to visualise and make connections, if we know the meaning of the words. However, … *the cold bites through your coat …* is not a simple statement of fact. Here, the writer has used personification to emphasise the 'biting cold' that the narrator knows about and is asking the reader to feel. We need to ask 'Does this have more impact than simply stating 'you are cold …'?'

As teachers of writing, we are constantly seeking those published pieces of writing, regardless of subject matter, that have some impact. And, in turn, we seek those pieces of writing from our students that will have some impact. What makes this kind of writing compelling to read are the images provided for the reader.

Other stories that describe hiding may be shared. Ones that have been used successfully with older students include: 'A Special Stone' by Patricia Grace (1991) and 'A Summer's Day' by Elaine Crowley (1992), and there will be many others.

> *Tania ran round to the back of the house. There was a small space between the back wall of the house and the wood that had been stashed there. She squeezed into the space and lay still. She heard her father start up the car because they were taking Darron to the doctor. Darron was going to lose all his blood and die. She heard her mother go inside and begin calling her. Then Mum came outside and started looking everywhere. After that she went away. Some time later her father returned, then her mother came back and said: 'She's gone. I can't find her.'*
> *They began calling and searching through the house and under the house but Tania kept quiet and still. You went to jail for throwing stones.*
> *Soon the neighbours were looking for her too, searching their houses and calling her name. Her father went off in the car to look along the main road and her mother went into the house again, opening all the cupboards and calling. Later her father came back. 'Didn't see a sign of her. Asked people but no one's seen her.'*
> *'What'll we do?' Tania heard her mother ask. 'We'd better ring the police station.'*
> *It was quiet for a moment then Tania heard her father dialling; they were getting the police on to her now. She moved a little further along the gap behind the wood and lay still.*
> (from 'A Special Stone' by Patricia Grace 1991)

> *I ran away, around the corner into the alley. I climbed the hill and lay down in the grass that grew near the top of the wall …*
> *… I lay for a long time. It seemed a long time, anyway. It began to get dark. My mother would be looking for me, calling me …*
> *… Then I heard the whistle. It was my father, whistling the way he did to call me in. Then I heard him call my name. His footsteps came nearer. I could see him now.*

My sobs grew louder, each one hiccupping through my body, choking me so that I couldn't call out. He saw me and started up the hill. 'Thank God, oh thank God. I've looked everywhere for you.' He wrapped me in his coat and carried me down the hill. I clung to him and cried all the way home.
(from 'A Summer's Day' by Elaine Crowley 1992)

It must be clear that teachers of writing allow time for their students to actually write. We don't get better at writing if all we do is talk about it. While sharing stories and exploring models of text are an essential part of learning about writing, we must ensure that we plan time for the talking, time for the reading and time for the writing – every day. Teachers have to make professional judgements at which point they will provide the opportunity for students to record the memories we have led them to recall. The professional judgements must include:

- clarity of purpose – where am I going with this topic?

- components of the lesson(s) – students need a chance to engage with the text (a model or an orally shared story), make personal connections – and write ... we will explore the text in more detail during a reading session ...

- pace – how do I ensure they are all engaged with me for this thirty minutes?

When the first draft has been written, it is a good idea to allow the students time to share their pieces (see Chapter 2 – *The Writing Classroom – Responding to the writing of others*). Sometimes the writing is left there; sometimes it is appropriate to encourage further work, crafting and shaping into a finished piece.

Here are some student examples:

My hiding place is in my wardrobe. It smells like clothes. I feel cold wood. I curl up in a ball. I hear footsteps.
Boy, Year 2

Eighteen, nineteen, twenty
'18 19 20 ready or not, here I come,' my sister said. I was squeezed and squashed like a ball in my sister's playhouse. I was feeling stiff and sore. I was quiet as a mouse. I said 'Ooh'. I could hear my sister's shoes scratching on the

concrete. Finally she opened the door and gazed around. When she walked out of the playhouse and into the house I ran out and screamed, 'I won!'
Boy, Year 4

I am squashed into the wall with my heart beating fast. I can smell the rabbit I kept in here two years ago. People talk and yell as they get caught. Minutes pass and I'm still laying here. Still. Silent. The minutes feel like seconds. I can hear someone coming.
Whispering. Breathing. They are coming towards me. I can almost feel them walking. I am motionless. The cane basket is now poking into me. My heart starts beating fast again like my chest is going to burst. Beside me is a blanket. I quickly cover myself with it. I cannot feel anything except the warmth of the blanket. I see her peering in. She looks around a little while, then she walks away. The blanket saved me.
Boy, Year 5

Dark and creepy,
Black as ink
Rustling of the wind under your bare feet
Hear them muttering
'Where do you think he is?'
Smell the rat poo. Might stinky rats slink?
Breezes sweep
Gritty sawdust drifts
Settles on the hard cold floor
Floorboards creak
They're getting closer, but will they find you?
You mustn't speak.
Curled up in a tight ball to keep yourself warm
Muscles cramp
Uncurl
Stretch
Crawl out
But they have gone!
Boy, Year 6

There are countless universal experiences to draw from. Teachers should watch for models of text that describe everyday experiences that students will be able to relate to, as well as sharing personal stories that will act as springboards for student writing. The following examples are from published novels, periodicals, unpublished diaries and classrooms, drawing on various topics and experiences.

Friends and family

I enjoy watching my dad shaving. He gets any towel out of the cupboard, it doesn't matter to him if it's a good one or not, he still uses it. He ties it around his neck like my grandmother at the dinner table. He gets his shaving kit with razors and shaving cream and other bits and pieces in it. He gets an odd shaped brush and dips it into the bottle of shaving cream. He rubs it round and round and when his face is covered in the white foam he looks exactly like the man's beard who lives next door. Dad always starts from his ear then down and up to the other ear and he lifts up his nose and shaves his upper lip. His razor leaves a track like a motor mower until he shaves the rest.
(Chris H from 'Passwords' edited by J Rose and P Young 1975)

Dora and I had some grand times together before they were put a stop to. We chased about the streets, Dora clutching at her stockings as she ran, her red hair flying, urging me on to goodness knows what. The streets round our house were all quiet and cannot have held much excitement, but we were excited.
(from 'The Other Day' by Dorothy Whipple 1950)

School Days

Swimming Lessons

Now and then, but not often, when the day was warm enough, Mr McLeod took us swimming in the lake. I dreaded swimming lessons and always tried to come up with a sniffle or a sore leg that might excuse me from going.
It didn't matter how hot the day was, the water was always cold. If you tried to get in slowly, you couldn't; the stones would take you before you were ready. As you slid in, the icy water rose quickly to your chest and snatched your

breath away. I would try and float a bit, but it was hopeless and all I wanted to do was get out again. So with wriggly macaroni legs, prickly with goose bumps, I would stagger back onto the beach. My soggy woollen togs would be sagging almost to my knees. A driftwood fire and a melting moment from my lunch tin were the only things that could help a little to warm me up.
(from *Piano Rock* by Gavin Bishop 2008)

Illness

There's a sore at the top of my nose between my eyebrows, grey and red and itching. Grandma says, Don't touch that sore and don't put water near it or it'll spread. If you broke your arm she'd say don't touch that with water it'll spread. The sore spreads into my eyes anyway and now they're red and yellow from the stuff that oozes and makes them stick in the morning. They stick so hard I have to force my eyelids open with my fingers and Mam has to scrub off that yellow stuff with a damp rag and boric powder. The eyelashes fall off and every bit of dust in Limerick blows into my eyes on windy days.
(from *Angela's Ashes* by Frank McCourt 1996)

Home
My street

Just remembered, suppose I ought to tell you something about where we used to live. Well you know these big estates, well it was one of them. They were really wide streets with big grass verges and that. We'd only lived there since just before I was born. It was all new, and even now they were still building bits on it all over the place. Down at the bottom there were some new houses that no one had moved into yet. We used to go down there on Saturday after-noons. There were splashes all over the walls where we'd been throwing mud balls, and all the fences had footmarks where all the kids from the catholic school had been seeing how high up they could kick.
It was like that all over. There were big lawns all over with these little fences round, only most of the fences had been pulled up when we went chumping for bonfire night, and the lawns had all paths worn across them where people had been taking short cuts.
(From *There is a Happy Land* by Keith Waterhouse 1964)

Fast Food

Fish and Chips

Sometimes, but not very often, when we had been in town, Mum would say we could have fish and chips for tea. The fish and chip shop always had a big long queue, and there was a man wearing a white coat standing at the fryer. The woman who served us looked as if she ate more chips than she sold, and she wore a hairnet over her hair.

The shop was a long way from our house, so when we had bought the fish and chips, Dad would drive straight home as fast as he could. It was my job to hold the parcel, which seemed to get hotter and hotter on my knee.

When we pulled up at our house, Mum unlocked the door while Dad put the car in the garage. My sister and I wanted to eat the fish and chips straight-away, out of the paper, but Mum always liked to put a table cloth on the table, and even put mats and plates out, like a proper meal. My sister grabbed the tomato sauce from the cupboard, and I got the vinegar. Dad loved vinegar on his chips.

When the parcel was opened, it was steamy and smelled so good! Mum used to tip all the chips into a basket, and gently lift the pieces of battered fish onto each plate. Sometimes my sister and I would get a sausage or a pineapple fritter instead of a fish, and we would all have a little pile of chips from the basket.

Mum said it was nice not to have to cook and Dad said he was glad he would not have many dishes to wash. Everyone loved fish and chip night.
(by Sally Muir 2003)

Holidays

No matter how broke he was, Dad always got us away somewhere for the Christmas holidays. Mostly, we took the bus and went camping at this special beach spot. We'd put the tent up and cook on an open fire for a week or two. I learnt to cook all sorts on the open fire - chow mein, spicy fried rice with lots of garlic and curry, or whole fish roasted in silver paper on the hot coals. We spent the days swimming, fishing, walking through the bush, or just sunbath-ing on the sand.
(from 'The Blue Humber 80' by Jack Gabolinscy 1991)

Sensory perception

Just as you start picking up speed on the down slope you get this great whiff of pigs. Poo. Pigs. It makes you want to laugh and shout it's such a stink. And as I go whizzing down the stretch on my bike I do a big sniff up, a great big sniff, and get a full load of the smell of pigs. It's such a horrible great stink that I don't know how to describe it.
(from 'Beans' by Patricia Grace 1980)

I remember the smell of sea and seaweed, wet flesh, wet hair,
wet bathing dresses, the warm smell as of a rabbity field after
rain, the smell of pop and splashed sunshades and toffee,
the stable-and-straw smell of hot, tossed, tumbled dung, and trodden sand,
the swill-and-gaslamp smell of Saturday night ...
(from 'Quite Early One Morning' by Dylan Thomas, from THE COLLECTED STORIES OF DYLAN THOMAS, copyright © 1954 by New Directions Publishing Corp. Reprinted by permission of New Directions Publishing Corp.)

The seasons

That was Summer

Have you ever smelled summer?

Sure you have.

Remember that time

When you were tired of running

Or doing nothing much

And you were hot

And you flopped right down on the ground?

Remember how the warm soil smelled

And the grass?

That was summer.

Remember that time
When you were trying to climb
Higher in the tree
And you didn't know how
And your foot was hurting in the fork
But you were holding tight
To the branch?
Remember how the bark smelled then
- all dusty dry, but nice?
That was summer.

Remember that time
When the storm blew up so quick
And you stood under a ledge
And watched the rain till it stopped
And when it stopped
You walked out again to the sidewalk,
The quiet sidewalk

Remember how the pavement smelled
All steamy warm and wet?
That was summer

If you try very hard
Can you remember that time
When you played outside all day
And you came home for dinner
And had to take a bath right away,
Right away?
It took you a long time to pull your shirt over your head,
Do you remember smelling the sunshine?
That was summer.
(Marci Ridlon 1969)

This model has inspired many students at the beginning of a school year, and provides a satisfying alternative when recalling events of summers past – focusing on the senses aroused. Personal memories can be stirred from the commonality of experiencing summer, regardless of where we spent it. This framework allows the diversity of experiences to be articulated.

> *Remember,*
> *Lying on the couch*
> *Your clothes clinging to your hot, perspiring body?*
> *You raised yourself up on your elbows*
> *To catch the direct breeze from the fan*
> *You reached up and swept a strand of hot*
> *Sticky hair off your forehead*
> *Then sank back on the pillows*
> *Grateful for their support.*
> *That was summer.*
>
> *Remember,*
> *Diving into the icy fresh water?*
> *Moving your arms in an outward motion*
> *Away from your body*
> *Water pressure*
> *Forcing you to the surface*
> *Then Breaking through*
> *Gasping for air.*
> *That was summer.*
> Melissa, Year 8
> Inspired by Marci Ridlon
>
> *Remember that time*
> *When you spent every last penny on donkey rides*
> *And you got to ride your favourite*
> *Eleven times?*
> *And the smell of donkey droppings*

Mixed with the salt and the seaweed.
And on the pier you could smell
Candyfloss and toffee apples
And you couldn't have any
Because every last penny was spent.
That was summer.
Sally Muir
Inspired by Marci Ridlon

Summary - *Tapping into Universal Experiences*

- Sharing personal stories and anecdotes.

- Walking students through their experiences.

- Visualisation.

- Sharing of ideas written.

- Reading/writing links: exploring models.

- Specific teaching (close reading, Three Level Guide, language resources).

Appendix - *Tapping into Universal Experiences*

Hide and Seek

Call out. Call loud: 'I'm ready! Come and find me!'

The sacks in the toolshed smell like the seaside.

They'll never find you in this salty dark,

But be careful that your feet aren't sticking out.

Wiser not to risk another shout.

The floor is cold. They'll probably be searching

The bushes near the swing. Whatever happens

You mustn't sneeze when they come prowling in.

And here they are, whispering at the door;

You've never heard them sound so hushed before.

Don't breathe. Don't move. Stay dumb. Hide in your blindness.

They're moving closer, someone stumbles, mutters;

Their words and laughter scuffle, and they're gone.

But don't come out just yet; they'll try the lane

And then the greenhouse and back here again.

They must be thinking that you're very clever,

Getting more puzzled as they search all over.

It seems a long time since they went away.

Your legs are stiff, the cold bites through your coat;

The dark damp smell of sand moves in your throat.

It's time to let them know that you're the winner.

Push off the sacks. Uncurl and stretch. That's better!

Out of the shed and call to them: 'I've won!

Here I am! Come and own up I've caught you!'

The darkening garden watches. Nothing stirs.

The bushes hold their breath; the sun is gone.

Yes, here you are. But where are they who sought you?

(Vernon Scannell 1996)

Hide and Seek

In 'Hide and Seek' Vernon Scannell has achieved impact through –

- rhyme and rhythm – occasional rhyming couplet links words;

- 'putting the reader there' – providing clues and detail of what it was like;

- the sounds, smells, feelings – what your body was doing;

- written instructions in the second person (you);

- present tense for immediacy;

- direct speech/exclamation marks – childlike, adds credibility, heightens drama;

- use of senses (smell); cohesion: seaside/salty;

- minimal use of adjectives;

- omission of 'weasel' words – (It is) Wiser not to ...;

- concrete nouns: sacks, toolshed, feet, floor, bushes etc;

- abstract nouns: seaside, dark, shout, blindness;

- use of senses (touch) 'the floor is cold';

- strong verbs, showing cohesion – searching, prowling, whispering, stumbles, mutters, scuffle;

- use of senses (hearing) 'here they are whispering at the door';

- short imperatives, for impact (link to opening);

- use of senses (touch) 'Your legs are stiff, the cold bites ...';

- combining senses: 'smell of sand moves in your throat';

- 'show me, don't tell me' – we get clues about the dark and quiet;

- personification: 'the cold bites through your coat' 'The darkening garden watches' 'The bushes hold their breath';

- use of a question at the end.

To ponder

- Is the writer the person hiding?

- Why is it written as if it's instructing someone else?

- Can you feel the change of emotions – from determination to triumph to disappointment?

	Three Level Guide Hide and Seek by Vernon Scannell	
Level 1	*Literal*	
1	The person hiding decided to hide in the tool shed.	True/False
2	The others talked loudly in the shed.	True/False
3	The person hiding was glad to have a stretch after hiding.	True/False
Level 2	*Inferential*	
1	The person hiding really wanted to be the winner.	True/False
2	The others tried really hard to find the person hiding.	True/False
3	The sacks had been used to carry seaweed.	True/False
Level 3	*Applied*	
1	It is good to stay quiet when you are playing hide and seek.	True/False
2	Children can be unkind to each other when they are playing.	True/False
3	It is not safe to play in tool sheds	True/False

Hide and Seek: the bare bones

We played hide and seek. You have to call when you're ready. I was in the shed, under the sacks. The others looked everywhere. I heard them outside the shed but they didn't find me. It was dark. I stayed where I was in case they came back. I stayed there for a long time and I got cold and stiff. It was smelly. When I decided to come out it was getting dark and it was quiet. I called to the others that I'd won but I didn't know where they were.

How the writer may have crafted his ideas:

Raw idea	Crafted	Language Resources
I was in the shed, under the sacks.	The sacks in the toolshed smell like the seaside. They'll never find you in this salty dark. But be careful that your feet aren't sticking out.	*Putting the reader there:* - description of smell of sacks - abstract noun, with adjective, is poetic: 'this salty dark' - more detail of what body is doing
I heard them outside the shed but they didn't find me. It was dark.	And here they are, whispering at the door. You've never heard them sound so hushed before. Don't breathe. Don't move. Stay dumb. Hide in your blindness. They're moving closer, someone stumbles, mutters. Their words and laughter scuffle and they're gone.	- detail of sounds heard - cohesion: whispering, hushed, breathe, dumb, blindness, stumbles, mutters, scuffle - short imperatives: for impact; adds to the urgency and drama of the situation - 'your blindness' adds weight to the description of dark - present tense for immediacy
I stayed there for a long time and I got cold and stiff. It was smelly.	It seems a long time since they went away. Your legs are stiff, the cold bites through your coat. The dark damp smell of sand moves in your throat.	- added detail – legs are stiff - personification: 'the cold bites through …' - evocative description of smell - combination of senses: '… smell moves in your throat.'
… it was getting dark and it was quiet.	The darkening garden watches. Nothing stirs. The bushes hold their breath; the sun is gone.	- personification: 'The darkening garden watches …The bushes hold their breath …' - clues (show me, don't tell me' that it was quiet and dark)

Some ways that writers have described being **cold ...**	
It's cold ...	*Author*
Your legs are stiff, the cold bites through your coat ...	Vernon Scannell 'Hide and Seek'
The mountain air, misty and edged with snow, cut across my face and crept into my bones.	Sherryl Jordan 'Winter of Fire'
It's December and it's freezing and we can see our breath.	Frank McCourt 'Angela's Ashes'
... fog cruelly pinching the toes and fingers of his shivering little 'prentice boy on the deck.	Charles Dickens 'Bleak House'
Nipped by winter ...	Gareth Owen 'Winter Days'
... but that was at four in the morning when the temperature always dropped and his thin blanket failed to keep him warm.	Maurice Gee 'The Fire Raiser'
The winds announce it. *The leaves run and hide,* *Leaving the trees bare to shiver in The icy mornings.*	Kitty Garden 'Autumn'

6   Memoir
The polished lens of memory

Memoir as narrative

Most autobiographies are a series of memoirs. If they were merely a chronological list of events remembered, they would probably never get into print. There are the predictable authors of autobiography – the celebrities, who have led an extraordinary life – but there are also many written by people who have lived a life which is very ordinary. What makes their stories reach publication, and become eminently readable, is the way that the writers have recognised themselves, and the way they felt and reacted, in the most ordinary as well as in extraordinary circumstances. Other people's lives and their responses to the world interest us because we are part of that same world. We recognise sameness, even when the writer may have lived on the other side of the world and had quite a different upbringing from ourselves.

This recognisable sameness became a valuable instrument in leading a twelve year-old student of mine to becoming a fully paid-up member of our writing team. She had arrived from another school, and was evidently feeling something of an outsider as she observed the writers' workshop that was routine in our class: the jotting, the drafting, the sharing, the peer response, and so on. One day she decided that she too had a significant moment from her early years to recall in writing – a time when she had suffered the embarrassment of wetting her pants in the town's main street. As she tentatively offered a draft of her personal story and I began to read, I was instantly reminded of a published memoir of Maya Angelou I had just been

> *A memoir is not what happens, but the person to whom things happen.*
>
> Virginia Woolf (circa 1920)

reading. My student had recorded her own remembered event and had included the words *I felt so embarrassed.* I thought to myself, 'Amy now needs to know about *showing* rather than telling.' I reached for the copy of *I Know Why the Caged Bird Sings* (1984) – I always kept my own current reading visible and at hand – and turned to a description of a young girl wetting her pants.

> *I held up two fingers, close to my chest, which meant that I had to go to the toilet, and tiptoed toward the rear of the church. Dimly, somewhere over my head, I heard ladies saying, 'Lord bless the child,' and 'Praise God.' My head was up and my eyes were open, but I didn't see anything. Halfway down the aisle, the church exploded with 'Were you there when they crucified my Lord?' and I tripped over a foot stuck out from the children's pew. I stumbled and started to say something, or maybe to scream, but a green persimmon, or it could have been a lemon, caught me between the legs and squeezed. I tasted the sour on my tongue and felt it in the back of my mouth. Then before I reached the door, the sting was burning down my legs and into my Sunday socks. I tried to hold, to squeeze it back, to keep it from speeding, but when I reached the church porch I knew I'd have to let it go, or it would probably run right back up to my head and my poor head would burst like a dropped watermelon, and all the brains and spit and tongue and eyes would roll all over the place. So I ran down into the yard and let it go. I ran, peeing and crying, not toward the toilet out back but to our house. I'd get a whipping for it, to be sure, and the nasty children would have something new to tease me about. I laughed anyway, partially for the sweet release; still, the greater joy came not only from being liberated from the silly church but from the knowledge that I wouldn't die from a busted head.*
>
> (from *I Know Why the Caged Bird Sings* by Maya Angelou 1984)

Amy took the book, found a comfortable corner, and read. I kept an eye on her, and could see, quite noticeably, the flush of recognition as she took in the meaning of the selected excerpt. She returned, clutching the book. There was a glimmer of a smile on her face. 'That's cool, but it's sad,' she said. 'I know what she felt like. What happened to her?' Here was a teachable moment. We talked about the way the published author had described the event, showing her readers how it was for her – and without using the word embarrassed.

I explained about the author's technique of 'showing rather than telling', and we discussed together the effect it has on the reader. This was a monumental turning point for this student. When it was time for our Helping Circle, she visibly grew with confidence as she shared her own writing, and explained how she was going to craft the piece to take out the 'I felt so embarrassed' and choose words that showed, rather than told her readers how it was for her. She had been inspired by Maya Angelou – inspired in seeing that real writers share moments of their lives and in doing so provide feelings and responses we can empathise with, as well as inspired to try out a technique she had not previously been consciously aware of. The rest of the class applauded her, and she was well and truly embraced as part of our team.

It is unlikely that we will all have the time to devote to composing a full autobiography, which by definition covers an entire lifespan, or to lead our students into developing their own. However, by teaching the essence of memoirs, we will move students from their thin narrative attempts, or dreary personal accounts, such as in 'The sweat is pouring down my face' to exploring a remembered moment – realising why it is remembered, and capturing the significance within.

Personal writing that I see being composed in classrooms is often disappointing, disappointing for the writer and disappointing for the teacher. When children are just asked to recall events (remembering to include the 'who, the what, the where and the when'), there is little chance for them to see any purpose for the writing, and so they often view the activity as a school task that is to be completed solely for the teacher. Teachers often recognise the inadequacies of a dreary account but do not know how to lead students to more satisfying writing. At the same time, students who have not been shown how to draw from memory often recognise their own inadequacies beside effective texts. So how to develop and lead writers to compose effective text is the next question.

Memoirs do not need to be retrieved from a childhood of long ago. We don't need to reach old age before being able to write our memoirs. If we are of the view that it is only the elderly who dwell on moments from their earlier lives, I think we cannot be listening to what our youngsters are saying – what they bring with them every day to school. It seems to me that humans are intuitive about reaching for memories, and these memories, scraps of time that have passed, even if only hours ago, are triggered by any number of things: things that have touched us, things that others have said, sights seen, feelings experienced, stories read, and so on.

Memories triggered can lead to jottings in a notebook. They can lead to a perceptively drawn 'moment in time', or vignette. And sometimes, they can lead to a memoir, which is that memory developed into a personal narrative concerned with more than a moment. If we liken a vignette to a snapshot, then a memoir might be the written equivalent of a short film. In a memoir, the writer provides some background for the reader, enabling us to begin our relationship with the narrator as we imagine the setting, enough details for us to form sensory images, a sense of sequence that is easy to follow, and most importantly we will be able to see why the experience mattered to the writer. There may or may not be a whole sequence of events, but there will be significance in the moment that is the focus central to the story. It is these rich personal narratives that resonate for us, causing us to respond with recognition. Writers of memoirs need to know that they have something to say; they also expect their readers or listeners to have a response.

When we write from a personal perspective, in the first person, it does not mean that we ignore other characters: that 'it's all about me'. We can write about other people who come into the story, as many of our stories of 'I remember a time when …' have other people absolutely central to the account, but these characters, what they say and what they do, are described through the eyes of the writer. They cannot be in the minds of the other people involved, but can only describe what they perceive and how they react themselves.

The young writer of 'Dad Hates Carrots' knew about reaching into her own life, and her own memory, to share her observations. She knows that her recollections involve others, and she is able to record a happening that gives us an insight into the family dynamic.

Although everything that happens in these pages has truth in it, not every word is based on fact. I took my memories and rearranged them, filling in details as I went along. I do not really remember every word that I or others said so long ago. I do, however, know exactly how it felt and what we were likely to have said.

Jean Little (1987)

Her short piece gives us, the readers, a glimpse of a small, but significant, moment from her life, where she is the observer:

> **Dad Hates Carrots**
> *Dad just hates carrots so when we have carrots in our soup or in our gravy,*
> *Mum cuts the carrots up into little pieces so that Dad can't see them.*
> *But he does see them and last night Dad put it all on my plate and said,*
> *'Can I have some pud?'*
> *'NO!' he got back.*
> Melissa, Year 2

I have shared this piece from my own classroom with many teachers as it demonstrates for me the sincerity of voice of a young writer who has understood that her own life is filled with moments she can capture, record and share. It is satisfying in itself, and, in its simplicity, fulfils the criteria for an effective piece. I would not have suggested to Melissa that she develop this piece any further – I think she has succeeded in focusing on a few moments that demand our attention, demand a response from us. Within the space of a few carefully selected words, she has introduced us to three characters, put us in a setting we can recognise, provided us with the voices and actions of the selected characters, and through the selection of subject matter, has revealed something to us.

As our students mature, and our expectations include their being able to extend a personal memory into a rich narrative, I would begin to immerse them in effective memoirs. I would read to them and pose questions that would get them searching through texts. I would tell my own stories and invite them to tell stories of their own. As we search for meaning and sigh, cringe and laugh together, we find new meanings in our own stories.

In sharing 'Dad Hates Carrots' with teachers, discussion often flows around the development, over time, of this particular purpose. How do we lead students on as they mature, and what would we expect of a student-written memoir as they continue to develop expertise as writers? The following piece, which was published as a winning entry in a secondary school short story competition, is one that I have shared with many teachers as a model displaying all the qualities of an effective piece of memoir writing.

From the Back Corner

Winter sun falls in slanted rectangles across the worn green carpet and glints off the teacher's spectacles.

Someone has scratched 'Mr Ashford sux' into the wooden desk; I run my pen absentmindedly along the lines and curves.

There is a certain anticipation in the air that always goes with the last period of the day. Students tick off minutes until the final bell. They chat and check their watches. The teacher stands at the front, scratching chalk onto the blackboard, droning monotonously.

We are bombarded with words and numbers but the worst of the attack doesn't reach me, sitting in the back corner of the class. I begin colouring in the desk where the navy blue paint has been chipped off.

An air of accusation, a new sharpness comes into the teacher's voice all of a sudden. He is speaking louder, loud enough to invade my space in the back corner.

'It's always yabber, yabber, yabber all over the class, isn't it?'

He gestures violently around the room. 'It used to be a pleasure teaching sixth formers, but this is no PLEASURE!'

There is heavy emphasis on the final 'pleasure'; however his tone of voice warns us not to giggle. He glares at us over his spectacles.

'It's a right pain in the arse actually! So why don't you all keep QUIET and save your chatter for your own time. Think about it from up here, yabber yabber all the time.'

He pauses for effect and seems to be trying to decide how seriously we are taking him. The entire class has looked up with interest and a silence descends on the room. No-one dares be the focus of the teacher's wrath. Hearing him swear has knocked them back.

I am faintly amused.

'But sir, if we want to ask a question we have to speak,' reasons a scrawny attention-seeking student.

I wait, almost excited, to see the teacher's reaction. The class is still hushed; Mr Ashford is stuck for words.

As the silence grows longer, tension mounts like electricity in the air, everyone almost leans forward, they are so eager to see what will happen. Tension in the air ripples like the muscles of a lion waiting to pounce.

'And my answer to that is, after you've asked, you should shut up to hear the answer.' But the long pause has taken the edge off Mr Ashford's statement. In a way he has been beaten. He coughs and then resumes his stream of words and numbers.

One by one students relax again; they pick up pens and re-check watches.

I proceed to retrace the lines and curves of the inscription: 'Mr Ashford sux'.

Margo Baars, Year 12

Memoir poetry

While memoirs are written as a narrative, the essence of them – that reflective recalling of moments passed – can be captured in poetry. A memoir poem can reveal remembered scenes or events in fewer words, where the images might be fragmentary. These ten lines of a James K. Baxter poem evoke scenes of a remembered childhood as the writer mentions places, people and activities enjoyed. Its strength comes with the opposition it creates: having dwelt on things important enough to be remembered, they are then labelled as being 'nothing important at all'.

Adult readers respond to this memoir poem with sighs of recognition, notably recognising that the innocence of childhood contrasts with the self-importance of adult lives.

Writers need listeners –

listeners who will respond

with silent empathy, with

the sighs of recognition,

with laughter and tears

and questions and stories

of their own.

Lucy Calkins (1994)

The town was usual enough; it had
A creek, a bridge, a beach, a sky
Over it, and even a small tin church
I never went to. My brother, my cousins and I
Did what boys do – dozed in the hot
Schoolroom, made bows and arrows, dodged the mad
Boatbuilder, crept like rabbits through the black
Under-runners with a weak torch,
Burnt dry rushes, wrestled or swam
Doing nothing important.
('The Town Under the Sea' by James K. Baxter 2013)

It may be tempting to imagine that we need to be nearing retirement to appreciate this nostalgic looking back, or even to emulate the writer as we have a go ourselves. However, primary students introduced to the poem were more than able to find meaning and significance in the lines, and were also able to draw from their much shorter memories to reveal something of their lives in the same way:

Otama was usual enough; it had
A school, a hall, and even a small white church
With stained glass windows
That I always went to.

My brother, my friends and I did what boys do,
Climbed the trees, biked down the road,
And swam in the pool, playing tig with a ball,
Doing nothing important at all.

Robert Gregory, Year 7-Inspired by James K. Baxter

The waterfall was usual enough; it had
Water, a bridge, a path like a road and
Some rope to walk across between the hills.
And it even had three fish in a little pond nearby.

My cousins and I did what boys do –
Got wet, ran up and down the path by the waterfall,

Blocked the water into a dam,
Caught the fish with a bucket while trying to push
Each other into the water, threw stones
And played super sleuths.
Doing nothing important.

Ben Light, Year 4 – Inspired by James K. Baxter

The bush was usual enough
It had trees, a creek, bark, bugs
And even a dead rat.

My friends and I did what boys do –
Made huts, climbed pine trees,
Fell in the muddy creek,
Made swords and shields,
Dozed in the hot bushes,
Got stung by wasps and bees.
Doing nothing important.

Samuel Tanuvasa – Inspired by James K. Baxter

The beach was usual enough
It had sand, sea, a bridge and sand dunes.
It even had a playground.

My brothers and I did what kids do –
Made sand castles,
Buried each other in the burning sand,
Threw big chunks of rock in the sea,
Played on the playground,
Wrestled, raced with each other
And swam in the blue sea.

Tyler Leuta Year 4 – Inspired by James K. Baxter

The street was usual enough; it had
Houses on both sides, a bit of graffiti, parked cars, a zebra crossing
And a shop on the corner I always went to.
My brothers and I
Did what boys do – raced each other to the shop,
Bought sweets and ice creams,

Counted the cars on both sides and told each other jokes.
Doing nothing important.

Edward, Year 6

The museum was usual enough; it had
Old relics, paintings in oils, statues of people
I'd never heard of, glass boxes
you could see through
and even a café for the visitors.
My classmates, teachers and I did what schools do -
looked at everything we could see,
Wrote in our notebooks, posed for photographs with a statue,
Listened to the man in the uniform,
Doing really important things.

Paige, Year 4

Sometimes we are so successful in our guidance of children bringing sensory images to mind as they observe and notice and remember that their notebooks are filled with poetic descriptions:

Wind ... shiver with fright ... howls like a wolf ... echoing animals ... fade away ...
Tractors bouncing along, bunny hopping.
Big racing tractors speeding along.
Tears glistening on Mum's cheeks, Nan's house cold and empty. Quiet as a
grave.

If our students have managed to come up with these seeds of ideas, they will need support to see how they might craft the images into a narrative. If we are asking them to try producing free verse, then a list of images may be effective. A narrative poem will require more than a 'picture in words' - it will tell a story, allowing the reader to follow the sequence of events. To write a narrative memoir, in prose, they must have some understanding of the form and structure of sentences (see Chapter 11 - *Using Models - Sentences*).

Developing a memoir

Nancie Atwell's class list of the qualities of a memoir (Atwell 2002), Ken Macrorie's list of what makes good writing (Macrorie 1984), my own exploration of memoir, and my experience in leading students in developing memoirs of their own, have provided a checklist of the features we can expect in a written memoir.

The writer has something to say: a story to tell

As with most writing, children will need an opportunity to respond, first in their thoughts and then articulating those thoughts. If we are going to ask them to reach into their own minds, their own memories, we need to guide their recalling, to avoid their getting lost among the myriad of experiences, events and feelings within those memories. Sometimes this can be done very simply, such as 'Think of a time when ...', when we are certain that the time we are asking they recall is a universal experience (see Chapter 5 - *Universal Experiences*).

Many memories will be triggered by another story: a shared anecdote from the teacher of another child, a story read and shared. Gavin Bishop's autobiographical *Piano Rock* (2008) provides a wonderful variety of remembered scraps of childhood. One of the many excerpts I share with teachers and students involves another universal experience: making huts.

Experience to date has shown that making huts (or dens) transcends geography and era - it seems that children the world over, now and eons ago, get involved in making huts. These huts can be indoors - under dining tables, beds, in stairwells or hot water cupboards, or outdoors - in paddocks, the bush or at the beach. One teacher, schooled in the northern hemisphere, even recalled a hut-building frenzy at primary school that resulted in rival igloos, after a particularly heavy snowfall. We need to be mindful of the variety of experience and variety of shapes that huts may take as we probe and prompt our students. We won't all have made the same sort of huts, but we will all share the feeling of being hidden, or designing and building a 'secret place'. It might be as simple as hiding under the bedclothes. We can share Gavin Bishop's memoir, we can demonstrate how that has prompted our own memory, and then we can invite our students to draw from their own remembered experiences. I have not met a group of students yet who are not keen to share their own hut-building time. (See Appendix for lesson plan, model and student texts.)

My Hut

We push the couches far enough apart to fit two of us in between and lay a blanket over the top as a roof. While one of us stacks the brightly coloured pillows high like a tower, the other pulls the sheets off the bed and drags the mattress towards our town leaving silver springs and red base bare.

The cluttered room becomes a city of bright pillows towered upon each other with a toy at the point of it as if it were a monument. More and more shops begin to open until there is no space left to build on. The only thing left to do is take some off the other two girls. As we creep up to the blue cloak door Perry yells, 'Oi! Get off our half of the room!' and before we know it war breaks out. Sheets fly around the room; soft bricks tumble down and mattress walls are bulldozed over. Our once city becomes a flannelette dump.

Mum storms in questioning the screaming. 'You all need some fresh air. Go outside and play.'

'What are we going to do outside?'

'I know, we can build a hut.'

Cory, Year 8

Sand Hut

We lifted the huge piece of driftwood that must have been washed up onto the beach after the storm.

We continued to collect wood until our pile was big enough. The plan was simple; collect wood then build a hut in the sand dunes. We put two big pieces of wood at the top of the dunes in each corner then two at the bottom corners. Every so often we would run down to the ocean and grab a bucket of water to pour over the sand that we had pushed up against the wood to make it more stable.

A shovel or spade was the next piece of equipment used to make this magnificent hut. We dug stairs, we dug steps, we dug couches, we dug all sorts of things to make this hut a luxury apartment.

The final step was to put the roof on to shelter us from the rain and the onlookers from above. We used flax for the base of the roof then piled lots and lots of sticks to make the roof big enough.

As we relaxed in our hut I heard Mum call, 'Lunch time!' So we raced off for lunch.

Matt, Year 8

Sometimes the range of topics will be evident, even if the initial remembering has come from the same starting point. For example, Margaret Mahy's picture book *A Summery Saturday Morning* (1998) can lead to discussions around summer days, trips to the beach, Saturday mornings, dogs, bikes, to name but a few. When the teacher reads such a book to a class, it can be enjoyed purely for itself, with the expectation that students will respond to the story, the language used, the rhyme, the illustrations, or it can be used to lead a discussion that might focus on something depicted.

> *I enjoyed seeing what these children were doing on their summery, Saturday morning ... it made me think about the time when I ...*
>   - *got chased by a dog ... I was quite small and not really used to dogs. I was walking ...*
>   - *went to the beach ... we didn't live near the beach so I didn't get to go very often. One time that I remember was when we all piled into Dad's rattly old car ...*

Or

> *I love Saturday mornings. One Saturday I decided to visit my auntie. She lived ...*

Or by simply asking children to make connections:

> *Bring to mind a Saturday that you can remember clearly ...*
> *Close your eyes and let your memory bring thoughts of a summer that you remember ...*

Of course it will be important to be checking that all students do have a time when ..., but I have found that as they become accustomed to reaching into their memories, there is always something, in any story shared, that will prompt something for everyone. They may not be the same, but the stories will be there, especially when based around very ordinary everyday things.

The writer recognises why this story has been remembered and has a sense of its significance

As we acknowledge that each child has settled upon a particular time from their own lives, we need to question, to lead their recall into a multi-sensory image. This involves questions around the sights seen, and sounds heard, along with the other senses, but the important questioning will be around 'So how was that for you? What were you feeling at that time? What were you thinking?'

The writer knows how to hook the reader in with a beginning that engages

Mini lessons can focus on beginnings that engage. A simple research of published books can be undertaken in the school library or classroom bookshelf. Each child can be directed to read the opening sentence of picture books, short stories, novels. Each opening sentence can be responded to – with the expectation that we recognise what the writer has done, and what invites us to want to read on. In traditional narrative, we are introduced to the main character very early – very often in the opening sentence. As authors introduce their protagonist, the relationship between the reader and that character begins. If the character is introduced in an engaging way, which often includes a situation or problem being faced, the reader is likely to want to develop the relationship further, as they come to know and care about the character. In memoirs – first person narrative – writers often begin the same way, by introducing themselves. For example:

> *When I close the gate behind me …*
> (from *A Land of Two Halves* by Joe Bennett 2005)

Sometimes other characters that are central to the story:

> *Dad just hates carrots …*

Sometimes it is direct speech that gives us the first clue to the characters we are about to get to know.

> *'Dad.'*
> *This was my older son Lois, then aged eleven.*
> *'Yes?'*
> (from *Experience* by Martin Amis 2000)

The other most common opening for a narrative is to reveal the setting before introducing us to characters:

> *Winter sun falls in slanted rectangles …*
> (from 'From the Back Corner' by Margo Baars 2000)

Whatever the device employed, writers who engage us in what they have to say inevitably provide us with an opening sentence that invites us to read on. Students will become fascinated with noticing what a writer has done in their very first sentence as they strive to engage readers of their own.

Writers select the best words to say what they mean – they do not waste words

One of the greatest challenges, and one of the most rewarding aspects of writing, is knowing that, as a writer, you are the one in control of selecting what you want to say, and which words will best say what you mean. The difference between saying out loud what we have to say and recording our message in writing is that we can, and often do, change what was first written. We become adept at noticing whether we have included what we wanted to, whether we have been specific where we needed to be, whether we have made our meaning clear, or, in contrast, whether we have been suggestive or have implied meaning. We also need to know whether the verbs we have chosen describe the action we want described and whether the senses we appeal to will evoke the response we hope for.

Writers, from the earliest stage of learning, need to know that they are in control, and, as their vocabulary increases, decisions about what to include and what to leave out are vital.

There is satisfying closure and a sense of wholeness about the piece

Just as writers control the words to best say what they mean, they also have control over the structure of a piece as a whole. They learn about beginnings that engage, and they learn about endings that satisfy. They learn about ways in which writers make connections and links, as a remembered time is recorded. Endings have posed problems for learner-writers as they sense the need to 'round things off', and exploring how published authors manage it is the simplest way to develop understanding. Traditional narrative has the protagonist ending up in a 'better' place than he began, with whatever problem that he was faced with being resolved. In personal memoir, the writer is able to end a piece with some resolution or evaluative comment that assures the reader the moment or events described have been reflected upon, and the significance understood.

The background information that a reader needs is woven into the story - the 'who, where, what, when, why, how' are embedded in the narrative

We often see examples of students' attempts at writing a personal account where they have included all the essential ingredients in the opening sentence.

Last Saturday (when) *me and my brother* (who) *went to the park* (where)
to play rugby (what).

While this provides the reader with all we need to make sense of the piece, it will often result in a less than engaging beginning, which requires skilful linking to personal comment and elaboration. Memoirs that work will provide us with the information we need, but given to us as it is required – not all in the opening sentence or even the introductory paragraph.

The reader can see, hear and feel the experience because the writer has included sensory details

Empathising with an experience that belongs to someone else becomes much easier when the writer appeals to our senses. We need to feel and hear, smell or taste an experience, as well as to see it, through the sensory details and our corresponding emotions.

The writer 'puts the reader there' - makes him/her believe

Through the inclusion of specific details, sensory images, comments and carefully selected words, a writer re-lives an experience, with all its components. The writer needs also to become aware of how readers respond to writing through being able to live the experience alongside the author. In a memoir, truthfulness and sincerity are noticed by the reader. We feel we can believe what the writer is telling us and identify with the recollection of something human. The reader knows what the writer thinks and feels, through the inclusion of thoughts, reflections, comments and observations. Many learner-writers move from action to action without any indication of how they feel about the experience. They leave no time or clues for the reader to form a picture in the mind. Readers lose interest when a mere chain of events is recorded.

The piece asks something of the reader – it causes things to happen for the reader as they happened for the writer

When we know how the experience affected the writer, we are able to align ourselves much more closely with the events described. And, as we align ourselves, we find our response matches the sincerity of the writer. If the writer has been moved to include thoughts and reflections, comments and observations, we as readers are more likely to respond on a similar level.

Building the writer's toolbox

As we work with our student writers, it is unlikely that we will be expecting them to fulfil all the criteria for a successful memoir from their first attempts. There will be a gradual accumulation of skills and strategies that our young writers will recognise as they are supported in their understanding of how writing works. We will have opportunities for conferring with them as they draft their memoirs, posing questions that ask of them: 'What is your piece actually about?' The student who had wet her pants was able to recognise that her significant memory was more than mere recall of the incident. She learned, as she was exposed to other writers, that she too was able to describe the way her body and her mind reacted. She skilfully provided her readers with carefully selected words, implying her extreme humiliation and embarrassment. This young author had expressed the deep-felt significance of this moment in time in a way which touched her audience – just as Maya Angelou had done.

If we believe that it is human to recall and share events and moments remembered, we need to support our students primarily through responding as humans – showing them that their memories are precious and worth recording.

As with other purposes for writing, memoirs can be an end in themselves. But as students are on their way to independence as writers, they should become increasingly confident in transferring what they know about writing across a range of purposes and forms. The rigour required in crafting an effective memoir will stand them in good stead when they are developing an expository essay. Even though the purposes of these two types of writing are very different, what students

are learning about conveying significance in a personal memoir, about clarity, economy, sentence structure – the control and manipulation of language for effect – can be applied in just the same way when faced with choosing how best to structure an essay. A child who writes a 'thin', loose narrative will most likely also write an ineffectual persuasive essay.

For very young writers, the understanding of deciding what they have to say (about a personal memory) and choosing the best words to say what they mean, should continue to develop in choosing the words to use when they come to write for an entirely different purpose. The writer's 'toolbox' that students are building up will have the tools they need for every writing task they are faced with – but teachers of writing will need to help them to make the connections.

Summary - *Memoir*

- The genre of memoir.

- Lifting the dreary recount into vibrant memoir.

- Retrieving memories.

- Developing sophistication in memoir writing over time.

- Memoir poetry.

- Developing a memoir.

- Qualities of an effective memoir.

- Building the writer's toolbox.

Appendix - *Memoir*
Features of a memoir

The memoir often tries to capture certain highlights or meaningful moments in one's past, often including a contemplation of the meaning of that event at the time of writing. It is usually written in familiar style from the first-person point of view.

The writer has something to say.
The reader is able to sense the significance (of the event) for the writer, the 'So what?'
There is an engaging beginning; the reader gets 'hooked' right at the start through such devices as: direct speech, monologue, dialogue, question, command, scene-setting by showing not telling, problem outline, tension.
Background information that the reader needs is woven in - the '**who, what, where, when** ... is embedded in the narrative.
There are thoughts, feelings, reflections, comments and observations. The reader knows what the writer thinks.
The pace is appropriate - it helps the event unfold, bringing the reader along with it and also gives the reader time to reflect, visualise and respond.
The reader can see, hear and feel the experience because the writer includes concrete, sensory details and descriptions.
There is dialogue when appropriate, to show something about the people involved in the memory.
The language is carefully selected for the purpose - it says exactly what the author wants it to say: specific nouns, strong verbs, etc.
There is a satisfying closure.
There is a sense of wholeness in the piece as a 'stand-alone'.
The reader is aware of credibility and sincerity from the writer - 'This is how I remember this time; this is how it was for me.'

Guided Writing Plan

Model text: 'The Town' by James K. Baxter

Purpose for the lesson 'We' refers to our team of writers: teacher and students	We are reading as writers. We will: • read and respond to a published work; • borrow the framework to create a personal image as a memoir poem.
Learning focus	We are learning to identify the purpose, the structure and devices used by a writer, and create our own poem by using the same structure and language patterns.

Leading the learning
Reading, thinking and talking
	• Discuss what we are learning and why.
	• Read the poem.
	• Ask students for response.
	• Check for understanding.
	Example
	• Any unfamiliar words? Unfamiliar line (under-runners - bringing up the image of wood, timber).
	• There is a list of ideas, of discrete elements.
	• What is the writer trying to do? (give a flavour of his carefree day, the summer holidays)
	• What are the clues to it being hot?
	• Count the actions - find the verbs *dozed, dodged, crept, burnt, wrestled, swam*
	• What is the purpose? Do we have a description?
	• What has the author done to position us?
	• What are the clues that tell us it is a small town? *church, creek, schoolroom*
	• What have we got in the town? (*sky, bridge* etc. Perhaps the mad boat builder signals a small town character.)
	• Did everyone manage to bring up a visual image? Has the writer been successful in giving us an image? How?
	• What has the author done?
	  - specific names of things
	  - a group of boys

Leading the learning *Reading, thinking and talking*	- the characters are limited – the boys and the mad boatbuilder - actions; verbs - any comments about where the line breaks are? (to surprise the reader, to provide humour, e.g. dozed in the hot schoolroom) • What about the last line? (We can get a sense of wonderment from something not so important, an understatement.) *Walk students through the process of constructing* • select a place that is personally significant • check that all students have a place • partner share • make a spider map with the selected place in the centre and ideas radiating from it • share to ensure all students are 'with you' • instruct students to take a new line • begin with *The _____ was usual enough* • pick 5 nouns related to the place • share • pick 5 actions using strong verbs • share and support • include *Did what boys/girls do* – between the nouns and actions • conclude with *Doing nothing important*
Success criteria *How will we know that we have been successful?* *Co-construct with the students.*	• selected a place that is personally significant • begun with *The _____ was usual enough* • listed at least 5 nouns related to the place • listed 5 actions using strong verbs • included *Did what boys/girls do* – between the nouns and actions • concluded with *Doing nothing important.*
Challenges for writers	To transfer the skills to other writing such as a memoir (prose) where the writer is able to convey to the reader a variety of visual images through using strong verbs and specific nouns.

*Most of all though, we liked making huts. We made huts in the shed at home;
we made huts in the willows along the creek; we made huts under the pine
trees at school. There, we heaped up the needles into low walls. Each day the
huts got bigger. We worked in groups of three or four adding more and more
rooms – vast roofless mansions spreading in every direction under the trees,
until someone would shout,*

'Our hut's bigger than yours!'

'No it's not!'

'Yes it is!'

'No it's not!'

'Yes it is!'

*This would go on and on until someone ran forward and booted a hole in the
wall of one of the huts. That would shut us all up. Then, quietly, the builders of
the damaged hut would set about rebuilding the broken wall until Mr McLeod
called us inside for afternoon school.*

(from *Piano Rock* by Gavin Bishop 2008)

Making Huts

When I was little (and I still am) I used to climb trees, play tiggy, and slide down the fire-pole at the park. But most of all, I loved making huts. Me, Cumorah and my two best friends, Madelyn and Sophie, used to use blankets and curtains and rocks and sticks, but most of all an old tree with overgrown branches would be our favourite. We would split into two teams and fight over who would have the tree, and who would have to find or make another one. The competition would be on.

'We get to have it this time!'

'Yeah, only for two minutes!'

It seemed it would go on forever! Finally, one group would go off, red in the face, trying to find another good spot. After about half an hour, the tension would rise.

'Don't look!'

'You were!'

'Were not!'

'Were so!'

'Were not!'

Someone would end up storming through the other person's hut, stealing ideas. But it wasn't always like that. We used to make lamps out of old beer bottles, or walls out of towels. Sometimes we made beds out of boogie boards - we used to joke about them a lot.

Whether it was an old avocado tree or a tunnel leading to the secret room full of gold, we all had fun, until we were told it was time for dinner.

Jeshua, Year 6

Guided Writing Plan
'Making Huts'

Purpose for the lesson	We are writing a memoir to record a moment in our lives. *We will bring one of our personal stories to life with the use of direct speech and lists.*
Resource	Text from 'Piano Rock' *by Gavin Bishop* Chapter 11 Playmates and Pastimes P49 'Huts'

Learning focus	We are learning to know, and to use, the rules of dialogue in our memoir writing.
	
	 • *speech marks – around what is spoken*
	 • *new line for each new speaker*
	 • *the place of an exclamation or question mark within speech*
	 • *we don't need to say 'who said what'*
	 We may also explore:
	      • *the use of a list in the text*
	      • *the use of a semi-colon in the list*

The wider learning foci that we are keeping in mind	• We are learning to use literature to make connections with our own lives and to gather possible topics for writing • We are learning to look closely at the choices an author has made in order to involve us in his story • We are learning to *notice* how punctuation is used in a text and the effect it has on the meaning

Leading the learning

What tasks will I need to design?

• Introduce book and excerpt
• Discuss the topic of making huts (and/or other playground games) Connect student and teacher experiences.
• Teacher tells own story…
• Students have a copy of the passage and a highlighter and as aspects of language are discussed, students are directed to mark and highlight, eg
  • *Who is the 'we'?*
  • *What words provide the picture? Language use - explore 2nd sentence: a list of places (adverbial phrases)*

- What is the effect of the repetition?
- Why the semi colons?
- Who's talking?
- Do we need to know who?
- How has the writer set it out on the page?
- Why?
- How does the speech add to the sensory image?

- Check the sort of huts we have made... indoor/outdoor... the sort of conversations we might have
- Ask students to bring up a memory of a time when they were building a hut with a friend
- Lead a visualisation (including the talk with friends about building the hut)
- Share with a partner
- Share one or two individual student images with whole class
- Prepare for writing by co-construction of criteria for success (what needs to be included)
- Write
- Guided revision in 'The Helping Circle'
- Peer response for effectiveness, checking in with success criteria

Success criteria	Write to describe a time when you built a hut with friends – which includes at least two people speaking.
What am I looking for in my writing? How will I know that I am successful?	I <u>will</u> have • included the words spoken/shouted • included the speech marks • started each speaker on a new line I <u>may</u> have used • adverbial phrases • semi colons in a list
Challenges for writers	• To make decisions about what to include and what to leave out • To be conscious of parts of the sentences as they write • To think about the cohesion of the piece: linking ideas effectively with appropriate sentence structure and punctuation
Transfer to other writing	Link the sentence structures and punctuation used, to a wide range of texts and purposes.

Grass Hut War

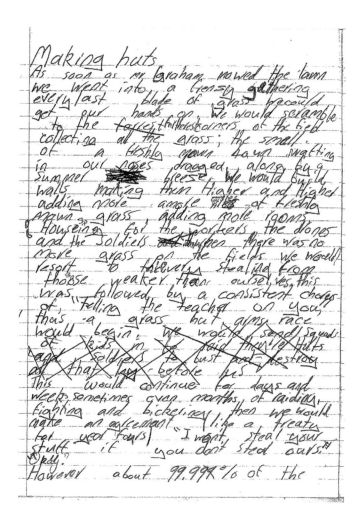

As soon as Mr. Graham mowed the long green grass of the school field we went into a grass fuelled frenzy gathering every last blade of grass we could get our little five year old hands on.

We would scramble and scatter to the distant corners of the school field collecting all the grass we could find; the smell of a freshly mown lawn lingering in our noses dragged along by a summer breeze. We would build walls, a vast fortress making it bigger and bigger adding more and more rooms, housing for workers and soldiers.

When there was no more grass to be found we would resort to thievery stealing from those weaker than ourselves. This was closely followed by a consistent chorus of, 'Telling the teacher on you!!!' Thus a grass hut arms race would begin. This would continue for days, weeks and even months of raiding, fighting and bickering and when the once small quarrel escalated into an all out war we would come to an agreement (like a treaty for little kids) 'I won't steal your stuff if you don't steal ours.'

However about 99% of the time it was an agreement most certainly short lived. So again the screaming and fighting would be reborn with a vengeance and we would go back to the old ways of waging a war in a glorious conquest for grass (as pathetic as it sounds). Then operation killjoy would begin and teachers would dish out detentions and make us sit on the naughty step. Then the dagger in the back 'NO MORE HUTS!!!!!'
'Oh.'
'Understand?'
'Yes Miss.'
'Alright.'
'One more chance?'
'I said no.'
'But ...'
'No buts about it.'
Bu ...'
'NOOOOOOOOO!'
Oh well, maybe next year.
Liam, Year 8

7 Observing and Noticing
Describing what we see

If we are to make sense of what is around us, we need to be able to notice. Notice, wonder and be able to record. When we record what we notice, the significance of what is around us becomes more evident. The dictionary defines 'significant' as 'suggesting a deeper meaning'. I am not suggesting that there is something deep and meaningful in everything ordinary, just as I am not suggesting that we record every waking moment of our lives, but it is this aspect of being human, of being able to see significance, make connections, and thus make sense of our world, that separates us from other living things. With practice, we can all become proactive observers –

> *How can a tree*
> *Wear crimson and orange*
> *Together*
> *And get away with it?*
> *I gaze, in awe, at the beauty of it.*
> *My top is orange*
> *My shoes crimson.*
> *I gaze, in dismay, at the clash of it –*
> *And change my shoes.*
> (Sally Muir 2003)

Many observations can begin as simple lists – lists of things. The poet Rupert Brooke recalls, in a list, the things that he loves, in 'The Great Lover' (1914).

These I have loved

White plates and cups, clean-gleaming,
Ringed with blue lines; and feathery, faery dust;
Wet roofs, beneath the lamp-light; the strong crust
Of friendly bread; and many tasting food;
Rainbows; and the blue bitter smoke of wood;
And radiant raindrops couching in cool flowers;
And flowers themselves, that sway through sunny hours,
Dreaming of moths that drink them under the moon;
Then, the cool kindliness of sheets, that soon
Smooth away trouble; and the rough male kiss
Of blankets; grainy wood; live hair that is
Shining and free; blue-massing clouds; the keen
Unpassioned beauty of a great machine;
The benison of hot water; furs to touch;
The good smell of old clothes; and others such –
The comfortable smell of friendly fingers,
Hair's fragrance, and the musty reek that lingers
About dead leaves and last year's ferns …
Dear names,
And thousand others throng to me! Royal flames;
Sweet water's dimpling laugh from tap or spring;
Holes in the ground; and voices that do sing;
Voices in laughter, too; and body's pain,
Soon turned to peace; and the deep panting train;
Firm sands; the little dulling edge of foam
That browns and dwindles as the wave goes home;
And washen stones, gay for an hour; the cold
Graveness of iron; moist black earthen mould;
Sleep; and high places; footprints in the dew;
And oaks; and brown horse-chestnuts, glossy-new;
And new peeled sticks; and shining pools on grass;
All these have been my loves.

While some of the language of this piece may be unfamiliar to our students, it provides a framework for personal lists of things, each thing being afforded a variety of descriptors – the sights, sounds, feelings, tastes and smells. But we must never underestimate the ability of our students to appreciate the chosen words. There is opportunity here for some in-depth discussion on the poet's decisions: the vocabulary used, the preferred word order and the effect that these have. You might ask your students whether it is easier to imagine 'the strong crust of friendly bread' or 'many-tasting food' to start a discussion on using specific detail. You might ask why Brooke describes sheets as having 'kindliness ... that soon smooth away trouble', and blankets that have 'the rough male kiss' to initiate discussion on personification.

This student has given some thought to the literary device of personification in his effort, inspired by Rupert Brooke:

> These I have loved:
> *The rain, as it trickles down the trees;*
> *The dew, as it hangs for its life on a nearby tree;*
> *The sun as it creeps through the window;*
> *Boats on the water;*
> *A bug, as it runs for safety;*
> *The wind as it blows through the trees;*
> *A rainbow.*
> Paul, Year 7

The things listed involve retrieving memories – past observations – and as we recall them, our memory enables us to bring to mind the sensory perceptions that accompanied the sights.

This may be a starting place for our students to understand that the images as well as remembered events that they have in their heads, are valuable – worthy of recording.

Going from what is already inside their heads to noticing what is presently around them necessitates close observation. This will come more naturally to some than others. If we ask students to record what they can see around them, we will undoubtedly be presented with a range of observations, from the languid to the energetic. If we use a model of text, such as Frank Kendon's 'The Looker-On' (1976), we can support students in recognising just what this writer has done, and see what makes it an effective piece.

... And ladders leaning against damson trees,
And idle spades beside old garden walls,
And broken sickles covered up in leaves,
And baskets wet with dew, waist deep in grass,
And spider webs across half-open gates ...
And memory of a moon, a giant rolling,
And, brown in moon's noonday, prolific oaks,
Glint of moonsilver on their solid acorns ...
And a fierce sun melting the fringed horizon,
Cold grass, hard apples fallen and forgotten,
And dew-logged thistledown ... and crackling beechmast,
And plump matt mushrooms – beggar's harvest – white
As chalk, bland as a nut, and pink to break ...
And bonfire incense, and bracken gold as beech,
And bearded hedges, latest blackberries,
Half-ploughed stubble and dusty threshing yards,
And early nights, cloud multitudes on firs ...
Dry noons, drenched dawns, deep scents, bright stars, lost thoughts ...
And empty orchards and wide open fields,
And robin solos in deserted woods,
And chimney smoke, and starry candlelight,
And far-off fields, and distances like the past,
And mossy silence, and the scent of leisure,
And spider webs across half-open gates,
And broken sickles buried under leaves,
And idle spades beside old garden walls,
And ladders leaning against damson trees ...
(Frank Kendon 1976)

Many of the images listed here indicate that this is not a New Zealand landscape, but kiwi kids have been quick to spot the pattern of Kendon's list, with the repeated

lines, in reverse order – all beginning with '*And ...*' and quick to recognise that this poem is simply a list of things, with descriptors – probably noted from standing in one spot – and noticing. Just as this poet may have spent time standing in a piece of rural England, and taking note of what he sees, so can our students be made aware that what they see around them in rural New Zealand can be recorded in a similar way:

> *And the waves thundering down,*
> *And the soft footprints of early walkers,*
> *And the breaking of the sun,*
> *And crabs running to the sea for safety,*
> *And sticks washed up,*
> *And the soft footprints of early walkers,*
> *And the waves thundering down.*
> Rosanna, Year 8

There are numerous specific teaching points to give students confidence in playing with language and imagery, which has taken this student writer beyond the list of nouns: waves, footprints, sun, crabs, and sticks. By giving her a framework from the Kendon model, she is supported sufficiently to allow her to play and experiment.

Similarly, students from different environments have been able to use the rural English scene to describe their own setting.

Urban setting

And the cars lining up one after another,
And the people waiting at bus stops,
And the traffic lights flashing red, amber and green,
And the shops all opening their doors.
Ben, Year 5

Holiday

And the people all speaking so fast,
And the colours and smells at the markets,
And the crowds pushing and jostling,
And the birds that look so different,
And the food that was too spicy,
And the colours and the smells at the markets,
And the people all speaking so fast.
Georgia, Year 6

Sport

And the stadium packed full,
And the crowd roaring,
And the red scarves waving,
And the players doing their best,
And the crowd roaring,
And the stadium packed full.
Will, Year 4

All of these examples have been created very swiftly, with young writers quickly identifying structure and content, and seeing how we can 'borrow' Kendon's structure to hang our own ideas on.

War poet Wilfred Owen wrote 'From My Diary, July 1914' – also a list of things, things in their places, and very specifically structured. It has some delicious lines:

Boys

Bursting the surface of the ebony pond.
Flashes
Of swimmers carving thro' the sparkling cold.

Fleshes
Gleaming with wetness to the morning gold.
(Wilfred Owen 1914)

This structure can form a framework for our students' own attempts at listing what they see, noun followed by a descriptive line. This student has taken note of the natural elements around her on an ordinary school day, but can't resist mentioning a human aspect – her somewhat scathing perceptions of the way boys behave!

Wind
Whistling and riding along, spreading ice throughout the land.
Branches
Reaching out to the hills, stretching.
Air
Muffled, brittle, sweeping the sea's surface.
Sun
Its rays diving down, stealing the sea's water.
Boys
Acting their part, but always forgetting their lines.
Nikki, Year 8

The real subject matter of much truly creative language is the inner life of the child with its reflections, attitudes and beliefs. It is also concerned with the child's place in the environment and reaction to it.

Stan Boyle (1986)

Good description is essentially a question of mentioning the right things, and we can encourage our students to jot down a list of things they can see, feel, hear, smell and even taste. How they respond to each thing noted is personal – and within the comfort of a given framework, they can experiment with their own response in words. Of course we must be mindful of the over-reliance on copying form. Models of texts, including poems with an easily identifiable structure, have their uses for learner-writers to 'borrow' a framework to hang their own ideas on, and can lead to a quickly satisfying result. This reliance on the structure or form of another writer should always be acknowledged as such – if learner-writers understand that they are borrowing someone else's ideas to play with, and

are satisfied with their own attempts, their confidence to move from that reliance and form their own style will come.

Our junior students will understand the features of a list, long before they are able to explore the works of Wilfred Owen or Rupert Brooke. One Year 3 teacher had identified the effect of listing poems for herself, and noticed how her young writers were closely observant. She led her students to notice their immediate environment, and to jot down a list of four things that they could see. She then encouraged them to extend each thing listed, by directing them to record what each thing looked like, or was doing:

> *Pine cones – scattered around*
> *Sand – with wrinkles*
> *Shells – all different colours*
> *Sticks – washed up*
> Stacey, Year 3

> *Picture books – waiting to be opened*
> *Posters – telling us where to look*
> *Cushions – colourful and soft*
> *Computers – always busy*
> Jonny, Year 3

From simple lists, we can ask our students to 'zoom in' on a particular thing that is observed. This can often be instigated with observational drawing. Bill Clarkson, in *Observation at the Outset* (1992), describes observational and 'memory' drawing as a process that develops observational skills and fosters children's natural curiosity about their world, prompting questioning from the observer. The examples overleaf, are taken from a class booklet, arose from a trip to the mangroves, sketching pencils and pads in hand.

In Liza's poem 'Frog', it is clear that she was a close observer of the creature she describes, and could well have produced a drawing of it. Her poem gives a powerful picture in words:

Frog

It sits, a moist ball of flesh in my hand.
Vulnerable, pressed belly close to my pink palm,
The ball of putty croaks,
Blowing out with care, his throat balloon taut.
He lets it go shrivelling back into limp folds
Like worn material.
He hangs his skin cravat under his chin and smiles.
Suddenly his head jerks up
Sending black warts colliding down his back.
His eyes swivel
Full of wet black wonder
Exaggerated by the thin circlet of gold he wears around them.
Regally he stands
In wait for the worm, long pale pink innocence.
Then tongue whips the air and satisfaction slips down
His throat.
He presses his eyes down and shuffles his membranous feet.
He smiles and rests his head flaccidly on my thumb.
Liza Robinson, 13 years
(from *The Forms of Narrative* by Abbs and Richardson 1990a)

The Mud Flats

The sun is hidden behind gray clouds
A breeze ripples the salty water
reflecting the dark shadow of a mangrove
Separated from its owner, a
ruffled seagull feather lies in
the oozing mud
Near a horse shoe of driftwood
In the distant mudflats lies a
stranded trawler
The chill wind blows a piece
of plastic across the desolate
mud

Jarrod - Year 7

Mangroves

The mangroves twist in a
maze
Human litter tangles around
their trunks
Seagulls hover, scavenging
for food
A rotted log, covered with
green moss lies half sunken
in the sand
I trudge through the oozing
mud
Gumboots squelching and
sinking
The air smells salted and
sandy
I love the beach

Wayne - Year 7

There can be no doubt that Liza has looked closely at a frog, but not only looked; she has captured the image, including her personal perceptions and responses to the experience. Observing something closely does not always produce a skilfully crafted poem. Observation with all of our senses can result in a vivid description that is written as prose. This young writer must have looked, touched, smelled and even tasted a dead holly leaf:

> *This dead holly leaf has been dead so long that it has turned into a kind of*
> *skeleton. You can see the veins clearly. It is a very light brown. In some places*
> *rotted remnants are still clinging to the skeleton. These are a greyish brown. These*
> *patches break up the clearness of the leaf. It is very fragile, and just a little jerk*
> *will break it. It is so thin that you can feel your skin on both sides when you pick it*
> *up. The larger veins are divided between each other by hundreds of smaller veins.*
> *It looks very dilapidated and dirty. It tastes of nothing in particular except earth*
> *and grass. It smells faintly of proper holly. The leaf was fixed to the holly bush by a*
> *slender, light-brown twig. This tastes like the wood they use for making pencils.*
> Andrew
>
> (from *Feelings into Words* by Copeman and Barrett 1975)

We don't always have the opportunity for literally holding the things we respond to. A while ago I was standing at my kitchen sink and noticed a native wood pigeon, feeding from the kowhai tree. The sight of this bird with its myriad of vibrant colours held me in awe for some time, prompting many thoughts and wonderings. I wondered about it, remembering stories of Hatupatu and the meals he made of Kereru (native wood pigeon). I recalled that my neighbour grumbled about the pigeons damaging his kowhai ...

Day after day the visitor returned, always alone, and always to the same kowhai tree. I watched, fascinated, and continued to wonder. Why is it always alone? Where does it go after feeding? How far does it fly each day? I reached for a camera, and captured some beautiful close-up shots. I also reached for a reference book, to find out more about our native kereru. This is what it said:

New Zealand Pigeon

H.n. novaseelandiae (GMELIN, 1789)

Description

Adult: Sexes alike. Head, throat and upper breast metallic green with gold reflections. Nape, mantle, back, scapulars and upper wing coverts, purple with

coppery green sheen. Lower back, greater wing coverts, primaries and sec-
ondaries, metallic grey-green. Tail brown-black with green lustre. Underside
of tail grey. Lower breast, belly, feathered upper legs and undertail coverts
white. Iris dark red. Bill crimson, slightly yellow towards tip. Feet dark red.
Claws black. H.n. chathamensis has purple head and breast with bronze and
green reflections, pale grey lower back, bronze-green undertail coverts.

Immature: Similar to adult but head, neck and upper breast dull grey-green
rather than bright golden green. Iris and bill dull red.

Nestling: Sparsely covered with yellow-brown down. Undersurface and area
around eye bare. Iris brown. Bill and feet grey-brown.
(from Readers Digest 1985)

I thought it very interesting to note the precise, yet very poetic descriptions used in
this textbook. So description is used in all kinds of writing? A teacher of writing would
note the fact and set about helping students to observe, notice and describe accurately.

Amid our wonderings, Sally and I explored where these wonderings might lead us
in a classroom setting. As the most enthusiastic learner in the room, a teacher will
inevitably lead students into similar wonderings, with an infectious enthusiasm.
There will be talk about what has been seen, and no doubt diving into reference
books, just as I had done myself. There may be models of text that we are reminded
of while we are observing a creature. Such musings prompted:

> ### Pigeon
> *It sits, bending the branch of the kowhai tree*
> *Pompous, settling to feed.*
> *The feathered finery*
> *A myriad of hues*
> *Like the cloth of the crowned.*
> *Suddenly the head jerks up*
> *Sending colours merging one with another.*
> Sally Muir

As we watched the pigeon feed, we were reminded of a prose passage, describing a hen:

Hen Feeding

The clocking hen puffed out her feathers and sounded a sharp, throaty cluck. With her mottled tan and white plumage raised from her body she seemed twice her real size. As she strutted a few steps forward in an attitude of special author- ity she clucked again and called her scampering brood of chicks in behind her. With a single movement of her claw she scratched the earth vigorously, then danced back two rapid steps, bending her beak and eyes quickly to the ground. Finding an earthworm, she raised her head and began a monotonous sequence of high insistent peeping noises, calling her chicks to the food. Only when they had all gathered in to her did she bend her beak again, seize the worm and begin tearing it apart with rapid shakings of her head. A plain white hen, hearing the shrill sounds, abandoned her scratchings a few yards away and ran over to join the meal - unwary! Quickly the clocking hen puffed herself out even more broadly than before and, whirling suddenly, raced at the white hen, pecking at her head and crying out menacingly as she did so. As the white hen fled in alarm the clocker turned her back to her brood and led them a few steps further off ...
(from 'The Hired Man' by Robert Bernen 1978)

Reading closely, we can make connections between our own viewing of the pigeon, and the hen, as depicted by this writer. He has provided us with sensory images and, as a reader, we can notice the writer's use of descriptors, providing images of colour, sound and movement. This piece, in turn, inspired a description where we attempted to capture the image of the pigeon feeding, hunting for the best way to portray the colour and movements:

Pigeon Feeding

The plump kereru lurched clumsily as the branches bowed with his weight. His head stretched down, then further, as he searched for the food. His back gleamed, with the oily mix of petrol shades. His head and neck were sleek as he strained forward, then jerked upright once more. The white of his chest, in stark contrast to the surrounds, proclaimed his presence. His red-rimmed eye took in the view and, satisfied that he was the sole claimant of the kowhai flower, he resumed his meal.
Inspired by Robert Bernen

Just as we practise noticing the things around us, so we practise noticing what pieces of text provide for us. When we lead our students to examples of rich text which serve a particular purpose and discuss what the writer has done, we are providing them with a model that inspires – perhaps providing a structure that can be improvised upon within the context being explored. As Sally and I played with the pigeon ideas, we 'robbed' particular ideas from the texts – even robbing certain phrases. Children will enjoy being 'robbers' as they experiment trying on another writer's shoes for a while. The learner-writer in *Love That Dog* (Creech 2001) writes:

> *I was very glad*
> *to hear that*
> *Mr. Walter Dean Myers*
> *is not the sort of person*
> *who would get mad*
> *at a boy*
> *for using some of his words.*

The 'creative' response to literature is twofold in its effect. Pupils are able, through reading and responding to literature, to develop an understanding of and control over an ever-widening range of written forms. The experience of writing creatively, or imitating the characteristics of a particular writer's style, leads also to an increased critical awareness of literary technique in the writing of others.

Peter Abbs and John Richardson (1990a)

And thank you
for typing up
my secret poem
the one that uses
so many of
Mr. Walter Dean Myers's
words
and I like what
you put
at the top:
Inspired by Walter Dean Myers.
That sounds good
to my ears.
Now no one
will think
I just copied
because I
couldn't think
of my own words.
They will know
I was
inspired by
Mr. Walter Dean Myers.
(from *Love That Dog* by Sharon Creech 2001)

The pigeon at my kitchen window also provided a context for playing with the structure of haiku. A Japanese poetry form, haiku is a three-lined poem containing five syllables in the first line, seven in the second, and five in the third. Containing just seventeen syllables, haiku cannot capture a 'big picture'. Instead, this form depicts, with mood and emotion, tiny images of natural beauty that might have been missed had the writer not taken the time to illuminate with carefully chosen words. There are many beautiful examples to share with students, and a specific observation may provide an opportunity for careful selection of words - attempting to mention one particular aspect - in this case, the sound the pigeon makes on its sudden arrival or departure:

Visitor

The thwack of the wings
like a dragon in chain-mail
splinters the silence
Sally Muir

Wondering about a pigeon at my kitchen window, or indeed anything that we might notice from our classroom, may lead into a variety of forms of expression in writing. It is not necessary to explore each and every one. Close observation of a pigeon could lead into poetry, poetic description, factual report, diary jottings, or a host of other forms of writing, but it would be tiresome to attempt to use the same subject for many forms. While encouraging our students to lead more wide-awake lives, and helping them to use their writing to make more sense of their world, we don't want to bore them rigid through drawn-out, 'ploddy' lessons.

Even very young students may use a notebook to record their thoughts, on any number of things – and these thoughts may remain as simple jottings. These Year 3 students have a teacher who is actively providing a lens for the students to notice significances in what is around them, through the expectation that we reach for our notebooks to jot things down as we observe:

Autumn

Trees almost bare. Leaves to kick. Leaves to throw and catch. The leaves are nice when they are dry and sometimes crunchy.

Beach

Blue and shiny, curving tunnels. Lights flicking. Golden sand and shimmery stones. Birds chattering. Sticks of different sizes everywhere. Shells spinning on our world, around and around. A big blue milkshake. A blue and white sky reflects into the mirror sea. The clouds, sand, sky, moana. Keep our beach safe.

Bird's Nest

Twigs stuck to the nest. It has a sort of bowl shape. Mud stuck together to keep the twigs on.

Blossoms
More and more stems getting ready for summer.

Zoo
Two elephants standing close. Giraffe reaching over the fence. Baby monkey cuddling his mum.

These five year olds have been encouraged to notice and articulate what they are seeing, and are able to record their noticings:

Water gets washed out of the rocks like a vacuum cleaner.
Waves search inside rocks.

Any of these observational jottings may be crafted into, or form the basis for, a satisfying piece in any particular form.

'The Sea', by Laura Ranger (1995), has been used with students of all ages as a framework for describing a scene in a particular season. As the lesson plan in the appendix shows, students are led to identify the specific nouns and the way the writer has activated those nouns, to provide the reader with satisfying and precise imagery. The poem is beautifully crafted, and students of all ages have been able to borrow the structure and create their own selected scene. Taking groups of students outside on a spring morning can lead to identifying specific signs of spring:

Selected nouns for spring
blossom   ducklings   willow   sun

Once the nouns have been selected, we need to look closely in order to see what each noun *does*:

> *The willow sprouts*
> *The sun warms*
> *The blossom covers*
> *The ducklings waddle*

We need to ask questions of the activated noun – 'The willow reaches what? Where?'

> *The willow sprouts a new green*
> *The sun warms the porch, inviting us for lunch*
> *The blossom covers the tree like a new dress*
> *The ducklings waddle across the grass behind their mother*

Once one context has been explored, the door will have been opened for further observations and responses:

It is our job as coaches of our teams of writers to seize teaching opportunities as they arise: such as noticing the wonders of a bird alighting outside the window, or the stretching shadows of the late afternoon ...

Wonderings, as we see with the pigeon, can lead into scientific investigation as well as poetic response, when we ask questions. These questions can be straight, fact-finding

If you give a child the gift of seeing the intricate patterning of bare trees etched against the monochromatic world of snow and twilight, you have added richness to every winter of his (her) life ...

(Mary Harbage, source unknown)

questions, or, for some students, the poetic form of a letter poem allows their thoughts to wander. A group of students studying the rocky shore had opportunities for researching facts, making observational drawings – and wondering:

> *Dear Shell*
> *How I admire your smooth twists and curves.*
> *Your bumps are like the ripples in a swimming pool.*
> *The black that covers you*
> *Mingles in with patches of vanilla.*
> *Let me ask you this one thing: How do shells come about?*
> Mara, Year 7

> *Dear Sea*
> *I notice your coming and your going*
> *The water's edge is sometimes near and sometimes far*
> *It's a ritual, day after day*
> *In and out, in and out.*
> *I read somewhere once that it's because of the moon*
> *How can this be?*
> *How can the moon, so far away*
> *Affect what the water does?*
> *Please reply on the next incoming tide.*
> Josef, Year 8

There can be times when we introduce our students to a writing task that supports writers noticing what is around them, and yet fail to take them further in their understanding that we need to record what we actually **do** notice. One group of Year 6 children I was working with, on the first day of autumn, had evidently 'done' autumn before – probably every year they had been at school.

I set them up with a task: they were to go outside, have a look around and return to the classroom when they could come up with a sentence to **show me** that it was autumn, without using the word 'autumn'.

Out they went and it was clear that, for most of them, looking closely at their surroundings was not a familiar activity. I called them in.

'Did anyone come up with a sentence to show me that it's autumn?' I inquired.

One very eloquent girl was clear about what she thought I wanted to hear: 'The red, orange, brown and yellow leaves are fluttering to the ground.'

'Are they?' I replied, casting my eyes to the window. I hastened to point out that her suggestion had certainly made some connections for us regarding what we might expect to read of autumn, but we were going to make connections between what we could *actually notice* and how we might articulate that. On this calm, still day, there was not a leaf to be seen fluttering anywhere.

'Let's have a think about the way writers behave; how writers observe and then select the most suitable words to describe what they see.'

The students stood at the window.

'Have a look,' I said. 'Look closely. What do you notice?'

'There's a bit of yellow on top of that tree over there,' volunteered a child.

There was general agreement; there was indeed a bit of yellow to be seen at the top of the closest tree.

'We could say the tree is **tinged** with yellow,' said another.

'Yes, the word 'tinged' gives us the idea that autumn colours are beginning to creep into the leaves. Now, how could we be even more specific about the tree itself? What kind of tree is it?'

All the students were aware that the tree was an oak. The sentence, to show me that it was autumn, without using the word 'autumn', had been crafted: *The oak is tinged with yellow*. This exercise took quite some time – but I believe it was valuable time. Once students understand the importance of observation, as well as the deliberate selection of words, in learning to describe anything, they are on their way to independence.

A teacher friend was concerned about her Year 5 students' lack of knowing why the leaves changed colour in autumn. 'My long-term plan has three topics for the last three weeks of this term: The Goat Farm, Self Esteem and Electrical Energy. And these kids don't even know why the leaves change colour in autumn!' I believe that the next three weeks became one of the most memorable learning times in the lives of those particular students. They had a question to answer and with the foresight of a very thoughtful teacher they set about discovering some answers to the question, 'Why do leaves change colour in autumn?'

The entire classroom was transformed into a scientifically accurate representation of a leaf, with stomata doorways and chlorophyll-charged pupils. With the help of a secondary science teacher, the students explored and acted out how photosynthesis works. This enabled them to understand, internalise and articulate the process. They produced meaningful explanatory pieces of writing about why leaves change colour in autumn, alongside an aesthetic point of view expressed in a variety of poetry forms. Not only were they learning facts about the subject and their personal responses to it, they were learning to collaborate in groups, develop their oral language skills and integrate their learning across the curriculum. These students will never forget how and why leaves change colour in autumn because of a teacher who believed that they should deeply know and respond to the world around them. There is no need for any conflict between scientific exploration and poetic expression - both are valid human responses, and both can be recorded in writing, helping us to work out the stuff of life.

Summary - *Observing and Noticing*

- Becoming observers.

- Seeing the significance in what is around us.

- Listing observations.

- Being inspired by writers.

- Description.

- Close observation.

- Where wonderings might lead.

- Choosing a poetic form, e.g. haiku, letter poem.

- Show me it's autumn, don't tell me.

- Why leaves change colour - scientific exploration and poetic expression.

Appendix - *Observing and Noticing*

Guided Writing Plan	
Model text: The Sea, from 'Laura's Poems' by Laura Ranger	
Purpose for the lesson 'We' refers to our team of writers: teacher and students	We will: • record observations from our environment in the form of a poem; • provide the reader with imagery - by thinking and crafting deliberately.
Learning focus	We are learning to: • include specific details in our writing, giving the reader a clear picture of what we are describing; • identify the structure a poet uses; • identify the literary devices a poet (Laura Ranger) uses to describe a scene; • activate nouns as a language device.

Leading the learning

Reading, thinking and talking

- Read Laura's poem about the sea - there is a copy over the page.
- Question for response and meaning.
- Ask students what Laura needed to do to write that piece (she needed to look closely).
- Draw attention to the pattern in the writing (four activated nouns).
- Go outside and find signs of spring – lead the talk around what the nouns are doing.
- Record observations (four nouns and what they are doing).
- Extend each line to include the *who, where, when, what, why, how*, as appropriate.
- Co-construct criteria.

OR

- Invite students to look closely at a seed pod - talking about it in terms of appearance, smell, texture.
- Frame the responses in terms of activated nouns - *the stalk holds ... the ridges stretch.*
- What does it remind you of? (simile/metaphor)
- Draw the seed pod.
- Jot observations.
- Look at the model - Laura's poem.
- Pull up nouns from the seed pod.
- Co-construct criteria.
- Write according to the criteria.
- Revise against those criteria.

Success criteria *How will we know we have been successful?* Co-construct with the students	We have: • included four nouns (from observation); • made the nouns do something; • started each new description on a new line; • extended each line to make more sense (it may include a *who, where, why, what, when*).
Challenges for writers	• to find writing possibilities in the environment • to look closely enough to require precise, original language • to make decisions about what to include and what to leave out • to order the words and phrases so that the poem reads well
Transfer to other writing	awareness of, and the use of activated nouns in all forms of writing

The Sea

the mist smudges out
Kapiti Island

the hills curve and rise
like loaves of bread

the sun sprinkles glitter
on the sea

the wind is writing
what it knows
in lines along the water

Laura Ranger 7 years

8 Inside or Outside
Describing the place

From lists of things remembered, or things around us, and describing 'the thing' itself, we, as artists, are also able to capture the place itself. Being able to write a vignette – a word-sketch – about a particular place, an interior or exterior scene, is as satisfying as capturing that scene with paintbrush or camera. Our powers of observation will still need to be finely tuned, and it is sometimes the specific detail that is captured, but sometimes it is the mood or atmosphere of a place that is recalled and described.

> *We are all observers. Whatever we are doing or saying, wherever we are going or have been, we are noticing the world around us and the world within us. Our experience is our own, unique, but what makes life interesting is our passion for describing and explaining it ... Descriptions are everywhere. We find them in every conceivable conversation and in every type of writing. Every picture and every photograph is a frozen description of a specific place and moment. The poet and the scientist are both concerned with exact descriptions through very precise use of language, yet how different their writing can be. Sometimes you can say categorically 'that is a piece of description' but even then that piece may be part of a larger text containing many forms of writing. No description, however plain and simple, need be dull; no description how-ever detailed and elaborate need be confusing.*
> (Janet and Andrew Goodwyn 1992)

As we share descriptive texts with our students, they will see how the writer is able to provide details of sights, sounds, smells, tastes and textures, which appeal to our senses as we read or listen. We can practise 'imaging our own scenes' from personal memory retrieval, and we can practise picturing what other writers have intended by responding to their sensory images. Children need to know that making pictures or 'imaging in their heads' is not only a normal function of the brain, but absolutely necessary. There are many things that stimulate healthy brain activity, and 'imaging' is one: every image we create for ourselves connects the neurons of our brain, which will enhance learning and memory. Concrete objects are the easiest images to create, and children will enjoy having their brain function 'tested' as you offer suggestions for them to picture in their mind: 'Picture a red car ...' invariably produces an assortment of shiny, racy sports cars when the students are asked to elaborate on their images. Talking to senior students about the way our brain works, especially our subconscious, will provide a lively discussion on what is going on in the heads of our students as they participate in imaging. With the instruction *'Don't* think of an orange ...' it is likely that the image of an orange will be created, *before* the word *'don't'* is acknowledged. When demonstrating how this works with a group of students, I said: *'Don't* think of a pink elephant ...' 'Too late!' came a cry from the back of the room. This was confirmation for this group of students that our brains are very good, and very *quick,* at making the pictures, prompted by words or thoughts.

In today's world, we are surrounded by ready-made images, with narratives often portrayed on screen as well as in print. It is interesting to draw children into discussion around the production of a film from a known book. It could well be the greatest challenge for filmmakers to re-create a well-loved book into a movie, when children, worldwide, have already successfully made the pictures in their heads. They will be quick to criticise, disregarding the poetic licence of a film producer, if they think that the characters or the setting do not quite match their own images. We need to be mindful, then, that in our 'imaging' every personal response is valid. There is no 'wrong' image. When we lead a visualisation, we don't voice our own image suggestions - we leave it open for all students to respond individually.

Descriptive texts which describe a place are common. We can find excellent examples in novels and short stories, as authors provide settings for their stories. Interior scenes, particular rooms, will often provide the specific detail readers require, as we build up our image of the happenings of the story.

From the opulence depicted in *Cold Comfort Farm*:

> *It was square, and unusually high, and papered with a bold though faded design of darker red upon crimson. The fireplace was elegant; the grate was basket shaped, and the mantelpiece was of marble, floridly carved, and yellowed by age and exposure.*
> *Upon the mantelpiece itself rested two large shells, whose gentle curves shaded from white to the richest salmon pink; these were reflected in the large old silvery mirror which hung directly above it.*
> (Stella Gibbons 1932)

to the poverty of Limerick:

> *... we find the kitchen empty. The table and chairs and trunk are gone and the fire is dead in the grate. The Pope is still there and that means we haven't moved again. Dad would never move without the Pope. The kitchen floor is wet, little pools of water all around, and the walls are twinkling with the damp.*
> (from *Angela's Ashes* by Frank McCourt 1996)

or the imagined:

> *It had a perfectly round door like a porthole, painted green, with a shiny yellow brass knob in the exact middle. The door opened on to a tube-shaped hall like a tunnel: a very comfortable tunnel without smoke, with panelled walls, and floors tiled and carpeted, provided with polished chairs, and lots of pegs for hats and coats - the hobbit was fond of visitors. The tunnel wound on and on, going fairly but not quite straight into the side of the hill - The Hill, as all the people for many miles round called it - and many little round doors opened out of it, first on one side then on another ...*
> (from *The Hobbit* by J.R.R. Tolkien 1937)

As described in earlier chapters, the use of models is important; they serve to demonstrate 'what writers do', and thus can be called upon for inspiration, or to borrow ideas by our student writers as they experiment with their own language power. As students become familiar with the experience of examining models, they will begin to identify interesting passages in their own close reading – developing their skills in 'reading as writers' as well as developing the skill of acknowledging the images we create for ourselves. Reading as a writer becomes second nature when we have been given the signposts to appreciate what is there, and to recognise specific literary devices.

Visualising a place: sensory images

Being able to 'image' a room described by an author is a good way to lead into writing a description of a room known personally. As we walk our students through their waking up in the morning (*Chapter 5 – Tapping into Universal Experiences*), we can draw their attention to specific aspects of their waking place. As they retrieve a familiar image, they may choose to give an 'impression':

> *To my left I see teddies, huddled together like bears hibernating in the winter.*
> *To my right I see my bed, looking like a bomb's hit it.*
> Anna, Year 7

or be much more specific as Mara has been:

> *The door creaks open as I step onto my smooth varnished floor. To my left a*
> *timber-framed window gives me a view right across the valley ...*

Of course it is not always a bedroom that is described – there are other interior scenes that leave an impression on us. I have found that putting students mentally into a favourite room, which may be a kitchen filled with the smell of Grandma's cakes, a room at a friend's place, or a hobby-filled garage, they will produce a sincere depiction of their feeling of enjoyment from that place.

Using our senses

Sensory language helps to create images, as we can appreciate from these excerpts:

> *And it was Sunday morning, and I could smell the church. How I could smell*
> *it! You know the smell that churches have, a peculiar, dank, dusty, decaying,*
> *sweetish sort of smell. There's a touch of candle-grease in it, and perhaps a*
> *whiff of incense and a suspicion of mice, and on Sunday mornings it's a bit*

overlaid by yellow soap and serge dresses, but predominantly it's that sweet,
dusty, musty smell that's like the smell of death and life mixed up together. It's
powdered corpses, really.
(from *Coming up for Air* by George Orwell 1939)

While making connections with the written word is the most significant aspect
of making meaning from text, there are sometimes things described that are
unfamiliar. Not everyone will have experienced the dusty, musty smell of a
church that Orwell describes. Nevertheless, in his choice of words he attempts
to illustrate for the reader a past experience which has been triggered by a smell
remembered.

John Betjeman (1958) also remembers past smells of his childhood:

Nose! Smell again the early morning smells;
Congealing bacon and my father's pipe ...

Classrooms of the 1950s can be recalled by the middle-aged, and it is often the
smell that is the most memorable. Chalk, plasticine, ink wells and blotting paper,
wet newspaper, discarded shoes and pot-belly stoves will no doubt strike a chord
for those of a certain age. It is interesting to initiate discussion with students
today to see what smells they associate with their immediate environment.

In a similar way, sounds and textures can be explored as well as the sights and
smells within a room. There are definite sounds associated with a working kitchen,
but specific detail of the actions producing sound will provide the reader with a
more precise image. Similarly, mentioning that there is the sound of a CD in a
living room will only hint at the scene: 'the staccato notes of the flute' or 'the
earthy tones of the soul singer' will provide a much clearer picture.

Be Specific
Don't say you saw a bird; you saw a swallow,
Or a great horned owl, a hawk or oriole.
Don't just tell me that it flew;

That's what any bird can do;

Say it darted, circled, swooped, or lilted in the blue.

Don't say the sky behind the bird was pretty;

It was watermelon pink streaked through with gold;

Gold bubbled like a fountain

From a pepperminted mountain

And shone like Persian rugs when they are old.

Don't tell me that the air was sweet with fragrance;

Say it smelled of minted grass and lilac bloom;

Don't say your heart was swinging;

Name the tune that it was singing,

And how the moonlight's neon filled the room.

Don't say the evening creatures all were playing;

Mention tree toad's twanging, screeching fiddle notes.

Picture cricket's constant strumming

To the mass mosquitoes humming

While the frogs are singing bass deep in their throats.

Don't use a word that's good for all the senses

There's a word for every feeling one can feel

If you'd want your lines terrific;

Then do make your words specific,

For words can paint a picture that is real.

The messages brought by senses

Are among life's greatest recompenses.

(M. Applegate c. 1950, source unknown)

In your mind's eye ...

To get your students to write about their remembered place, walk them through this imaging:

> Close your eyes and bring this place to your mind's eye.
>
> Look around – what colours do you see? Textures? Shapes?
>
> Look at the furnishings – is there anything on the wall?
>
> Take note of where you are in the room.
>
> What are you wearing? Doing?

Note the time of day. What season is it?

What sounds do you hear? Any voices?

Any distinctive smells?

Are there any windows you can see out of?

Explore the room with your senses for a minute ... then open your eyes.

Quickly record the details you recall.

The jottings that will come from this activity may be crafted into a prose vignette, or a poem, that will stand alone. The following piece evokes a room remembered, drawing on the list above, in an effort to describe. Each aspect of the room (in this case, a cellar that had become a haven for teenage years) was jotted down, with some thought to activating each concrete and abstract noun, resulting in an 'instant poem'.

Room For Fifteen

Whitewashed, windowless walls.

Cool to the touch:

Underground moisture seeping through.

Cool to the eye:

Graffiti, blatantly breaking the rules.

Candlelight flickers, interrupting the gloom.

The deep bass thud of 'The Best of Cream'

Urging us towards primeval thoughts.

Flagons of wine,

Carefully made and carelessly drunk

Cheap cigarettes,

Secretly lit and innocently inhaled.

Upturned crates, that once held beer,

Offer seating for languid teenage limbs.

Limbs clad in denim, Levi Strauss,

And loose, muslin tops.

We are individuals: we dress the same.

But what comfort this damp cell extends

What secrets ...

Eight stone steps

Take us to where we want to be.
The fusty, musty air pervades
Those whitewashed, windowless walls.
(Sally Muir 2003)

And this piece, from a student, written in prose:

My Room

Burning incense tickles your nose as you enter the room. The dull wallpaper with brown flowers is mostly hidden with cat posters. White frilled curtains hang across the wooden French door as well as the large window. The panes have been decorated with colourful stickers. Glass crystals hang in front of the glass. A bright Balinese quilt, with drawings of fish and water lilies covers the bed. Many of the shelves are filled with various things on display, mainly stuffed toys and dolls. A miniature doll's house with delicate furniture sits on some rather old drawers. Inside the wardrobe hang many flowers in the process of being dried. Fixed to the wall next to the wardrobe is a mirror with a ballet bar across it. Ballet shoes dangle on the end of the bar.
Micah, Year 8

Moving outside

Creating an instant poem can be a satisfying activity, and a starting point for further exploration of descriptive writing. Using a model of description of a place outside, 'The Old Alley' has provided many students and teachers with a framework for a descriptive poem.

The Old Alley

Soaked papers cling to aged stone,
Dustbin lids rock to and fro in the light wind,
Milk cartons, beer bottles and newspapers
Squeeze through holed, rusty and overloaded bins.
Broken drainpipes hang from decaying and depressing walls,
Thieving rats raid abandoned houses.
'Mick for Trace' chalked onto a wall
Now blurred and hanging limply

As specks of drizzle touch the writing.
A malodorous smell reeks from open drains,
Shattered windows reveal dark and musty places behind.
Shadows hang dolefully on cracked brick,
The echoes of children playing bounce back off
Each alley wall.
A homeless dog limps in the gutter,
Sniffing at the drains - whining for food.
The drizzle stops.
Rays of sun try to grope their way into
Sheltered corners of this dark, musty, alley-way.

I look on, thinking of the past,
The good old past,
I feel no emotions,
I can't,
Ghosts can't.
I am just an old forgotten stranger,
Drifting through this wise abandoned alley.
(Richard Partridge)

There are several mini lessons contained in this piece, but, like most pieces of text offered, professional judgement will decide what to do with it. Always the first step is to gain thorough meaning and a shared impression of the piece through discussion and questioning, involving every member of the class. Students come to expect that text rewards them with meaning. The author of 'The Old Alley', Richard Partridge, has returned to a place from his childhood and the poem describes what he finds and how he feels. It is important that we never skip this step of making meaning behind the words.

Now we are ready to examine how the poem is constructed. One activity that successfully makes the structure explicitly clear involves arming each student with a copy of the poem and a few coloured pens. As we re-read through the beginning of the first few lines together, we can identify nouns, underlining or highlighting in one colour, adjectives with another colour, and verbs with another.

> Soaked **papers cling** to aged stone,
>
> **Dustbin lids rock** to and fro in the light wind,
>
> **Milk cartons, beer bottles** and **newspapers**
>
> **Squeeze** through holed, rusty and overloaded bins.
>
> Broken **drainpipes hang** from decaying and depressing walls,
>
> Thieving **rats raid** abandoned houses

For teachers, it is advisable to browse through the pages of a reliable grammar book to be reminded of our responsibility to be secure in our own depth of knowledge and understanding of language. This poem is a good example for debating whether a word is an adjective or not: in lines two and three, we have 'dustbin lids', 'milk cartons' and 'beer bottles'. In each of these cases, we have words that are normally used as nouns appearing in the position associated with adjectives (dustbin, milk, beer). They are no longer nouns, but not strictly adjectives either. They may be referred to as having a 'descriptor function', but for the purpose of this activity, I will be content to identify the word classes simply:

nouns, adjectives, and **verbs**.

Once identified, we can examine what the writer has done; he has described some of the nouns with an adjective, and he has activated them – making them *do* something:

> the papers are soaked, and they *cling* …
>
> the dustbin lids *rock*
>
> the milk cartons, beer bottles and newspapers *squeeze*
>
> the drainpipes are broken and they *hang*

The nouns at the end of each clause are also described with an adjective:

> *aged* stone
>
> *light* wind
>
> *holed, rusty* and *overloaded* bins
>
> *decaying* and *depressing* walls

Students will be able to appreciate the effectiveness of activating the nouns, rather than using auxiliary verbs. 'Soaked papers cling to aged stone' works better than

'Soaked papers are stuck to aged stone', or even 'Soaked papers are clinging to aged stone'. This is a useful device to call upon when supporting students in descriptive prose, not just poetry.

Often we find writing too static with too many auxiliaries, for example: 'The bed is in the corner. The curtains are pulled back. The painting is hanging on the wall.' We might demonstrate how these basic observations can be brought from the inert to the more animated: 'The unmade bed sits in one corner. Faded blue curtains allow shafts of sunlight into the room. The heavily framed painting dominates one wall.' All that has changed is the addition of adjectives and the nouns being activated. However, the choice of verb here might then lead into discussion about personification, where the chosen verb not only activates the noun, but also gives some human trait to a non-human object: curtains allowing sunlight into a room suggests the idea of inanimate curtains having some choice in the matter.

You, as the teacher, will have some authority over guiding the discussion in the direction you wish it to go; you may want to continue identifying word classes throughout the poem, you may want to discuss specific literary devices as shown in the opening lines. You can move into creating an instant poem after the opening lines have been discussed. Take the students back into their own special place, where they 'bring it to mind', picturing that place that is particular for them. Get them to:

- jot down four nouns – concrete nouns, naming items that they 'see' in their visual recollection;

- activate these nouns;

- extend their nouns with appropriate, specific adjectives.

One student's attempt at describing a hut included:

tin, branches, axes, spider-webs
When each noun was activated, she wrote;

- tin clangs;

- branches lay;

- axes sleep;

- spider-webs cling.

The adjectives added:

- old rusty tin; sad branches; tired axes; holey spider-webs.

Adding appropriate adjectives to the selected nouns, and extending the image with adverbial phrases (which give us more information about the verb – telling us how, when or where) produced:

> *Old rusty tin clangs on the hut wall,*
> *Sad branches lay dying slowly,*
> *Tired axes sleep after a hard day's work,*
> *Holey spider-webs cling to yesterday's dust.*
> Ahna, Year 8

And from the junior room, this 'shared writing' was created:

> *Trees bend*
> *Leaves dance*
> *Doors slam*
> *It is windy.*

Junior writers can be introduced to the effect of such description with careful questioning, without their having to be aware of the term 'activating nouns'. As we guide them in their observations, with the expectation that they can articulate what they see, we can provide young children with alternative ways to describe. One young writer, well on the way to being 'a noticer', was intent on recording the movements of the trees as the wind howled outside the classroom. The teacher chose to use this learning opportunity to create a poem collaboratively, as she posed questions to activate selected nouns.

> 'The wind is making things happen.
> Let's make a list of some of the things that the wind is affecting …
> … what do the trees do on a windy day like today?' Some responses were:
> *trees lean, trees bend, trees talk.*

We can support our students to be able to depict an outdoor scene, either from memory or through observation, and by exposing them to models of published texts where writers have described a place. We may have students in our classroom whose regular experiences include observation of a cityscape:

> *People hustle through the city, anxious to get to their destination. A bus pulls*
> *up and people crowd on and off. Everybody breathes in fumes and breathes*
> *out steam. A traffic jam clogs up the city; people quickly cross through the*
> *stopped cars. People in the cars bang their horns and look at their watches, a*
> *look of pure frustration on their faces. A man on the sidewalk begs for spare*
> *change from passers-by. Buildings tower like a giant wall on each side of the*
> *road. People hustle through the city, anxious to get to their destination.*
> Liam, Year 8

We may have students who observe a seascape and play with the use of metaphor:

> *How calm you can be, sea.*
> *Calm and as clear as glass.*
> *So innocent looking,*
> *Like a little girl in a blue dress,*
> *Tugging at Mother Earth's green skirt.*
> *Next then, a rowdy teenager*
> *Pushing, pulling, eroding.*
> *Killing, strangling all who infuriates it.*
> *A little girl in a blue dress keeps whales and dolphins,*
> *A teenager plays loud, crashing music.*
> Elizabeth, Year 8

Junior children, too, guided in observation and introduced to the concept of a simile to support their efforts to describe, can produce effective comparisons:

> *The rain is like drums on the roof.*
> Billy, Year 1

It is useful to take particular notice of the way writers describe scenes by mentioning small details. Sometimes it is the use of colour that seems significant, as mentioned in William Carlos Williams' 'Red Wheelbarrow', in Chapter 1. The red of the wheelbarrow and the white of the chickens are very important in helping us picture this scene, as are the colours in Alan Ross's (1976) description of the River Thames:

> *A zinc afternoon. The barges black,*
> *And black the funnels of tugs nosing*
> *Phlegm-coloured waves of slap-slapping*
> *Stone wharves. A smell of sacking*
> *And soot. Grey chimneys, and statues*
> *Grey with cold, and grey lifebelts.*

Because of the picture he creates, he doesn't entice one to visit London in winter. A mild summer evening sounds much more appealing:

> *The sun was melting in the pale blue sky (the light is softer than that of*
> *the southern hemisphere), creating a rose-tinted horizon. Walking from*
> *Bayswater Road through Hyde Park to Knightsbridge, I stopped on the*
> *bridge that crosses the Serpentine.*
>
> *Looking east, I took in a distant view of shimmering river, lined with rows of*
> *leafy tree-tops and bordered with majestic stone buildings.*
> (from Travel Footnotes by Lynn Bryan, *The Listener* 1998)

Or the technique could be a magnification of a sense. Patricia Grace does this effectively in her story 'Beans', when she portrays the voice of a young boy as he rides down a hill on a Saturday morning. There is no mistaking that there was a horrible smell ...

> *Just as you start picking up speed on the down slope you get this great whiff*
> *of pigs. Poo. Pigs. It makes you want to laugh and shout it's such a stink. And*
> *as I go whizzing down the stretch on my bike I do a big sniff up, a great big*
> *sniff, and get a full load of the smell of pigs. It's such a horrible stink that I*
> *don't know how to describe it.*
> (from 'Beans' by Patricia Grace 1980)

Spanning the centuries

There are countless examples of written description - once alert to the images they provide, and the effectiveness of the language chosen, teachers become skilled in seeking out models for their students. The one that follows may not seem an obvious choice to use today. How do we find relevance for our twenty-first-century kids in text written in the middle of the nineteenth century? And when those kids are from the other side of the world, it may seem an even bigger stretch to make connections.

What had prompted the choice of text was yet another example of an everyday wondering, which led to notebook jottings. We had been travelling to Taupo, New Zealand, very early one morning in late autumn. As it gradually became light, the usually scenic route was partly obscured with patches of fog. We noticed and wondered out loud why the fog appeared in some places and not others - and a notebook entry was made:

> *... autumn mist ribbons through poplars in roadside paddocks.*

We discussed where these wonderings might lead, and the variety of ways to describe fog and mist, from the poetic to the scientific. Sally later researched radiation fog and was able to satisfy a 'wondering' with a precise, scientific explanation. She also recalled a literary description of a foggy scene - from Dickens. The excerpt that interested her and was, in turn, to interest her students, was this description of fog:

> *London ... November weather. As much mud in the streets as if the waters had but newly retired from the face of the earth ... Smoke lowering down from chimney-pots, making a soft black drizzle, with flakes of soot in it as big as full-grown snowflakes - gone into mourning, one might imagine, for the death of the sun. Dogs, undistinguishable in mire. Horses, scarcely better; splashed to their very blinkers. Foot passengers, jostling one another's umbrellas, in a general infection of ill-temper, and losing their foot-hold at street-corners, where tens of thousands of other foot passengers have been slipping and sliding since the day broke (if this day ever broke), adding new deposits to the crust upon crust of mud ... Fog everywhere. Fog up the river, where it flows among green aits and meadows; fog down the river, where it rolls defiled among the tiers of shipping ... Fog on the Essex marshes. Fog on the Kentish heights. Fog creeping into the cabooses of collier-brigs; fog lying out in the yards, and hovering in the*

rigging of great ships; fog drooping on the gunwales of barges and small
boats. Fog in the eyes and throats of ancient Greenwich pensioners, wheezing
by the fireside in their wards; fog in the stem and bowl of the afternoon pipe
of the wrathful skipper, down in his close cabin, fog cruelly pinching the toes
and fingers of his shivering little 'prentice boy on the deck.
Chance people on the bridges peeping over the parapets into a lower sky of
fog, with fog all round them, as if they were up in a balloon, and hanging in
the misty clouds.
(from *Bleak House* by Charles Dickens 1852)

This group of eight and nine year old students would have struggled to read this passage unaided, or even to listen to it being read, without a starting point that they could
relate to. A supported reading lesson came first, with all the questioning, prompting and
scaffolding required. What did they know about fog? Living close to the shores of Lake
Taupo, and being late autumn, fog was definitely a phenomenon familiar to them. The
writing of Dickens was not at all familiar, so they were pre-warned that this piece had
been written about a hundred and fifty years previously, so some of the words used,
and the order in which they are written, might seem unusual. The setting was explained.
None of the students had actually been to London, but all of them knew whereabouts in
the world it was - about as far from Taupo as you can get. They knew, too, that Novem-
ber in London would mean a winter, not a summer, was approaching. Feeling secure that
they knew what to expect, and that they would be helped to work out what was meant
in the text, the students dived in. They unashamedly identified unknown words using
highlighters, and happily accepted definitions or clarification, questioned and grappled
with the metaphors until they understood, made all sorts of connections to what they
knew about (drizzle, rivers, boats, horses, dogs, mud and so on) and reached the end of
the piece feeling very satisfied. They agreed that Mr Dickens had succeeded in describing such a scene very well. The success, they deduced, was in the way he had included
specific details, elaborated the ideas, and talked about what the fog was doing. Before
the lesson was over, Sally directed them back to the list of where the fog is found, and
what it is doing. The kids grabbed highlighters and were quick to find all the examples of
where *fog* had been activated:

Fog creeping ...
fog lying ... and hovering ...

> *fog drooping ...*
> *fog cruelly pinching ...*

Lesson over, they were sent on their way with the promise of trying on the shoes of Charles Dickens the following day. The same group of students gathered again – this time to see if they could come up with their own descriptions of fog, in twenty-first-century Taupo, using what they had learned the day before. As they took their seats, two of the group were anxious to share their thoughts:

'I've brought my own highlighters today,' announced one small girl, proving beyond doubt that she was as keen to get stuck into a challenging piece of text as any literary scholar. 'Mum helped me look up that Charlie Dickenson guy on the internet,' offered another, a nine year old boy. 'He's written lots of books and he's really famous!'

Their enthusiasm was acknowledged, and the writing lesson began.

The children were directed back into the text, and discussed the effect of the list that Dickens had provided: the word *fog* being repeated, with a variety of actions ascribed to it. The students had remembered that the word 'fog' is a noun, and the activating words are verbs. They even remembered that the '-ing' words are called present participles. It was explained that they were about to have a go at describing a late autumn image of Taupo, using the same structure: a 'weather' noun, activated with a present participle. They agreed that they needed more than the '-ing' words; they would need to extend the image by including something about where the action was taking place, and what it looked like.

They worked collaboratively at first, drawing on what they had experienced of foggy days in Taupo. The combined thinking produced the following suggestions:

> *Fog creeping over the lake*
> *like dragon's breath.*
> *Fog stealing*
> *the view of the mountains away.*

They had got the idea and, secure in the criteria for success, each student was asked to create their image, with a noun that depicted a typical weather pattern for this time of year. They were delighted with their efforts, and especially delighted to think that they had 'done a Charles Dickens'. They took their written images away and filed them with previous jottings, material which may or may not have been crafted into a fuller descriptive piece at a future date.

Rain	Frost	Wind
sliding down windows in shiny, wet trails	*crisping the ground with frozen icing sugar*	*howling round corners whipping my legs*

We are reminded of the perceptions of junior children, and their appreciation of the rich text that Katherine Mansfield (1974) provides in the story of the creek (see Chapter 1 – *The Teacher of Writing*). Juniors have also enjoyed this excerpt from Virginia Woolf's *To The Lighthouse* (2004 [1927]):

Step outside the classroom, that is where you will find the most exciting teaching resources. There, the smells, rich experiences, treasures for eye, ear and heart are all the catalysts you could ever want to motivate artists, scientists, writers and Lovers of Life.

Pennie Brownlee (2010)

The sails flapped over their heads. The water chuckled and slapped the sides of the boat, which drowsed motionless in the sun. Now and then the sails rippled with a little breeze in them, but the ripple ran over them and ceased. The boat made no motion at all.

Small children with experience of boats knew exactly what the writer was saying by describing the water as chuckling and slapping. It is important to note that in recognising the purpose of this particular piece as being to describe, it is the writer's deliberate choice of verbs that provides the impact. When we are teaching children about effective description, it is important to have a deeper knowledge of descriptive devices rather than simply encouraging our students to use 'describing words', as we have often found that to mean the use of adjectives. Woolf's excerpt is a good example of sensory imagery, with only one adjective employed. Junior students will attempt to describe their environment quite simply, but with no less sincerity than older students:

> *I was so hot when we went to the creek I couldn't wait to get there. The water was sparkling and you could see reflections of the trees. It was icy cold when I got in.*
> Hera, Year 2

> *The sea is rough today. There's big waves so we can't go on the beach.*
> Nick, Year 1

> *The tree has dropped all its leaves on the ground. The branches are like sticks. I hope it will get some more next year.*
> Amy, Year 2

It is important to remember, as we reinforce the value of our students' writing to help them make sense of their world, that the most exciting teaching resources any teacher will ever need are right there, a few steps outside the classroom door. At our fingertips are all the visual aids, experiences and motivators that a perceptive teacher could ever wish for.

Summary – *Inside or Outside*

- Descriptions are everywhere; they are in every type of writing.

- Descriptions – capturing the place.

- 'Imaging' – making the pictures in your head.

- Be specific.

- Reading as writers.

- Description of a room.

- Specific teaching from a model – 'The Old Alley'.

- From London to Taupo – using *Bleak House*.

Appendix - *Inside or Outside*

Fog explanation

Where Does Fog Come From?

Fog is cloud in contact with the ground. Like clouds, fog is made up of condensed water droplets, which is the result of the air being cooled to the point where it can no longer hold all of the water vapour it contains.

For every bit of sunlight that reaches Earth, the same amount of heat must radiate from the earth back to outer space. Everything emits radiation, and although it can't be seen, it can be felt. For example, if you hold your hand over concrete at sunset, after a hot day, you will feel more warmth coming from the ground than you do from the air above. This is because at that time of day the sky is emitting less infrared radiation than the ground is.

In autumn, the weather is cooler and the nights longer. The land and water surfaces that have warmed up during the summer are still evaporating a lot of water into the atmosphere. This makes the air humid. The longer nights allow the ground to grow cold enough to condense water vapour in the air above it, which is seen as fog. This is called radiation or ground fog.

The fog usually disappears soon after sunrise as the sun's warmth evaporates it.

Fog legend

How Autumn got its Mist

Sally Muir

The Four Seasons of the world were arguing.

'I am the most loved,' boasted Summer. 'Everyone and everything looks forward to the warmth I bring. I adorn the world with beauty, for every flower provides colour and every tree is in leaf. Nothing can match the splendour of my season!'

'You may be the most loved!' snapped icy Winter. 'But you have no power! I carry my own low temperature always about me; I ice the trees and the lakes and the mountains, the landscapes, the cities and the homes, and I don't thaw it one degree at Christmas!'

'But when I come along,' said Spring, 'I warm your ice, and make it melt. Your wintry weather does not chill me! And when your chill is gone, and my warmth is felt, why – all the peoples of the world leave their homes once more, and new growth greens the earth once more. That surely makes me more powerful than you! And more loved than you, Summer – for everyone is so grateful of my power, to chase the foulness away that Winter brings!'

Only Autumn was silent. He listened to the boasting of Summer, and could not find it in himself to disagree. She was lovely: so sunny and bright. He cowered as Winter snapped, like the very icicles that he formed so readily, and accepted the power of his word. He gazed on Spring: so youthful and filled with hope – a visual contrast to himself. What use was he? Why, only the tiresome chasing away of Summer's heat.

And he, in turn, would surely scurry away as soon as Winter's icy blasts were felt. He sighed an Autumn sigh.

Sun was listening to the argument and the boasting. She knew that Autumn was filled with despair.

'Autumn,' she whispered. 'Why are you so sad?' Autumn sighed once more.

'I must be sad,' he said, 'for my purpose is one of sadness. I cannot compete with the heat of Summer, nor the chill of Winter. And surely the promise of Spring is far greater than the warning that I bring.'

Sun smiled fondly at Autumn, for he was her favourite of all the seasons.

'You forget, my son,' she said kindly. 'You forget the glorious colours you bring. Why, poets turn to their pens when their eyes fall upon the leaves as you turn their green to gold.'

'But that is surely not enough,' replied Autumn. 'They know that the gold will turn to brown, and then the leaves will fall - to rot while Winter ices the ground.'

'Then I will give you more,' Sun promised. 'You will bring mist to the world, a warning more severe of the gloom that is Winter.'

'What is this mist?'

'I will make you a promise,' said Sun. 'And my promise will be to shine upon the earth with all my might, all the summer long. And the earth and the seas will warm.'
'But that is always your cause! Each and every year!'

'Ah, yes, indeed. But this year will be different. This year you will be praised for the beauty that you bring, and respected for the mystery that will be yours.'

Autumn listened.

'The warmth that I provide the earth,' continued Sun, 'must be given back to me. And as the earth gives back my warmth, so I receive it. But as summer ends, and before winter begins, the people must be warned most strongly to take heed of the change of seasons. As I reduce my rays, and the air cools, the earth's warmth will form a mist - a cloud over the ground - which will fill them with wonder, and hasten them to prepare for Winter.'

Autumn looked doubtful.

This mist,' he said. 'It will not make me more loved, I feel.'

'Ah, but some will admire your mists,' promised Sun. 'Some will wonder at the beauty of it. So you will be loved. And others - they will curse as your mist will prevent them from going about their way - for they will be as blind men, so you will have power. The season of Autumn: beauty and power!'

Autumn smiled and was happy, and kept his mist mysterious.

Where does fog or mist come from?

Comparing the language of transactional explanation and poetic myth.

In autumn, the weather is cooler and the nights longer. The land and water surfaces that have warmed up during the summer are still evaporating a lot of water into the atmosphere. This makes the air humid. The longer nights allow the ground to grow cold enough to condense water vapour in the air above it, which is seen as fog.

- *impersonal*
- *objective*
- *specific, technical terms*
- *timeless present tense*
- *passive voice*
- *scientific processes - verbs*
- *links ideas of cause and effect*

'The warmth that I provide the earth,' continued Sun, 'must be given back to me. And as the earth gives back my warmth, so I receive it. But as Summer ends, and before Winter begins, the people must be warned most strongly to take heed of the change of seasons. As I reduce my rays, and the air cools, the earth's warmth will form a mist – a cloud over the ground – which will fill them with wonder, and hasten them to prepare for Winter.'

- *personification*
- *present tense*
- *direct speech*
- *modal verbs, indicating obligation*
- *sentence beginnings using conjunctions*
- *sentence structure: poetic word order*
- *... so I receive it*
- *... must be warned most strongly*
- *'old fashioned' verbs: to take heed, hasten*
- *'fill them with wonder ...' evoking mood*

9 Character Portrait
Describing people

Readers want to see people on the page, hear them talk, watch them in dramatic action and reaction with people. They like to read anecdotes, the little scenes in which people reveal both themselves and the subject. Readers want to meet people with whom they can identify, and often readers become, for a few moments, the person on the page, and so extend their experience by living another life. Readers also enjoy a strong sense of place and time: they like to see the people they read about in their world - to be shown as well as told.

(from *Learning by Teaching* by Donald Murray 1982)

As we are coaching our students in their mastery of language, we find in our own reading that we become more finely attuned to what writers do in order to tell their story, or to inform or to entertain. Our students, in turn, will notice the importance of what a writer has included, once we show them. Learning to describe a character can be an end in itself, or it can be a major component of an extended narrative. When we read novels or short stories, watch movies or plays, our main interest is with the characters: what they are like, how they behave and how their experiences affect their lives. We respond to these characters, and like them or not, develop relationships with them. All human beings can be discussed on any or all of a range of levels, from a simple physical level through to a more complex level of thoughts and actions.

Portrayals of characters in narrative, in written or dramatic text, need to give the reader or viewer enough information to make the relationships satisfying: we need to feel that we get to know them. Novelists and playwrights may be criticised if they fail to provide this information; critics may note that they were left feeling that they knew about the characters, but they didn't *know* them. Even our very youngest writers can write a character sketch depicting a person with the sincerity of voice that enables us to get a sense of knowing that person. It is for this reason that I ask them to think of someone who has some meaning in their life, rather than dream up an imaginary character; this will ensure sincerity.

Each writer brings to their writing the sum of a life's experiences. When writing about an event, an issue, or a character, no matter how good the work, it can only be a representation by one particular person at a given time. The view will reflect life's influences on the writer, while another entirely different view will be expressed by another writer. So too in art. One day I took a vase of my spring flowers into the classroom for a still-life art lesson. The result was eighteen very different representations of the same subject, all at different skill and knowledge levels, yet all beautiful in their own ways.

When we write about a character we look for ways to portray the essence of that person. So our concern is with how we craft the gathered information and observations so that the character comes alive for the reader and serves the purpose for the writing.

Teacher Sheryl May demonstrated this in her piece about her relationship with an old Maori kuia.

'Come here Pakeha Girl.' I felt the whiteness down to the very tip of my toes. I felt the coldness of my colour engulf me and I was terrified. With my eyes looking at the ground and tears welling up inside me, I tottered over to Nanny Waho.

'Sit down love,' said Mrs Waho. 'Nanny won't bite you. She has no teeth now.'

'Pakeha Girl, Pakeha Girl.' What power Nanny Waho gave to the word 'pakeha'. I had never been called that before. The coldness began to creep out of me and a wonderful warm feeling filled my very being. A large brown bony hand clutched my small white one and I gently turned my face to look at Nanny Waho. The brown skin stretched and smiled. Warm brown eyes danced and talked to me and sent messages of love. Nanny had strange black lines on her chin; they looked like the scribble pattern I had drawn at school. I loved Nanny Waho. She was my real Nanny. I was proud, proud that I had a brown nanny. No other primer four pakeha had a nanny like mine.

Each afternoon I would sit on a stool at Nanny's feet and peel her an apple. We would share in the delight of the taste. Sometimes nanny would let me have a puff on her pipe. The smoke would make me splutter and choke. Nanny would chuckle and call me her pakeha girl. She never called me by my christian name – ever. Often though, she would sing to me – songs that I had never heard before. I couldn't ever join in because I never remembered the words, but my heart would sing with her – and that song in my heart became my favourite. I learned about the scribble pattern on her chin. We would practise a hongi, but my pakeha nose was too pointy. My nanny used to chuckle at my attempts. 'You pakeha girl – you no Maori, but you'll do okay for this nanny.'

It changed. I had to let go of my nanny. Pakeha girls don't hongi, don't sleep in one room with everyone else and they sure as hell don't puff on pipes. I never said goodbye to Nanny. I would walk past her house and look over her fence, but I never saw Nanny on the porch again. I cried for Nanny. I wrote her a letter. I love you Nanny Waho. I felt Nanny inside of me. We moved from Ohakune. Nanny Waho sent me a message. 'Your nanny will always sing for you Pakeha Girl.'

Over the years the songs have faded in and out and Nanny's Pakeha Girl still hears them, but still can't sing them. But Nanny, the words are getting stronger and the song is beginning to sing in my heart where it has never really left. Once there was a maori nanny who loved a pakeha girl and there was a very pakeha girl who loved her Maori nanny.
(May 1990)

The bridge from expressive to expository writing

A structured character portrait is a very natural way to lead students from expressive poetic prose, as they have practised in their personal memoir writing, to a more structured expository form: they are still writing about something which is very familiar to them and drawing on snippets of narrative and colloquial text in their supporting anecdotes. We want our learner-writers, who have little experience in structuring a piece over time, to access and use information which they already have at their fingertips, although they may not realise it. My job as their teacher is to give them the 'lens' to find that information, to lead them on to discover insights about their character and themselves and to put it within such a framework as this:

A framework for character portraits

1	In your **first** paragraph, describe this person – how the character looks, sounds, smells. This is the **physical** description. Show, don't tell. Be specific.
2	In your **second** paragraph, you will deal with **behaviour** – how a character speaks and acts. What makes this person unique – a laugh, a way of talking, a way of moving.
3	In your **third** paragraph, discuss how the character affects other people. We are now dealing with **reputation**. Make the character come alive. Show, don't tell.
4	In your **fourth** paragraph, describe the character's **environment and belongings**.

I will outline *one possible* process to work through, one which has a deliberately structured framework for teachers to 'walk through' with their students. My directions for choosing a character, the sequence of activities, and the phrases and words I use are carefully selected to ensure the greatest support for every student to experience success. Of course the models and discourse would be adapted to the age and maturity of the students in a particular class.

All students in the class may be engaged in the same basic process, but there will be a range of achievements evident in the class results. As in other forms of writing, I can gradually drop the scaffolding for students who have internalised the basic process. Once clear on the 'rules' of the genre, these writers may go on to break the rules, combine, or invent forms and still come up with a piece of writing to suit their purpose. Others may continue to follow a clear structure.

Choosing a character

Students are asked to think about a person who has had a powerful influence on their life one way or another: a person whom they have loved, respected, admired, been fascinated by, or perhaps feared.

For example:

- *a specially loved relative or neighbour*
- *a favourite teacher*

(For this first attempt at character, I steer students away from choosing a peer or sibling, because they often become 'bogged down' in the emotion of the moment, 'I hate my brother because he is mean to me!' For the same reason, I initially steer adult learner-writers away from choosing a spouse or a partner – it may be that they are too close to the subject to write more objectively.)

This can be given as a specific homework task over a weekend so that students can discuss the person with family members:

Ideas to jot down tonight ...

Talk with your family about a person who has been important in your life. Think about why this person is special.

Jot down the things you want to remember in your notebook. Perhaps you might be able to find a photograph or a treasure that reminds you of that person.

Back in the classroom, as a starter, students can tell a partner about the person they have chosen and why. They can share any associated photos or artefacts.

Thesis statement or theme to be explored

With older students who are assembling a formal character study, in expository form, which includes at least four paragraphs as set out below, we can lead them to form a thesis statement about their character, something that sums up the person in a sentence. Everything that follows adds up to that thesis.

> *My father-in-law is the greyest person I know. Not only does he have grey eyes and slate grey hair (not silvery like some), but I think his soul is grey too ...*
> Teacher

Beatrix Potter does this well in *The Tale of Jemima Puddle-Duck* (1908). She writes: 'Jemima Puddle-duck was a simpleton.' Everything that Jemima does throughout the story adds up to her being a simpleton, right down to the act of providing the fox with sage and onions ... This thesis statement often opens the character study but it can also be embedded within the body of the text, or sum up at the conclusion.

Physical description

An extract from literature which describes the physical appearance of a character can be shared. For example:

> *Although he moved slowly, his pace was steady and deliberate. I guessed he must have been in his seventies at least. His skin was weather-beaten to a tan like an old leather wallet. Even the top of his head shone like a small polished table. Clearly he'd spent most of his life out of doors.*
> *His hair was white, thin and straggly. With the fringe around his bald patch and the clumps of hair escaping from his ears and nostrils, he looked a bit like a toy that's losing its stuffing.*
> *Although the whites of his eyes were a watery yellow, the irises were intensely blue.*
> *A three-day grey, black, silver stubble hung over the neck of his striped, flannel union shirt which he wore without a collar. His blue overalls were shapeless and the jacket which he wore over them had shiny patches which reflected the lamplight like the patches of ice I'd seen in the road.*
> (from *Moses Beech* by Ian Strachan 1983)

The literary and structural devices used in this extract or any other chosen, can be discussed:

- Can you see the character in your mind?

- Could we draw this man?

- What has the writer done to help us form a real picture?

Responses may include:

- Use of simile

  his skin was weather beaten to a tan like an old leather wallet
  the top of his head shone like a small polished table

- Use of clues, which lead us to assumptions about the life of the character

  clearly he'd spent most of his life out of doors

- Use of contrast

  although the whites of his eyes were a watery yellow the irises were intensely blue

- Use of specific detail

  striped flannel union shirt

This passage offers a range of language features, which could be the focus for mini-lessons. The choice of teaching focus would be dependent on the experiences, skills and needs of the writers.

Juniors have shown their skill in identifying physical characteristics through looking closely at illustrations in picture books when their teacher is prompting close observation to get specific detail. For example:

  Tell me about his face ... what do you notice?
  What colour are his eyes?
  What shape ...? and so on.

The skill of precise description can be practised by observing animal life closely, as shown in this piece by a five year old boy:

Seagulls

They have orange feet
A red beak
They drink up water
From the puddles.
They fly in circles
They are white.
And they have black
On their wings
Fletcher, Year 1

One of the skills of putting any piece of writing together is the deliberate selection of precise language, and crafting that language to say what we observe and want to record. While we are assembling an extended character piece, we can be practising those skills through incidental opportunities. These may present themselves in real terms, such as the day a litter of puppies was brought into our classroom, where children were able to sketch and observe. This activity had nothing to do with the character we were describing, but it did support the learning we were involved in. Opportunities may also present themselves when we notice relevant pieces of text to share with our students, as many children's books explore character through animals. Colin Thiele gives us this description of physical characteristics:

> *At first he was a disgusting sight, naked and floppy, with a bald head and little useless wings ... His beak was always open and pointing upwards, waiting for his mother or father to drop something into it ... His beak was a hungry noisy beak, stretching higher than his sister's and gobbling everything quicker than a wink.*
>
> (from *Magpie Island* by Colin Thiele and Roger Haldane 1979)

There are many examples in extended narratives that can be selected for younger students too. Teachers can read a short excerpt that is manageable and still offers a range of features to notice, for example, the following description of Doc Spencer from Roald Dahl's *Danny, Champion of the World* (1975):

> *He was a tiny man with tiny hands and feet and a tiny round face. The face was as brown and wrinkled as a shrivelled apple ... with wispy white hair and steel-rimmed spectacles ...*

Children can be encouraged to notice the use of descriptors, which give the image some clarity by providing information about size, colour and shape. Teachers can guide them to see how the details that a writer provides, brings to life the portrait we are able to visualise.

The skill of describing physical attributes can be practised by 'people-watching', as Laura Ranger did so well in her poem 'Mum'.

Mum

Her hair curls
like fern fronds.

Her eyes are like
speckled green birds' eggs.

Her glasses are two pools
of clear water.

Her nose is blunt.

Her hands are wrinkled and kind.
She reaches out to touch me.

I love my mum
forty four million
times around the world.
Laura Ranger 7 years

Start in your mind's eye

Having explored what other writers have done, in describing physical characteristics, and having chosen a person that has some importance to them, students can be walked through the following visualisation:

To get you started, close your eyes and put your character in your mind.
Is there anything special you notice about the face?
What is the hair like? (length, style, texture, colour)
Be aware of your character's body (size, shape, stance, height).
Are there any distinguishing features?
What is your person wearing? Look at the colours, textures, style of their
clothing. How do they wear their clothes?
Do they have particular gestures or ways of moving?
Take a minute to look carefully at all those aspects of your person.
Open your eyes. In non-stop writing, jot down all you can recall.

Guided revision

After ten minutes or so, have students share their jottings with a partner before bringing them to the helping circle for a guided revision. They come prepared with their crafting pens to make additions as they gather further ideas from their peers' contributions. This is an expectation from these sessions.

Teacher: *Who has something about the stance of their person?*
Student: *She stoops over the garden.*
Student: *He puts his hands on his hips when he's growling me.*
Teacher: *Who has something about the hair?*
Student: *You can see white hairs in a few places starting to show.*
Student: *Grandad's got a little bit of hair around the edge.*
Teacher: *Who has something about the way they wear their clothes?*
Student: *Mum has a favourite shirt and she always rolls the sleeves up.*
      And so on ...
Teacher: *What will you now add to your zero draft?*

At this stage, there will be enough information to work into a crafted paragraph. For students needing further scaffolding, the teacher may model the crafting process using a student's draft.

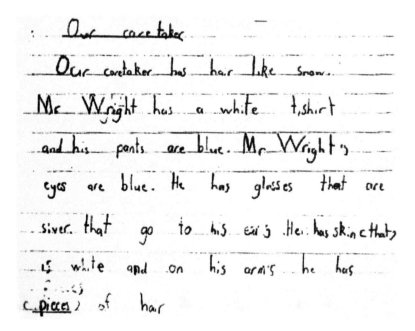

Our caretaker

Our caretaker has hair like snow. Mr Wright has a white t,shirt and his pants are blue. Mr Wright's eyes are blue. He has glasses that are siver. that go to his ears. He has skin c thats is white and on his arm's he has c.pices) of hair

Behaviour

When we respond to characters in narrative, either visual or written texts, we want to know what they are like, not just what they look like. Describing what someone looks like is an important part of the process of forming our observations into words, but we reveal more when we try to describe the way they behave. In an extended narrative, we have a need to get to know the sort of character this person is in order to predict the way they will respond to the situations as they arise. In a character portrait, we can select typical behaviours to include, giving our readers a sense of knowing our chosen character.

As in learning to describe the physical attributes, I begin by providing opportunities for my students to notice what other writers have done. I draw attention to the specific information given, and lead discussions around what we learn of a character by taking a close look at an aspect of behaviour.

> *I watched him pull the charred, stubby remains of a pipe out of his bib pocket together with a small, silver penknife which he used to carefully remove every scrap of dottle from the bowl of his pipe. Once satisfied he replaced it with brown curls of fresh tobacco plucked from a yellow, floppy rubber pouch which he pressed home with the end of the silver knife.*
>
> *After a few trial sucks, he lit the pipe with a paper spill from the crowded mantelshelf. The whole performance had an air of ritual about it, but the result was a vile smelling haze of blue smoke which fogged the lamplight and enveloped us both.*
> (from *Moses Beech* by Ian Strachan 1983)

Again, the description of human behaviour can be practised by 'people-watching', as Laura demonstrates with her delightful poem 'Nathan'.

Nathan
Nathan at my school
thinks he is
extremely cool.
He dances the be-bop
in the class,
and plays the fool.

Mrs Herman
has hands on hips
and tight fish lips.
She turns
and looks stern.
She makes an announcement
'Nathan does not listen,
so he will not learn'.
Laura Ranger 7 years

There are examples of character behaviour traits in any novel, short story or picture book. Sometimes it might be a sentence or two, sometimes a paragraph or two. As we find our models, we become more and more secure in being able to frame the questions needed to lead our students into noticing the writer's choices themselves.

When students are able to identify what has been mentioned by other writers, and to notice the effect it has for the reader, we need to bring them back to think of their own chosen character:

In your mind's eye ...

Close your eyes and take a few minutes to bring to mind your character.
Now have this person act in a way that would be very typical of them.
Where are they? Inside or outside?
What are they doing?
Do they have anything in their hands?
Are they alone or are they with someone?
Open your eyes and tell your partner what you had your character doing.

As well as sharing with a partner, it will be useful for some students to share their anecdotes with the whole class, so that they can build on one another's ideas. The discussion should always lead to students considering the effectiveness of their own language choice.

Listen to what Emma had to say about her Grandad ... let's see if we can tell
what sort of person he is ...
You said that he's always 'making stuff', Emma ... tell us more about that –
what sort of things does he make? What does he use?

Has that helped us get to know more about him, now that we know he's always going to the beach to get driftwood, to make sculptures for the garden?

It is important for students to make connections and apply the principles and techniques of these discussions back to their own writing so that crafting and re-crafting becomes part and parcel of a day's writing – it is what we do.

How has this helped you with your own description?

At this point, provide a quiet writing time for students to record their personal tale of their character's behaviour.

When students have made their first draft, they can share what they have written, have their peers respond and subsequently do any revision they feel necessary, to make sure they have chosen the words which say what they mean.

Monologue and dialogue

What the character says, and the way it is said, reveals something about that person's make-up, temperament, background and values. This may be a quotation in a character portrait, but in narrative it is often the dialogue that adds depth to the characterisation. Sometimes it is the briefest of extracts from the story, which

gradually builds up clues about the character, using direct speech, often in an exchange. This is a solo dad, talking to his young son:

> *'Get your chops around this,' he said, shoving a peanut slab at me.*
> *'Couldn't afford any ice cream this week,' he told me while we put the groceries away. Still he had that big smile on his face. 'Can't afford ice cream as well as petrol ...'*
> (from 'The Blue Humber 80' by Jack Gabolinscy 1991)

This one, a mother to her daughter:

> *She yelled loudly, 'Get up off that road, my girl. There's nothing wrong with these togs. I didn't have any togs when I was a kid and I had to swim in my nothings. Get up off your backside and get to school.'*
> (from 'It Used to Be Green Once' by Patricia Grace 1980)

Monologue, as well as dialogue, provides detail of character. Here we see A.A. Milne's Rabbit, full of self-importance:

> *'After all,' said Rabbit to himself, 'Christopher Robin depends on Me. He's fond of Pooh and Piglet and Eeyore, and so am I, but they haven't any Brain. Not to notice. And he respects Owl, because you can't help respecting anybody who can spell TUESDAY, even if he doesn't spell it right; but spelling isn't everything. There are days when spelling Tuesday simply doesn't count. And Kanga is too busy looking after Roo, and Roo is too young and Tigger is too bouncy to be any help, so there's really nobody but Me, when you come to look at it. I'll go and see if there's anything he wants doing, and then I'll do it for him. It's just the day for doing things.'*
> (from *The House at Pooh Corner* by A. A. Milne 1928)

This device is often more revealing of the character than reported speech, as we can actually 'hear' the character speaking or thinking. Reported speech can give us clues to the character being quoted – and often clues about the character who reports:

And Mrs. Bradwick who was the Chair Person of the Governors … said
she didn't blame it on Mr. Kerney personally, but blamed it on the Sixties when
teachers stopped caring about Janet and John and Nip the Dog and long
division and the ten times table and all they ever did was finger painting and
dancing and the sort of poetry which made no sense and didn't even rhyme.
(from *The Wrong Boy* by Willy Russell 2000)

These extracts, of course, are from extended narrative, and although useful in discussing with students as we collectively learn to take delight in acknowledging the skills of writers, it is the concept of using the actual words spoken in building up character that we are noting.

Students of literature will no doubt spend much time analysing the content of Shakespeare's soliloquies, where we learn more of the character from the internal voice than from the dialogue. This is sometimes referred to as dramatic monologue, and can be used effectively as a 'stand-alone' piece, often accompanying a picture of the character.

Young people these days, they certainly live in a different world from the one I grew up in. No one rides ponies to school anymore like we did when I was a child, nor do they bike, and they don't even walk. My son takes his children to school in the car and their college isn't even a mile away. But what I can't get over is so many of them have phones, tiny little phones that fit into their pockets! My great grandson's phone plays music, sends messages, and it is a camera too. All that. In his pocket. Imagine trying to fit our old phone into a pocket. It was nearly as big as a microwave, and wired into the wall. Even our camera was bigger than two packets of butter. Yes, the world is definitely getting smaller.

There are many reasons for introducing a dramatic monologue as a writing task for our students. Again, it is not a random activity but one that allows our young writers to practise and build on what they are learning about portraying a character.

We can expect that our students will be able to draw on their imaginations when creating a dramatic monologue for an imagined character, perhaps motivated by an anonymous photograph. It is interesting to see the variety of characters that students can draw from one picture, with a range of individual 'takes' on the same picture. We can also expect that what a writer makes a character say will be credible, even if imagined. Similarly, an image of a 'real' person may be used in composing a dramatic monologue. This requires some knowledge of the person portrayed to ensure credibility as we make some assumptions about what they might be thinking and the language they might use. This same technique has proved a useful exercise with students of all ages as they respond to new learning in a specific context. Imagined monologues from images of pop artist Andy Warhol, or a policeman during the controversial 'Springbok Tour' (a tour of New Zealand by the South African rugby union team), both provide students with a way to show their understanding of the unit of study.

'I didn't discover Pop – it's just there. It's all around us. Everyone is buying things and everyone buys the same things. Rich people drink Coke and poor people drink Coke. It doesn't matter how rich you are, you can't get a better Coke than the poor guy.'

'Standing behind barbed wire while my country destroys itself over a pointless tour. I hope nobody starts throwing bottles at me or tries to break through. I don't want to hit anybody. Why, oh why, did I join the police? I suppose I'm safe behind my shield and I have got a helmet and a baton so I suppose I'll be OK. What if my friends are in the crowd? What if I have to hit them? I can't hit them. What am I doing here? I can't do this. Help.'

In a character description, as opposed to characterisation within a story, we need a brief glimpse of the sort of things that are commonly said as we outline our chosen character:

In your mind's ear ...

Close your eyes and take a few minutes to bring to mind your character.
Now have them speak in a way that would be very typical of them.
It may be something you have heard them say more than once.
Where are they?

Who are they talking to?

What tone are they using? What is their mood?

Do they have a particular accent?

Open your eyes and tell your partner what your character was saying and perhaps some responses they would typically receive.

We might expect students to be sharing things like:

My Dad's always joking around. He always says 'C'mon, gorgeous!' to my mum. And things like 'Here comes trouble!' when I walk in.

When there has been opportunity for students to recall the voice of their characters, and to share the sorts of things they are saying, teachers again provide a time for writing, to allow students to focus on recording the words.

How a character affects others

How others respond to the character tells us something about their place in the world, their standing, or reputation. There are many examples in stories that show something of a character by describing the effect on others – in this case from the narrator's viewpoint:

Spit Nolan was a pal of mine. He was a thin lad with a bony face that was always pale, except for two rosy spots on his cheekbones. He had quick brown eyes, short, wiry hair, rather stooped shoulders, and we all knew he had one lung. He had had a disease which in those days couldn't be cured, unless you went away to Switzerland, which Spit certainly couldn't afford. He wasn't sorry for himself in any way, and in fact we envied him, because he never had to go to school.

Spit was the champion trolley rider of Cotton Pocket. He had a very good balance, and sharp wits, and he was very brave, so that these qualities, when added to the skill as a rider, meant that no other boy could ever beat Spit on a trolley – and every lad had one.

(from *The Goalkeeper's Revenge* by Bill Naughton 1988)

The discussions that can ensue around excerpts from stories can enhance the enjoyment and the appreciation of a shared novel with a class of students. In sharing the piece above, teachers can prompt talk of Spit Nolan's reputation, and what he had done to deserve it.

With thoughtful questioning, we can not only check on understanding, but lead students to think critically about what the writer has included, and how that helps us to build a three-dimensional image of the character we are getting to know.

When it's the students' turn to write, I would suggest the same format as described for earlier paragraphs.

In your mind's eye and ear ...

Close your eyes and bring your character to mind again.
Imagine your character doing something that is usual for them.
Are they alone or with someone?
Is there any talk going on?
Now stand back from the action and watch carefully from the sideline.
How are other people responding to the actions and words of your character?
What might they be saying about your person?
Open your eyes and tell a partner about the effect your character has on others.

Description of character's environment or belongings

If we are close observers, we can collect more clues to the personality of our character by taking note of the environment they set up for themselves, what and who they surround themselves with. Teachers need to be continually searching for suitable models of text that we can bring to our students' notice. In most narratives there will be descriptions of the surroundings of the characters.

The room, like his clothes, was more serviceable than comfortable. There was no carpet, just a rug which might have been any colour when new but was now mostly grey with dust ...The only other furniture, apart from a couple of

armchairs by the fire, consisted of an old treadle sewing machine with a bake-
lite radio sitting on it, a huge round wall clock above it, and the main table with
its oil lamp in the middle of the room.
'Pull a chair up,' the old man said as he slapped two steaming piled plates on to
it. The half we sat at had clean newspaper spread on it, like a tablecloth, but the
other half held everything you were ever likely to want during a meal, and a few
you weren't. Sauces, pickles and jam jars rubbed shoulders with a mousetrap,
some fishing line, a trowel, an odd collection of cutlery, a misshapen loaf and
some elderly fruit pies with enough mould on them to glow in the dark.
(from *Moses Beech* by Ian Strachan 1983)

When we share excerpts such as this, we can lead discussions about what we learn of the character, through being given a glimpse of their environment.

As outlined in previous examples, you can lead your students through visualising a description of a place they associate with their character, for example, a room, shed, or garden, and then repeat the writing process.

Putting it together

For very young writers we can be pleased with one idea recorded. This may be a physical description:

My Nana has baggy eyes and wrinkly skin.

or a description of personality that is often the most significant feature of an individual in a young person's life:

My Granny is the best Granny. She reads to me.

For our more experienced writers we may wish to have them combine or expand their vignettes, which they have composed one at a time, into a more comprehensive piece of writing. Of course, this will depend on the purpose of the writing and the age and experience of the writers.

Each vignette may be recorded as a new paragraph in the final 'putting together', which may entail some specific teaching about the layout and function of paragraphs.

The following piece came from a Year 4 class after their teacher walked them through each stage of the process.

My Special Grandma

Her short curly, grey hair bounces when she is in a hurry. Old lines like roads show her age as do her purply legs. She always wears faded dresses with brown shoes. Eyes glitter as she meets friends. Her tidiness makes her look lovely.

She is loving and caring towards other people and animals. She always takes one of her friends' dog for a walk every morning. A kind-hearted lady, always ready to help.

Though tired from working on pictures of mountains to sell, she never lets it out. Sadness from fear of our dying grandpa sometimes shows on her face. She works every morning in the rose garden that my grandpa planted.

I always feel she wants me when she writes to me and tells me about our little baby cousin and his mischief. I feel she loves me and other people. She makes me feel excited and special when she is with me.

Anna, Year 4

Dad

My dad is medium height with red hair, moustache, beard and a pink tinted face. His eyes glisten comically with the colour of hazelnuts. His arms and legs are freckled and hairy with big shoulders of muscle. Dad's teeth are yellowish from years of eating and you can see white hairs in a few places starting to show. The clothes he wears are dark brown, green, grey and black, generally shorts, T shirt, trousers and sweat shirt.

He has a jerking laugh and a rolling voice. He is the most joking person I know and teases anyone. Sometimes he is sad, but usually at home. He likes animals and hates killing them to eat, so there is usually a protest and ideas of breeding when killing our pig comes into the discussion. Classic cars are his main interest and he would put ours in a bed if Mum would let him.

Sometimes my dad is stubborn and childish. He is continually teasing anybody about anything, so nobody is safe doing something silly or funny. He is a TV lover so he gets grumpy if anyone blocks his view or speaks when he is watching the news. Dad is hot tempered and hates untidiness, but hates tidying.

Sometimes people don't know how to take him because he is very critical and joking, a weird mixture. He is fun and can think up ways to make chores enjoyable. He is very protective over his possessions, so people are often taken aback by his rudeness. He hates showing his emotions to other people and is ashamed of crying which he influences on my brother and makes my mum mad. Even though he teases me I love him.

Katrina, Year 7

Summary - *Character Portrait*

- Responding to characters in narrative.

- Structured framework for scaffolding students – a bridge from expressive to expository writing.

- Choosing a character and a theme.

- Physical description.

- Actions revealing personality and behaviour.

- Monologue and dialogue.

- How a character affects others.

- Description of a character's environment.

- Combining the paragraphs – putting it together.

Appendix – *Character Portrait*

Portrait of My Teacher	
My teacher is the most enthusiastic teacher I've known. The minute the classroom door opens, kids rush in to see what is planned for the day. She usually stands by the door, running her hands through her hair as she greets us, one by one. Her hair is feathery and stands on end: messed up from the wind or her own hand. Her fingers run through it continuously, drawing it away from her eyes. She needs to have clear vision to keep a watchful eye on the students in her care. She strides about the room, usually with a book in hand, pausing at chosen tables. Her dangling earrings bounce back and forth as she moves. Soft skin is dented from old smiles and her cheeks become flushed from embarrassment, laughter or anger. She dresses casually and her wardrobe includes a selection of coloured jeans and shirts. The muted green leather of her Doc Marten boots shows individuality and a holding on to her past.	Thesis Physical description
It is clear that she is dedicated to her craft. Each Monday morning we are greeted with a fresh display of art works, carefully selected books and the poetry we published last week. The tape deck is always in use, playing a selection from Mozart to The Beatles. 'They knew how to write a good tune,' she says. There is always a personal greeting at the door, 'Good morning Tracey,' she will say, 'How was your weekend? Come and have a look at this amazing new book I found.' Although her English accent is fading, it fights its way back when she gets mad.	Behaviour

School assemblies are the best when my teacher leads them. The little kids sit up straight, smiling up to the platform, knowing that there will be lots of singing and a few laughs. Even the seniors are unusually attentive, expecting more than dreary routine. Her musical plays have become a tradition in our school. The way she directs gets the job done, even though we get to see flashes of temper along the way. She seems relaxed around her colleagues – always joking and laughing, and always with a mug of coffee in her hand.	Reputation – how she affects other people
It is easy to see what her interests are. The shelves behind her desk are cluttered with her personal belongings. An ancient French violin is one of her treasures. She rarely plays it, but she polishes it with silk. Her collection of books, videos and CDs are the clues: beautifully illustrated volumes showing works of Andy Warhol and Escher; posters advertising opera and ballet, violinist Vanessa Mae. All these are the things she likes to share with us. She is generous with her time and with her possessions. My teacher expects us to think and work with the same enthusiasm she has, which is why I am always keen to get to school each day.	Her artefacts – what they say about her  Thesis confirmed 

Suggested Guide for a Character Portrait

Preparation

1 Explore examples of character portraits for
 	
  • purpose
  • a particular structure – how they link with what we already know about writing and what is new for us to learn
  • language features
 	
2 Think about a person who has had an effect on your life
 	
3 Homework tasks in notebooks - gathering material for writing - talking with our friends and family about our chosen character

Week One
• Share character preparation with partner   • Compose a thesis statement – *This person is the _____ person I know*

Physical (Paragraph 1)
  • Visualisation
  • Zero draft
  • Helping Circle - guided revision with crafting pen

• Explore text (*Moses Beech* – physical) for language features
  • Form a 'checklist for the writer'
  • Write a paragraph (physical description) from zero draft

Behaviour (Paragraph 2)
  • Mini lesson - the anecdote - explore examples
  • Visualisation
  • Zero draft
  • Helping Circle - guided revision with crafting pen

• Explore text (*Moses Beech* – behaviour) for language features
  • Form a 'checklist for the writer'
  • Write a paragraph (description of behaviour) from zero draft

The Character Speaks

Monologue

- Explore examples of monologue
- Use a photograph as a practice exercise
- Share class samples

Week Two / Three

Dialogue

- Explore examples of dialogue in texts showing the effect of the character's interactions with others
- Pull the character to mind to capture a typical way of talking
- Jot what comes to mind
- Plan to add where it might enhance the portrayal of the character

How the Character Affects Others (Paragraph 3)

- Explore text (Spit Nolan) for clues to how the character affects others and the language features that contribute to this
- Visualisation
- Zero draft
- Helping Circle - guided revision with crafting pen
- Talking with our friends and family about our chosen character

- Mini lesson - adding talk - share student examples
- Form a 'checklist for the writer'
- Craft a paragraph from zero draft

The Character's Environment and Belongings (Paragraph 4)

- Explore text (*Moses Beech* - environment & belongings) for language features
- Form a 'checklist for the writer'
- Write a paragraph (physical description) from zero draft

- Combine paragraphs
- Craft for excellence
- Present

Guided Writing Plan

Model text: excerpt from 'Moses Beech' by Ian Strachan

Purpose for the lesson	• We are describing a character, a person that we know well.
Learning focus	• We are learning to identify what language features an author has used in his description of the physical characteristics of his character. • What techniques has he used to give the reader a clear mind-picture of the person? • We will look particularly at the sentences which begin with a conjunction.

Leading the learning

Reading, thinking and talking

How are we going to do this?

• Read the physical description - *Moses Beech* p.12
• Question students to pull up the main content of the piece - what is described -

   walk, skin, head, hair, ears, eyes, face, clothes

• How has the author described those physical attributes? (Bring up prior knowledge)

Sentence beginnings - draw attention to the sentences that start with a subordinating conjunction ...

   Although he moved slowly, his pace was steady and deliberate.

   Although the whites of his eyes were a watery yellow, the irises were intensely blue.

or start with a preposition

   With the fringe around his bald patch and the clumps of hair escaping from his ears and nostrils, he looked a bit like a toy that's losing its stuffing.

Sentence structures - what effect on the sentence structure and meaning do these conjunctions make?

Comparisons - note how the conjunction at the beginning of the sentence creates a comparison

Activated noun - *stubble hung* - the noun *(stubble)* did something *(hung)*

Writing Task
- Ask students to think of an older person that they know well
- Students share with a partner the physical attributes of that person
- Lead a visualisation exercise to bring up physical attributes
- Students jot all that they can remember
- Use one example as a shared piece of writing
- Collaboratively form criteria for success
- Students write own physical description
- Guided revision
- Students asked to innovate on a sentence beginning with a conjunction - use own writing for the content
- Students add newly formed sentence to writing if it enhances the effect

Success criteria *How will we know we have been successful?* Co-construct with the students	We will know we have done this when we have included in a paragraph – • a description of four different attributes (parts of the body) • sentences starting in different ways (may include a sentence starting with a conjunction) • at least one comparison
Challenges for writers	• to make decisions about what detail to include and what to leave out • to select the most precise language to suit the purpose • to transfer identified techniques to our own character studies

10 Writing across the Curriculum
Writing to learn and writing to share our learning

Writing, like reading, forms an integral part of all curriculum areas in any classroom. As coaches of our teams of writers, we are ever mindful of the purpose for writing, and the most appropriate form that will serve that purpose. We can find textbooks which list suggested writing functions and forms. Many teachers have been diligent in their attempts to teach 'coverage' and expose their students to the 'range of genres' listed in these textbooks. This can be at the expense of helping our students see the real purpose for writing, and can result in teachers and students getting bored with the prescribed structure and features of a particular genre being 'taught' for weeks on end.

Of course it is essential that we provide frameworks for writing for our learner-writers. If we are aware of a responsibility to coach students in understanding the conventions of written language and to write confidently and appropriately for a range of purposes, we may be tempted to think that this would necessitate marching students through a list of genres. The march need not be dictated by a timetable, though. If we are open to the opportunities that present themselves in all learning areas, we will see that if anything dictates the type of writing we are to attempt, it is the purpose and the audience.

As the range of functions of writing are explored in a variety of text forms, the learner-writer will deliberately seek to employ specific language features of poetic or transactional writing, and mix both, as they become increasingly aware of purpose and audience. It is while exploring these functions, that students can be shown a variety of structural patterns and language features that suit the purpose of writing.

Very young writers write expressively, and will incorporate facts with personal opinion quite naturally:

This young writer has attempted to explain how a baby chick gets out of the egg, and is accurate in her knowledge. She manages to include a very personal connection with eggs. As we mature, we come to realise that expressing personal feelings may be inappropriate for an expository piece of writing.

Generally, we have moved on from the formal, 'encyclopaedic' language of former years in classrooms, when students were encouraged to remove the 'I' from trans-actional writing, to ensure that the information contained was objective and imper-sonal. We do still need to be able to equip our students with the skills required to write formally, of course. Formal or factual writing need not be dull; we can often still hear the writer's voice, regardless of the form being employed.

Teachers may feel some uncertainty with regard to getting the right balance of providing a specific structure for their students, and allowing them to write freely. It seems that there is a certain amount of instinctive behaviour here, which we can learn to trust, as we write to make more sense of our world and to present our thoughts and knowledge. Even the youngest of our students have a degree of understanding about what is the most appropriate form of writing to use. They know that a shopping list is just that – the list does not require lots of descrip-tors. Similarly, a text message doesn't require full sentences or even conventional spelling to get the message across. I remember, with some amusement, the notes I found on the kitchen bench on summer afternoons:

Gone up the
creake
p.s. it is 4 o'clock

The author of this note, immature in years and spelling proficiency, is mature enough to know that a poetic description, precise facts, or full sentences are unnecessary in this form of written communication.

When we explore published texts, in literature, journalism, advertising, and so on – in the 'real' world as opposed to 'school writing' – it is hard to classify a particular piece, and it is often this lack of clear criteria that gives the piece some impact. We can have some interesting discussions about what we think might be the author's purpose in writing. An article by a Sunday columnist about the finding of a prostitute's body on an inner-city section initiated such a discussion among teachers on a Monday morning. Was the graphic description and detail used to inform the reader of the facts? Or to shock an audience into the realisation that such horror can occur in respectable suburbs? Or was it to create interest in the upcoming exhibition of paintings by the deeply affected neighbour? The discussion was animated and thought-provoking, but no consensus was reached about its purpose. What everyone could agree on, was that the article drew a response. An itch was scratched ...

In Ken Macrorie's *Writing to be Read* (1984), the author describes 'The Alternating Current' in writing. By this, he is referring to the strategy used by professional writers, where they shift back and forth from a lowly 'kitchen' language to a 'bookish' or 'elevated' language.

He explains further:

> *The Alternating Current* isn't difficult to turn on in your writing. The secret
> lies in the genuineness of its juice, the speech you already have in your

unconscious memory. If you remember your native dialogue – the language
you learned at Mother's knee – and alternate that with the language of writ-
ing you've picked up through reading and listening to teachers in classrooms,
you'll find the current naturally coursing through your prose. Finding it again
is a matter of honesty. What is your voice? Do you hear how you speak when
you're not thinking of your language?
(Ken Macrorie 1984)

Professional columnists are usually interesting to read as they write in a compelling way; it is often use of the 'Alternating Current' that makes what they have to say compelling.

They are able to argue a point, get across factual information, offer explanations, and so on, with the credibility of some research in evidence, while putting a very personal slant on the issue being discussed. They often write in the first person, and are masters of persuasion, leaving us in no doubt of their opinion on a particular topic, even though it may have been only the facts that we were after. They illustrate the 'stream of consciousness' that we want to encourage as we help our students see significance in things around them, and respond, whether it be wondering about a scientific phenomenon, thinking about the artwork they have created or expressing their feelings about ... anything.

On the crossing at the bottom of Queen St in downtown Auckland, backpack-
ers wearing beige pants with pockets and zip-off legs are running amok. Legs
in the mall at St Lukes are awash with khaki and pockets. Down at the Victoria
Park skatebowl, teenage boys swarm and spin, finding new ways to crack open
their heads, and all wear the same uniform: sneakers, massive T-shirts and
oversize pants with pockets on the outside. The colours vary: grey, red, cam-
ouflage and denim blue, and an awful lot of beige. But there is no mistaking
the pockets, sewn onto the outside and billowing out from halfway down each
trouser leg. They are cargo pants, formerly known as army surplus or cammo
pants, and they are everywhere ...
(Bianca Zander 2000, excerpt from magazine column)

We do need to become familiar with the 'pure forms' that writing can take, and consciously support students in recognising the characteristics of different genres, so that they are equipped to make choices as they develop skills in creating meaningful text. Teachers in primary classrooms appear to have an advantage over secondary colleagues when it comes to teaching appropriate writing forms across the curriculum. As primary teachers are responsible for delivering all curriculum areas to their students, there is scope for one teacher to support the same students through a range of text forms, enabling them to investigate appropriate forms to express their ideas in all learning areas, all within the same classroom. There is some responsibility then, for primary teachers to ensure that their students are well grounded in the pure forms, and have had ample opportunity for trying out what makes a piece of writing effective in an appropriate form, and in a given context.

Writing to explain

In a primary classroom, if we take 'explanation' as a text form to explore, in a specific learning context, we can see how readily we might:

- write expressively, as we try out ideas and make connections with what we already know;

- explain things in a poetic sense, with the language of mythology;

- use explanation in a transactional sense, where the phenomenon is explained in a factually accurate way.

Moving between expressive and transactional writing

What are Volcanoes?

> *I think that volcanoes are like mountains that erupt sometimes. They would have a sort of tunnel in the middle that goes from underground right to the top of the mountain, and when it erupts, red hot lava comes out of the top and runs all down the sides. I have seen a volcano on a documentary. They filmed an eruption. It would be dangerous to be on the volcano when it erupts.*

Sam, Year 8

This writer has been given the opportunity to articulate his thoughts around the subject of volcanoes. Expressive writing is the closest written form to speech, and we can see how this writer feels comfortable to jot down his thoughts, as though he were having an informal discussion with someone. It is evident that he has noticed something about the way volcanoes work through watching a documentary, and it is likely there has been discussion at home and school. He has picked up information and specific vocabulary, like 'erupt' and 'lava', and used them appropriately, and it seems that he is comfortable with his efforts of communicating his thoughts, even though he may not feel particularly knowledgeable, yet, about volcanoes. When students are encouraged to write what they know, safe in the knowledge that their personal thoughts are valid, they will feel secure in their learning.

Very young children are concerned with 'self' and self interest gradually matures into interest in social and natural phenomena:

- What is going on around me?

- Why are things the way they are?

- Where and how do I fit into all this?

Part of our job is to encourage and support students to write outside themselves.

Explanation is thought of as a transactional or expository form, and can help children form and sequence ideas, clarify ideas and beliefs, and reflect on ideas and understanding.

Expressive writing, leading to transactional or expository writing, can provide scope for self-discovery through exploration of the world around us, in just the same way as expressive writing can lead to poetic forms, such as memoir and descriptions.

Sam's expressive writing may stand as it is, and may have been a response to personal wonderings, but it is likely that it was prompted by the teacher directing students to make some connections within a given topic before investigating further. He may be led to research, to discover more about the natural phenomenon of volcanoes, and may then be expected to write a 'formal explanation' on the topic. The following piece is a model of 'Explanation', which may serve to support Sam in his research.

How are volcanoes formed?

A volcano is a hill or mountain that has built up from the eruption of molten rock from the middle of the earth.

The temperature deep inside the earth is so hot it melts rock into a super-hot liquid called magma. It also builds up a lot of pressure. This pressure then pushes the magma, along with gases and steam, up through openings in the earth's crust. These openings become volcanoes.

When magma reaches the surface, it is called lava. It can be shot into the air in a fire fountain or just pour out of any of the volcano's openings. Volcanoes can erupt for a very brief time or they can erupt many times over millions of years. Sometimes they sleep for long periods (lie dormant) and people think they are finished, but they aren't.

Because hot lava is a liquid, it often flows like a river of fire down the sides of the volcano. Though lava starts as a super-hot liquid, it will become solid rock once it cools. Consequently it builds up around the volcano's opening, getting higher and wider, as long as the volcano stays active, until eventually

it becomes a mountain. Active volcanoes are a feature of the New Zealand
landscape. The North Island has a Volcanic Plateau, with the volcanic peaks
of Ruapehu (2,797m), Tongariro (1,986m) and Ngauruhoe (2,291m), with Mt
Taranaki (2,518m) to the west.
(Unknown source)

We need to ask ourselves what language features are included in explanations, and several models of this form of writing will need to be provided. If this piece is unpacked, teacher and students will be able to identify what makes it effective as an explanation. The language features seen in the Volcanoes model include:

- paragraphs;

- economical use of descriptors (although some are used, e.g. super-hot, fire foun- tain, river of fire);

- personal pronouns not used;

- timeless present tense used;

- topic-specific vocabulary;

- generalised non-human participants (volcanoes, magma, lava, rock, mountain);

- cause and effect relationships (consequently);

- time relationships (until, eventually);

- verbs describe material processes (melts, pushes, flows).

Specific teaching is necessary to support students in their understanding that a particular structure is useful in writing for a particular purpose – in this case, to explain the natural phenomenon of active volcanoes. This study may be part of a study of The Planet Earth – there may be a focus on the geography and geology of New Zealand. Whatever the curriculum focus, the intended learning will need to include how an explanatory text is put together. If we guide our students in identi- fying what makes explanatory writing effective, we are providing the scaffold that they need in order to write an effective explanation themselves. There may be opportunities that arise where an explanatory form can be practised to consolidate learning, but the order of thinking is important here:

We are going to find out how volcanoes are formed;
We need to be able to write to explain how volcanoes are formed.
So -
We need to find information about volcanoes;
We need to find models of explanation, and unpack them.

Rather than:

We are going to 'do' explanation writing;
We need to find a context to use, to practise explanation.

If your classroom offers learning opportunities in all curriculum areas, you will find that you have contexts at hand when explanatory writing will be the most appropriate for the purpose.

We can't leave explanation as purely formal, transactional writing, when our human history of legends and mythology is expressed in explanations. In a climate of learning to unpack texts and identify specific language features, students will be interested to see how explanations can be written in a poetic way:

The Legend of Taranaki
Taranaki, Ruapehu and Tongariro were three great mountains, shaped like per-
fect cones, who lived together in the centre of the North Island of Aotearoa.
All three of these magnificent mountains were in love with a pretty, smaller
mountain, Pihanga, who stood nearby. When Pihanga could not decide which
of them she loved the most, the three great mountains began arguing with
one another, and making angry rumbling noises. Finally, Taranaki and Ton-
gariro started to push and shove each other. Then, Ruapehu joined the fight.
He made the water of his crater boil, and threw it at Taranaki. Taranaki hit
back with a shower of boulders which broke the top of Ruapehu's perfect cone
and ruined his handsome looks. In a fit of rage, Ruapehu swallowed his cone,

melted it, and threw the red-hot lava all over Taranaki. Taranaki was badly wounded, and hurried to get away from Ruapehu. He fled far away to the sea to cool down. Ruapehu seemed to have won. But when he cooled down and looked around for Pihanga, he found she was not in her usual place. The little mountain had taken fright during the battle and gone to shelter beside Tongariro, the least war-like of the three giants. And while Ruapehu and Taranaki were fighting over which of them should possess Pihanga, Tongariro had won her heart.

To this day, Taranaki stands sulking near the sea, far away from the place where he was defeated. For Ruapehu, the hurt is even more bitter. He must stand forever within sight of his beloved Pihanga, who still shelters beside the mighty Tongariro.
(Unknown source)

This legend offers a poetic, narrative explanation of how and why these volcanic mountains came to be where they are today. Typically, the natural phenomenon of mountains and volcanic eruptions are personified – the mountains become the main characters of the story. The natural geological processes are described as human behaviours – premeditated actions – as the central characters are given gender and personality.

Teachers can lead students in being able to identify the deeper features within the language of legends, and a class will be able to discuss why myths and legends are universal - our human attempt to explain natural phenomena.

While myths and legends may be interesting to explore, and may be used in a comparison with scientific explanation, we are mindful of cultural beliefs and values - never undermining the beliefs and understandings of others. Gods have long been associated with the powerful and recurring wonders of nature - sunrise and sunset, thunder and lightning, frost and snow, earthquakes and volcanoes. And people everywhere have felt the need to appease the gods whose might controls these natural happenings.

> *And why should we know about mythology?*
> *Because we cannot afford to miss the opportunity to eavesdrop on the inner-most thoughts of mankind. Myths and legends are a universal human inven-tion. They have arisen at different times and different places as explanations of the problems that always face people. They tell of misfortune, success, cruelty, love, death, betrayal, magic, power, fate, war, creation and the nature of the universe.*
> (Unknown source)

There will be many contexts across the curriculum for students to be able to explain. I have seen students having a go at explaining:

- science observations;

- the rules of a game;

- life cycles;

- rules and laws;

- how an art work was created;

- why the tide comes in and out.

Finding the right words to explain something is valuable stuff as our learner-writers grow in their thinking about the world – in everything from purely scientific phenomena to the purely social.

Writing to persuade

Another text form to explore in primary classrooms is 'written argument'. This type of communication gives us a vehicle to be able to express personal opinions in a legitimate and effective way. Transactional in purpose, a written argument again provides student writers with a means to clarify their thoughts and make more sense of the world and their place in it.

The essential purpose for argument is to persuade a reader to the writer's point of view, and so the writer must convince the reader by including relevant points with some supporting evidence. The language features would include:

- the use of vocabulary that shows the writer's attitude;

- precise, factual details, to give credibility;

- specific, topic-related language, to add authority;

- emotive words that express feelings and persuade;

- conjunctions to link cause and effect.

While very young children can be opinionated and form an opinion on an issue, it is through maturity that we are able to justify the reasons for holding that opinion. Our young writers, then, might be expected to say what they think without qualifying their opinion. For example, after reading *The Little Red Hen*, a junior child wrote:

> *The little red hen is mean.*

As they mature, a simple opinion will be supported with reasons, not necessarily rational, which justify the stance taken. For example:

I think the little red hen was mean to the animals because she didn't share the bread.

Older students may well argue that the Little Red Hen wasn't mean at all, as she was justified in her decision not to share the bread.

Students will need to understand what makes an argument effective – what a writer should include in order to convince a reader. Discussions with students, and parenting experience, have shown us how children are masters of persuasion, particularly when it comes to trying to get their way with a parent, and they are quick to be able to articulate what is the most likely approach to work. They know intuitively that using 'polite' language works better than abuse and that good reasons (for whatever is being sought) must be provided. If they agree that this is the most effective tack to take in arguing a point or persuading verbally, it is likely that they will see that the same approach is appropriate for the written form. It is these personal issues that often provide a real context for persuasive words.

There are countless contexts for argument, but we need to remember that a topic which has some relevance for the students will be argued with some sincerity. It is difficult to be sincere about an issue that is irrelevant to our lives. Suitable contexts will arise in any school and home environment. Small children will be able to have their say on issues that affect them directly. Older children can be encouraged to debate not only personal issues, but look to local, national and even global issues that they may have some particular interest in. There will be opportunities for forming opinions and arguing a point through literature – from discussing the injustice in *The Little Red Hen* to complex social issues in teenage novels. The world of advertising is also a context which allows exploration of persuasive language features. Whatever the context, learner-writers will need to be clear about the purpose for their writing an argument, and that there are certain features that are common to persuasive arguments.

As with explanatory writing, the sequence in planning and teaching for writing argument would be:

- We have become aware of an issue or injustice in the world – and have something to say about it; we are going to clarify where we stand on **War**.

  Or

- we are going to persuade the Board of Trustees to build a skate ramp at school,

- and we need to be able to write a persuasive argument.

  So

- we need to discuss the pros and cons of the issue;

- we need to know how to construct an argument;

- we need to find models of persuasive argument, and unpack them.

The use of model texts will be essential in any exploration of written argument, along with opportunities for discussion and oral debate. The examples we put in front of our students might include such visually persuasive texts as advertising, picture books, poetry, columns, short stories, letters and editorials, as we lead the discussions around the impact of the writer's message:

- What is this writer saying? What does he feel about ...?

- How does it make us feel? How do we respond?

- Has he managed to persuade us to think along the same lines?

Or with visual text:

- What is this advertiser telling us?

- How does the advertisement prompt a response?

- Has it persuaded me? (to buy, to visit, to donate)

There will be features common to the diversity of texts, and after exploring several examples, the features which make a text persuasive might be identified. The list of language features outlined on page 222 may not be true of every text, but as we explore a variety, our students are able to develop an understanding of real purpose for writing. Sometimes a writer is drawing on an emotional response to a heart-felt issue to compose a poem, and sometimes expressing a strong opinion to the editor of the local newspaper.

To simplify things initially, and to provide a framework for learner-writers, we can deconstruct a simple argument which offers a thesis statement, showing the stance taken and some supporting statements:

> *Should sunhats be worn at school?*
> *Sunhats should definitely be worn during the summer at school. Children spend a lot of time outside during the school day, and are at risk of sunburn. We all know the dangers of sun damage to the skin. If our skin gets burnt, we can suffer from melanoma which can be fatal. Sunhats will protect children by shading their faces from the sun. It is essential that all children are encouraged to wear them.*

We can support our students to identify whether the piece 'works', that is, am I clear about how the writer feels about the topic? Does it persuade me to the writer's point of view?

Through questioning and noticing the effect of specific words, students should be able to see the importance of topic-specific vocabulary, factual information, declarative statements, emotive words and so on.

We need to transfer what has been learned about the way an effective argument is put together to the issue that prompted such exploration in the first place. Of course, we don't always wait with fingers crossed for an opportunity to present itself, to provide a context for learning about written argument. Sometimes we can engineer a context to serve that learning.

One successful topic that we have used many times is the zoo. Here's a subject that readily prompts an itch worth scratching. Most students I have come across have been to a zoo, and if there are any that haven't, they are aware of the concept of captive animals. Anthony Browne's picture book *ZOO* (1992) has been a thought-provoking introduction. This picture book can be shared and enjoyed, students noticing what the writer has done with his cleverly drawn illustrations, as well as responding to the words. We can infer what the writer thought about animals in captivity, through his deliberate choice of words and his cynical illustrations. Students respond with their own emotional thoughts about the wisdom of keeping animals in captivity. The debate can become heated as feelings run strong, with many justifications being aired. For example:

> *Some animals are endangered, so it's only the zoos that are keeping them from becoming extinct.*

Or

> *Zoos are unable to provide the natural habitat of any animal.*
> (See Appendix for suggested lesson plan.)

Combining language features

Sometimes we have the opportunity to combine language features of a particular poetic form with a particular transactional form. In teaching writing, we are always mindful of the generic features of text that create an impact on the reader, whatever the form. One such feature is that a piece of text must have an engaging beginning, to hook the reader in right from the start. While transactional pieces in a 'pure form' need not be dull, it is increasingly evident that contemporary writers of formal writing take heed of the 'Alternating Current' in order to engage their readers. It is interesting to browse through passages of text in magazines and newspapers. There will undoubtedly be good models of text to be found, where journalists have determined to engage their readers, often with a provocative statement, or have seduced them into reading further by the deliberate use of sensory description.

Stella Gibbons, author of *Cold Comfort Farm*, written in 1932, spent some years as a journalist before embarking on writing a novel. Her training in the newspaper industry worried her:

> '*The life of a journalist is poor, brutish and short. So is his style.*'

A journalist's training at that time included learning to say exactly what you meant in short sentences. This is a somewhat simplified summary of what journalism entailed. Economy of language is a skill in itself, in literature and poetry, as well as in transactional text. However, the skill of linking a poetic, sensory passage into a factual report, or explanation, or argument, is now often used to engage readers, and we can support our students in exploring language to incorporate such skills.

Typical of magazine articles, and columns, are beautifully crafted poetic passages:

> *Low cloud hangs over Lake Rotoiti as drops of rain fall softly on a black shag standing guard on a rock near the deserted foreshore. Overnight the scene changes as snow-spattered mountains shrug off an early mist to admire their reflections in the blue coolness of the lake ...*

Then comes the main purpose for the article writen in a more expository form:

> **... So why are the southern lakes under-utilised?**
> (excerpt from an article by Joanna Wane in *Pacific Way* inflight
> magazine 1995)

The thesis statement of the article is not stated until the reader has been given this image of a rather lovely New Zealand landscape. The article is persuasive, and argues that this particular location, although beautiful, is under-utilised, giving historical facts and proffering reasons why. The writer, a journalist, has deliberately chosen to use language features of poetic description before posing the question to be explored, or examining the facts.

This is a device used to strengthen the impact of a piece, and can be included in our teaching with young writers. Persuasion by sensory language as well as by credible facts is useful in written argument, as a class of youngsters discovered when they argued the case for retaining the roosters of Albany. This junior class was responding to a newspaper article which suggested that the roosters be culled. They were indignant, and felt particularly strongly because the Albany roosters feature on their school uniform. After much discussion, the teacher provided several models of argument writing, and supported the students through their unpacking of the texts, making sure that they could identify what language features were evident. When the students were able to see what it was that made the piece effective, they were able to build their own checklist for success.

The teacher provided a framework for argument, and they attempted to persuade the readers of the newspaper that the roosters deserved to stay. The arguments were rational, but not particularly strong, and so the teacher took a step backwards in order for her students to think what it is about a rooster that is so appealing. They watched the roosters, looked at pictures, drew roosters, and discussed the physical appearance, the teacher drawing on previous discussions around the use of imagery in descriptive writing. One student's attempt to hook the reader in, by first appealing to the senses with a descriptive sentence, resulted in:

> *He stands proud like a soldier as his scarlet red comb glistens in the daylight, and his green flax feathers hang from his tail. As he sings his early morning song he wakes the people of Albany Village. People enjoy coming and walking down to watch and feed them all. The roosters can wander around where ever they want to in Albany Village.*
> *They are lovely birds to see in Albany and if you went to another city you would not find them. They are unique to Albany School because they are on our school monogram.*
> *Please keep the roosters in Albany.*
> (Ministry of Education, English exemplar 2003)

Another began with poetic word order:

> *How he stands so proud in the golden sunshine. Walking like a soldier in the army he crows a beautiful song. With straight legs he struts over to the shadows to rest. His feet scratch the ground.*
> *We should have roosters in Albany because they were here first. We should never move them away from their home in Albany Village. If people are not enjoying the roosters they should move away from here. Some people like them. I do and I do not want them to go. It is unique for Albany to have them*

there. Some people have never seen roosters, but when you come to Albany
you will see one.
KEEP THE ROOSTERS IN ALBANY!

This writer has begun with a poetic description of a particular rooster, rather
than a generic group; by using the personal pronoun, the reader is drawn closer.
She has also attempted to argue the point with evidence, and offered a solution.
The ending, like the first example, is a childlike imperative – demanding attention
and action.

Another classroom scenario, this time in a secondary social studies class, saw how the
use of a poetic introduction to a transactional explanation elevated the piece, providing
the reader with a sensory image, before going on to explain the process. The students
had been required to explain how the temples of Abu Simbel had been saved. Dylan,
a Year 11 student, began with:

Rescuing the Temples at Abu Simbel
In the twentieth century, the population in Egypt has expanded rapidly,
and so river dams have to be built over the River Nile to cope with the

ever-increasing demand for water and electricity. The Aswan High Dam (actually called Sudd el Ali) was constructed between Cairo and Abu Simbel but it dramatically increased flood danger potential. The great temples at Abu Simbel were going to be flooded.

The United Nations Educational Scientific and Cultural Organisation (UNESCO) decided to help and appealed to the public of the world to aid them in saving the mighty temples. Scientists, architects, a workforce and special machinery were gathered to assist in this incredible task.

An aerial and ground survey was conducted over and around the temples and surrounding terrain. The relics inside the temples were removed and their positions marked. An entire map of the inside created for each temple.

The cliff rock above the temple had to be removed so bulldozers were employed. Scaffolding was put in the inner rooms to prevent parts of the temple from collapsing. They then covered and filled each temple with sand for protection. Saws fitted with special teeth designed to keep them from wearing down were found the most ideal tool for cutting the temples up. They were cut into blocks weighing up to 30 tons, then transported to their new home.

Finally, the process was reversed and the temples were re-erected. Concrete domes were created over each temple to make them seem to still be in a cliff setting. The temples had been saved.

(Ministry of Education, English exemplar 2003)

Dylan had grasped the structure of a formal explanation. After a class exploration of the previous example about the Nelson lakes, he had seen how a poetic introduction might enhance the piece by engaging the reader from the outset. So he had a go ...

The sun glares upon your back, stinging you and making sweat over your sunburn. Low grunts from other workers and the sound of metal colliding with stone creates an ever present background music that you ignore as you chisel away at the frustrating wall of rock. Are you enjoying your little trip to the 1960s? After all, rescuing temples is hard work.

He then continued with:

> *In the twentieth century, the population in Egypt has expanded rapidly, and so river dams have to be built over the River Nile to cope with the ever-increasing demand for water and electricity ...*

He was able to make a deliberate choice to begin in this way – exploring ideas for different purposes. It is useful to remember that it is always the purpose for the writing, along with the intended audience, which dictates the appropriate form. In these examples of argument and explanation, the purpose was transactional. Including poetic description does not alter that purpose.

While it may be difficult to find 'pure forms' of transactional text in published literature, there are many teacher resource books available which provide sound models for students. It is helpful for teachers to find a model that has been annotated, so that the text can be unpacked with students, identifying the language features that characterise a particular form. Students will need to know what makes up the text in order to create their own piece.

It becomes more and more apparent that, in equipping our students with the skills they need to write in a variety of forms, it is of equal importance that the most appropriate words be chosen, and written in the most appropriate order, whether it be a poetic text or a transactional one, or a mixture of both. Students can appreciate a writer's choice of particular words, deliberately chosen for effect, in poetry and poetic prose. They also need to see the importance of selecting exactly the right words for a transactional piece. Nowhere is the language more precise than that of a scientific description or explanation. If we look at one particular context, we can see how students mature in their writing proficiency as they become more sophisticated and more adept in their language power across all contexts.

Collaborative learning

In order to integrate literacy learning across the curriculum, we need to stay 'true' to the intent of all learning areas, while at the same time providing solid teaching and guidance in the reading and writing demands of that learning area. For example, if we were studying how living creatures thrive and survive, it would be important to study one that we can readily observe, such as the slater (woodlouse). I have used this context with students but more often as a model for teachers, where teachers become co-learners, and demonstrate to themselves, through active involvement, the possibilities to be found through collaborative learning in the classroom. Through pulling up prior knowledge and discussion, students (of any age) begin their deep study of a very ordinary, yet ecologically important creature.

This is how it can be approached:

Ask learners to draw a slater (woodlouse).
Students draw on prior knowledge of slaters and record their knowledge.

Share with a partner, discuss and make adjustments.
This activity inevitably prompts debate over the number of legs these creatures possess, whether they're insects or not, and so on. Students negotiate and question their shared knowledge.

Talk in the larger group about the discoveries.
Students pool their knowledge and make further adjustments to their drawings as they see fit: this is an expectation of the helping circle – we listen to the views and discoveries of others and we craft and adjust our own contributions accordingly.

Examine the actual creatures.
Because of the abundance of slaters in wood piles, learners can be provided with a specimen each, along with magnifying glasses and specimen dishes. (My husband is now practised in the collection of thirty slaters and making up a temporary home for them in a large plastic container lined with rotting logs and leaves.) With a class of children, there would be time made to seek out the slaters for themselves from the school grounds. Equipped with a magnifier and a slater, students examine the creature very carefully, comparing what they see with their original drawing, and making adjustments.

My experience is that when anyone looks this closely at a living creature, there is absolute engagement, an increased interest in what is simply a 'common garden bug', an instinctive respect for that creature, and a high level of constructive discussion and collaboration among learners.

Make a list of the sorts of things this creature would need to survive and thrive.

This list can be compiled in partner or group collaboration, drawing on hypotheses and prior knowledge.

List any questions which have arisen.

Teacher distributes pieces of informational text.

By this stage, most students are eager to find out more, and taking into consideration the age, abilities and reading needs of the students, the text can be searched for information and clarification through independent, shared or supported reading activities. This practical engagement with the creatures has always created an urgency and enthusiasm for reading the factual text. Students settle arguments, clarify, confirm or dismiss hypotheses, and discover many other fascinating details about slaters.

This process is a learning experience in itself and deserves to be reflected on. It lends itself to a variety of learning tasks to follow, depending on the desired outcome. If the culmination of studying slaters is to write an explanation about them, a framework can be provided. This might include an actual framework sheet to write on:

Title: How do slaters survive and thrive? 
Introduction: Definition - *Slaters are ...*

Explanation:
    - explanations are written in the present tense
    - use words like 'because' and 'as a result' ...

Summary:
    Say again what phenomenon you have explained.
    This is how ...

Results of a written explanation task might look like this from a young writer, attempting to explain how a slater survives and thrives:

> *The sat ets dut and wod to lv*
> *(The slater eats dirt and wood to live.)*

Or there may be greater proficiency with the addition of more factual ideas:

> *Slaters are little creatures that you get under wood.*
> *They like being in the dark and they like it to be a little bit wet. They eat rotten wood and rotten leaves. They will survive if they stay in the dark places that are damp and they have these things to eat. They have a hard shell so this will help them survive. They will not survive if they get too hot or if it is too dry. And they will not survive if they can't get something to eat.*

Still more details, with greater maturity and sophistication, and appropriate language features are evident in:

> *Some people think slaters are insects but they're not. They are crustaceans that are found on land.*
> *If slaters are going to survive, they need to have the right conditions. They need to live in places that are dark and damp. If the place gets too dry or too hot, they will not survive.*
> *They need to have the right food to eat, which is decaying wood or leaves, so they are found under wood-piles or bark. Did you know that they sometimes eat their own skin? Their skin splits down the middle and half of it comes off and then the other half.*
> *Slaters come out at night to feed because they like the dark. If you disturb them in the day they try to find something to get underneath.*
> *Slaters can survive and thrive if they are living in a dark, damp place with rotten wood and leaves to eat.*

The production of a detailed explanation, incorporating more sophisticated language features can be expected. This writer has used topic-appropriate vocabulary, cause and effect words, and has included details of the slaters' anatomy, environment, nutritional and mating needs, and particular habits, explaining satisfactorily how they might survive and thrive:

Slaters are crustaceans that live on the land. They are cousins to the water crustaceans like crabs and shrimps. They have a hard grey shell which is segmented.

If you find slaters in the garden, they will usually be found underneath wood, plant pots or dead leaves, as this provides the environment that they need to survive. They need to be in dark, moist places that are sheltered from predators. Because their shell is segmented, they can roll into a ball. This is a protection from predators and it is also a protection to stop them drying out. They moult their shell when they are growing which makes them vulnerable, so they try to hide when it is the time to moult.

They feed on decaying leaves and wood when they come out at night. They also eat their own shell when they moult and they eat their own faeces. Slaters are usually in groups and they need others so that they can mate. When they have mated, the female can have about 100 babies. The babies live in her pouch for protection because they have not got a hard shell when they are very young.

Slaters need to have the right environment to survive and thrive. This must be dark and moist. They must be able to mate and the babies must be protected by the mother slaters.

It is clear that, as the students mature, there are more details and a more secure grasp of grammatical structure and appropriate language features, but the essential framework of an explanation can be found from early writers too, from the single idea to a sequence of ideas.

Donald Murray in *Write to Learn* (1984) says that writing is the act of using language to discover meaning in experience and communicate it. When we understand this, we can encourage a climate of critical thinking, one where students will expect to 'go beneath the surface' in whatever area they are asked to think about. They will expect to 'wonder' and to be asked to write their responses to a multitude of learning experiences. We don't need to 'conjure up' topics – we need to be mindful of the opportunities – to think, wonder, talk and write that are present in all curriculum areas.

Overlapping

As already discussed, there can be some overlap in purpose. Some teachers have found that when they have asked students to explain a phenomenon, the students have lurched into persuading the reader, or have deliberately written a detailed procedure. When this happens, it only serves to highlight the importance of teachers being absolutely clear themselves, on two counts: firstly, that the topic lends itself to (for example) explanatory writing; and secondly, what the end result might look like, and the language features we can expect to find in an explanation.

Students were asked to explain a social phenomenon – Why do we have to wear seatbelts in cars?

The results were predictable: the teacher had done a good job in leading discussion about the merits of protecting ourselves while travelling, and children were keen to record the reasons. However, they all demonstrated the language features and shape of a reasoned written argument. These persuasive pieces all had credibility as personal responses to the topic provided, so would need to be acknowledged as such. It is not necessary to be critical of a piece that does not 'follow form', if the piece suits the purpose and the audience. If we get results that surprise us, we must ask ourselves if we were clear in our own thinking.

Why do we wear seatbelts?

Argument

It is essential that kids wear seatbelts in cars. Did you know that there are hundreds of innocent children hurt or killed every year, simply because they didn't get belted in? That's just about the same as child abuse. We don't need to kill our kids like this. Nobody knows when an accident is going to happen so it is very important to make sure that your kids are strapped into a seat belt every time they travel in a car. Clunk click every trip!

Explanation

A seat belt is a safety device used in a car or plane to hold you in your seat in case of an accident. Seatbelts are fitted in all cars and it is the law to wear a seatbelt when travelling. Parents take responsibility for small children and babies, making sure that they are strapped in before the vehicle moves. If a vehicle is involved in an accident, which causes it to come to an abrupt halt, the seat belt will prevent the passenger from being thrown forward. In accidents where seatbelts have not been worn, the passengers' injuries are likely to be much worse and often fatal.

Personal narrative

One time, when I was coming home from school, my mum's friend stopped her car to give me a lift. I hopped in the back but I didn't bother putting my seat belt on. There was only a short way to go. Just around the corner, just before you get to my street, a little kid ran out of his driveway and into the road. I think he was chasing a ball. Mum's friend jammed on her brakes and I got flung into the back of the driver's seat. I hurt my knee quite badly and one shoulder. Luckily I wasn't sitting in the middle or I could have gone right into the front, into the windscreen. I will always remember to put my seatbelt on from now on.

All of these pieces 'explain' to a reader why seatbelts should be worn. We could write a procedure which lists what needs to be done when we get into a car; we could describe a seatbelt; we could write a factual report about seatbelts. All of these writing tasks may be valid writing experiences. We must be clear in our own minds what it is we want our students to learn, and what we are going to design to ensure they will learn what they need to. In all of the examples above, the writer has something to say and has chosen the words deliberately to say what they mean. The writer must be aware of the purpose for the writing and who the intended audience will be. If we have got our students to the point of being able to make decisions about the way they will explain something to their readers, we have supported our students to be independent - and they must have skills and strategies at their fingertips to be independent. There is an analogy between writing, as one creative art, and music or painting. Music and art teachers will applaud their students' attempts to experiment with form and media, but the results of such experimentation will only be impressive if there are some basic techniques employed.

Many primary teachers seem to have swung, over recent years, between two approaches: allowing their students to write 'anything', in any way they

wanted, which often resulted in pages of poorly constructed prose, lacking in skills and techniques; or imposing set frameworks for specific purposes, resulting in prescriptive, formulaic pieces, lacking in voice or sincerity. If we are to develop writers in our classrooms, we, the leaders of learning, must be able to recognise what form of writing suits what purpose as well as being familiar with:

- what features to expect;

- what content to expect;

- what shape, or structure to expect in a variety of text purposes and forms.

Summary - *Writing across the Curriculum*

- Understanding genre.

- Moving from expressive to transactional writing.

- The 'Alternating Current'.

- Teaching appropriate forms across the curriculum.

- Exploring a framework for a written explanation.

- Language features of explanatory writing.

- Poetic explanation.

- Language features of a written argument.

- Combining poetic with transactional writing.

- Collaborative learning.

- Overlapping forms.

- The purpose determining the form.

Appendix - *Writing across the Curriculum*

Should sunhats be worn at school?

Sunhats should definitely be worn during the summer at school.	Thesis statement (shows stance taken)
Children spend a lot of time outside during the school day, and are at risk of sunburn.	Statements to support opinion
We all know the dangers of sun damage to the skin. If our skin gets burnt, we can suffer from melanoma which can be fatal.	Topic specific vocabulary
Sunhats will protect children by shading their faces from the sun. It is essential that all children are encouraged to wear them.	Drawing on facts to support opinion

Guided Writing Plan

Resources:

- *excerpt from 'Written on the Body' by Jeanette Winterson*
- graphic organiser
- model of argument
- *'Zoo' by Anthony Browne*

Purpose for the lesson	• We are learning how to write an argument. • Today we are exploring how to form an opinion, and to express a particular point of view.
Leading the learning	Long-term learning focus: the purpose of a piece of writing dictates the structure and choice of language used. • We are learning to take a stance on an issue and to justify our opinion. • We are learning how to frame the argument in writing.

Leading the learning

Reading, thinking and talking

Lesson One:

- Introduction – purpose for writing.
- Link to previous work.
- We are learning to …
- Link to students' prior knowledge about opinion and persuasion.
- Discuss: how do you persuade someone to your point of view?
- Introduce context through teacher reading Jeanette Winterson. (see page 246)
- What does she think about zoos?
- Read 'Zoo' by Anthony Browne.
- Discuss: what messages is the writer giving us?

  What do we know about zoos?

  What do we think about zoos?

  How does it make us feel about zoos?

- Discuss: (in pairs) pros and cons.
- Share the T shirt slogan '9 out of 10 animals prefer the wild to zoos'. Invite response.
- Agree or disagree with statement.
- Form an opinion: *Is it a good thing to have zoos?* or *Animals should not be kept in zoos.*
- Use a graphic organiser to sort ideas.

Lesson Two

- Review learning in Lesson One.
- Deconstruct argument text – use a model to annotate. What do we notice? Can we break it into parts? What sort of language is used?
- Identify qualities and features.
- Innovate on sentence structure around the language of reasoning – e.g. rhetorical questions.
- Writing task: expand on the framework, using the language of reasoning.

Success criteria *How will we know we have been successful?* Co-construct with the students	Lesson One • I have formed an opinion. • I have supported my viewpoint with at least two reasons. Lesson Two • My viewpoint is clear in my introduction. • I have organised my ideas, reasons and opinions into paragraphs. • I have made logical links between ideas using connectives. • I have used the language of persuasion including modal verbs, emotive words, rhetorical question, imperatives, passive voice.
Challenges for writers	Show awareness of audience through choice of content, structure and language.
Transfer to other writing	Example: in a memoir about a visit to the zoo, the writer is able to convey to the reader how they feel.

9 out of 10
animals
prefer the wild to
zoos

Hmm, what does Anthony Browne think?
And what do you think?

Title:

Thesis:

Supporting reasons:

-

-

-

Conclusion:
Restate your thesis

Framework for argument

Title:

Thesis:

Supporting reasons:

-

-

-

Conclusion:

Restate your thesis

I keen in the fields to the moon. Animals in the zoo do the same, hoping that another of their kind will call back. The zoo at night is the saddest place. Behind the bars, at rest from vivisecting eyes, the animals cry out, species separated from one another, knowing instinctively the map of belonging. They would choose predator and prey against this outlandish safety. Their ears, more powerful than those of their keepers, pick up sounds of cars and last-hour take-aways. They hear all the human noises of distress. What they don't hear is the hum of the undergrowth or the crack of fire. The noises of kill. The river-roar booming against brief screams. They prick their ears till their ears are sharp points but the noises they seek are too far away.

(from *Written on the Body* by Jeanette Winterson 1993)

11 Using Models
Where texts might lead us

'I'm not really sure what to do for this child, to help him improve ...' is probably one of the most frequent comments I hear as I work with teachers. Part of me loves to hear these words – as they signal willingness from a teacher to value and support their student in developing as a writer. For many of us, appreciating what is good in writing has been a hit-and-miss affair, much like the layman's approach to art: 'I don't know much about art, but I know what I like ...' When we read ourselves, for enjoyment, it is not always obvious what it is about a particular writer that we enjoy, but with practice, we can sharpen our reading skills to include an informed appreciation of what the writer does to give the writing the impact we respond to.

It is impact in student writing that provokes a response too, and in order to understand what has given the piece impact, we need to have an awareness of what makes writing effective, whether it is poetic description or transactional journalism, whether it is by a published author or a primary student.

We all have our favourite authors, or our favourite type of writing. While some of us enjoy classical poetry, others prefer contemporary thrillers. Many enjoy the diversity of written material that is available – from the weekend paper to the newly bought paperback. Often it is the reason behind our reading which colours our appreciation, and the reasons for reading are as many as those for writing.

> *Literature is the art of writing something that will be read twice; journalism*
> *what will be grasped at once.*
> (Cyril Connolly 1938)

Whether we read to be informed, to relax and escape, or to learn, we find some texts preferable to others. I am not about to suggest what is the best type of writing to enjoy, for that is largely a matter of personal taste, but regardless of our own preferences, I feel that there are aspects of written text which should be understood in order to heighten our recognition of 'good' writing. We can then exercise this in our teaching.

A piece of writing that is 'good' will leave a strong impression.

Poet Robert Frost says:

> What do I mean by a phrase? A clutch of
> words that gives you a clutch at the heart.

I've got the words,

but I'm trying to get

the music into them.

Lucy Calkins (1991)

While not every piece of writing will have the impact of clutching at the heart, there should be some impact. We, as teachers, are striving to help our students find that personal voice that gives a written text its sincerity and impact.

When we list the indicators of a 'good' piece of writing, they apply to all writing regardless of the age and stage of the writer – from new entrant to published authors – and regardless of the type of writing:

- it is legible;

- it 'hooks' the reader in, making them want to read on;

- it conveys a message that can be understood;

- the form suits the purpose;

- there is a sincerity of voice;

- it is constructed to read fluently;

- the vocabulary chosen is appropriate for the subject matter and the intended audience;

- (with more mature writers) there is evidence of deliberate attempts to include specific language features which enhance the telling, a sense of audience.

Earlier we looked at how a piece of text may be unpacked, and language features identified. Teachers have often said to me 'Can you give me a list of suitable models?' or 'Where can I find appropriate pieces of text to use with my students?' There is no answer to these requests other than 'You must seek them out for yourself'. This is not a deliberate attempt to be difficult or obscure, and I am happy to share what resources I have, but the simple fact is that we all need to develop the ability to recognise something in a piece of writing. Teachers constantly need to have their antennae out for texts, with possibilities for teaching and growing writers. There may be an unconscious recognition at first, as we gain satisfaction from reading a particular text, but if we are to help our students, then we must look again, with heightened awareness, and begin to identify what this writer has done.

What does this piece offer my students?

We choose a model because it speaks to us in some way. I chose the following piece because I felt a strong personal connection – I grew up in the same part of the world as Gavin Bishop and when I read his memoir *Piano Rock* (2008), I felt as if I was reliving my childhood. All of his descriptions were familiar, right down to the knitted togs and how the stones 'took' me into Lake Wakatipu. I also knew that today's students would be able to identify with getting into cold water – a connection triggered. That was my starting point.

> *Now and then, but not often, when the day was warm enough, Mr McLeod took us swimming in the lake. I dreaded swimming lessons and always tried to come up with a sniffle or a sore leg that might excuse me from going.*
> *It didn't matter how hot the day was, the water was always cold. If you tried to get in slowly, you couldn't; the stones would take you before you were ready. As you slid in, the icy water rose quickly to your chest and snatched your breath away. I would try and float a bit, but it was hopeless and all I wanted to do was get out again. So with wriggly macaroni legs, prickly with goose bumps, I would stagger back onto the beach. My soggy woollen togs would be*

sagging almost to my knees. A driftwood fire and a melting moment from my lunch tin were the only things that could help a little to warm me up.
(from *Piano Rock* by Gavin Bishop 2008)

If I want students to write a vignette that similarly describes an experience, I need to be clear what this text offers learners: I have to know what makes up this text before I can lead students to consciously compose their own. So, in Gavin Bishop's piece I found:

- sentences are constructed to provide the setting **before** the main message (clause)
    - *Now and then, but not often, when the day was warm enough ...*
    - *It didn't matter how hot the day was ...*
    - *As you slid in ...*

- the reader is provided with adjectival phrases (extra information between commas)
  So with wriggly macaroni legs, prickly with goose bumps, I would stagger back onto the beach.

- contrast is used within a sentence
  It didn't matter how hot the day was, the water was always cold.

- personification
  ... the water snatched your breath away.

- strong verbs
  dreaded, rose, snatch, stagger, sagging

So far, we have identified deeper features, but it is also important that we recognise the deliberate use of punctuation to enhance the meaning. This gives us opportunity for teaching specific punctuation use within a real text. The text also demonstrates the:

- use of a semi-colon to divide two main clauses while keeping them connected
  If you tried to get in slowly, you couldn't; the stones would take you before you were ready.

- use of commas to add extra information
  So with wriggly macaroni legs, prickly with goose bumps, I would stagger back onto the beach.

We want to help students understand that punctuation affects meaning. If we can lead them to this understanding while they are getting satisfaction from writing about a piece of their lives, the correctness of the punctuation learned has much more chance of being remembered – much more effective than a random lesson on semi-colons.

This short model, like many published texts, has many features worth noticing, all of which contribute to the overall meaning and effect of the piece. We can't teach all of the features in one lesson, so we must decide which ones to draw out for learning. This one text provides many opportunities, which can be revisited – hence the reason for students pasting the model into their draft books.

Because the identified learning need for these students was 'to add detail' to their writing, I chose to explore the descriptors between commas (after the noun).

> *So with wriggly macaroni legs, prickly with goose bumps, I would stagger back onto the beach.*

We have an adjective and a metaphor acting together (*wriggly macaroni*) to describe the legs, but the author has chosen to add further information with an adjectival phrase *after* the noun (*prickly with goose bumps*) and has then carried on with the main part of the sentence, *I would stagger back onto the beach.* This demonstrates a way of adding more detail without a string of adjectives preceding the noun. I also made the decision to draw their attention to the use of the semi-colon.

> *If you tried to get in slowly, you couldn't; the stones would take you before you were ready.*

So I have a wonderful context (getting into cold water) from a rich text that I am sure the students will connect with, and I have identified the focus for learning. I expect them to write a vignette about their experiences in cold water, including a sentence which has added information between commas. They may also include a sentence with a semi-colon. Now I need to design the lesson which will lead the students to that learning.

As described in previous chapters, before we do anything else, the text needs to be read, understood and enjoyed. Meaning must be established through the stories told by the teacher and students. Then the text may be discussed in terms of effectiveness:

- How has he made it sound like a child talking?

- Which part stands out for you?

- How do you get a picture of the character/scene?

- What do we know about the boy?

- What tells us how he is feeling?

- What senses does the writer appeal to?

Framing learning talk – *for explicit teaching*

When we are sure that students have gained meaning from the text, which may even happen the day before the writing, we can then lead students to the point of learning through our careful framing of statements and questions. Of course, this will differ between age groups and abilities so what I offer here is merely an example of how to lead students directly to what you want them to notice. It is about giving them a challenge to search, to discover and to make connections that lead to new learning.

Adverbial clauses and phrases – leading students to notice the adverbial clauses and phrases and their functions

Read the first sentence to students.

> *Now and then, but not often, when the day was warm enough, Mr McLeod took us swimming in the lake.*

Which part of that is the main part of the sentence?
So put a line under <u>Mr McLeod took us swimming in the lake.</u>

What is the rest of the sentence doing?

What does *Now and then* ... tell us? *But not often* ...? *When the day was warm enough* ...?
Oh, so we've got three things that tell us *when*.

That's interesting, where else in the text has he told us *when*?
> *As you slid in, the icy water rose quickly* ...
As you slid in ... What does that do? It tells us something about the *when* too.

Adjectival phrases
Read the sentence.
> *So with wriggly macaroni legs, prickly with goosebumps, I would stagger back*
> *onto the beach.*
What do you notice about the sentence?
What do the words *wriggly* and *macaroni* do in the sentence?
What do you think *prickly with goosebumps* does in the sentence?
Would it make sense if I took that bit out?
> *So with wriggly macaroni legs* ... <u>*I would stagger back onto the beach.*</u>
Yes, it does make sense. So *prickly with goosebumps* is extra information for effect.

So we're talking about the legs – put your finger on that word – there are two descriptors before the noun (one adjective and a noun with an adjectival function) and some information after it. What effect does that phrase have?

Semi-colons
Have a look at the sentence.

> *If you tried to get in slowly, you couldn't; the stones would take you before*
> *you were ready.*

There's a special punctuation mark in there – what do you notice? I wonder why Mr Bishop put that in there. That's called a semi-colon – what job does it do in this sentence?

If I put a full stop there instead –

If you tried to get in slowly, you couldn't.

Does that make sense by itself?

The stones would take you before you were ready.

Does that make sense by itself?

So Mr Bishop could have used a full stop there, but he made a decision to separate the two ideas with a semi-colon. That's interesting. A semi-colon can be used to join two separate sentences which are closely linked; it can be used instead of a full stop, and has a different effect.

Drawing out students' stories

After we've explored some of the devices that Gavin Bishop has used in his text, it is time for students to tell their own stories of getting into cold water: the first connection triggered. This would lead on to a visualisation, as explained in Chapter 5.

From there, it's a question of telling their own story using some of the devices explored – how might we tell our own stories, deliberately using some of the effective strategies that we have talked about. We are all prepared to have a go at using some of Mr Bishop's techniques, inspired by what we have read and noticed. When I'm sure that all students have a place and a story in their heads, and they have told it to someone else, I ask them to visualise and pick three nouns around the scene they have in their heads. In order to model the process, one child's noun selection from his swimming place, *bridge, creek, bush,* was used:

Teacher: *So let's take the noun 'bridge'. Tell us a little bit more about the bridge. So, it was an old swing bridge? What did it do?*

Student: *It shook when I jumped off.*

Teacher: *Okay, we've got The old swing bridge shook when I jumped off. Let's go back to Mr Bishop's sentence, where he added information after the noun. If we were to add some more information between commas after the word 'bridge', what might that be? What else can you say about the bridge?*

Student: *It was riddled with rust.*

Teacher: *How might we put that extra information between commas?*

Student: *The old swing bridge, riddled with rust, shook when I jumped off.*

Teacher: *So we now have a sentence with extra information between commas. We've added an extra descriptor after the noun. That's effective. Now let's all have a go with one of your selected nouns.*

Students are supported to come up with a sentence including extra information between commas. Feeling secure in knowing how to include the extra information, and therefore secure in knowing how to succeed, students record their own stories. They will be aware of what they are expected to include and what they have been invited to attempt (see lesson plan in the appendix).

The following first draft examples from these Year 9 and 10 students show the effect of the lesson on the choice of language, the choice of sentence arrangement and the deliberate use of commas and semi-colons.

A rough grey rock, <u>tall and towering</u>, sat like a giant on the other side of the lake. My brother was already swimming towards it, carefully avoiding the teenagers jumping recklessly off the top, but I stood shivering in the shallows.

<u>It wasn't often that we came here; my mother hated swimming; she avoided it like the plague</u>. I waded into the chilly water, screaming as the sand gave way and icy water hit my chest. My mother was still sitting on the shore and I called for her to follow, not noticing my brother creep slowly up behind and duck silently under the water.

I am taken by surprise as a hand grabs my foot and I am pulled from the summer air into a murky green world that swallows me whole. Cold seeps into my arms and legs, <u>now bumpy with goosebumps</u>, and spreads upwards, turning my lips blue. My arms flail uselessly in the water, desperate to reach the top. I break the surface and race after my retreating brother, leaving only a trail of bubbles behind.

Emma, Year 10

The sun was stretched over our bare shoulders as we ran, the scratchy summer grass tickling our legs. Soon we were down the bank, staring into the rushing green stony water. I sidled across the rocks, putting one foot, then the other, into the ice cold river. The water wove its treacherous fingers around my toes, trying to pull me into its speeding depths. Stepping onto the next slimy stone lurking just under the surface, I looked back at Lisa.

'You go first,' I said. The cold seeped through my legs, right into my bones. She shook her head.

'We'll go together on the count of three.' I nodded. I stepped onto the next rock which I knew lay just beneath the surface. It betrayed me, shifting wildly under my weight. My scream turned to laughter as I was suddenly thrown into the wild current with powerless limbs flapping …

Amber, Year 10

Reflecting on what we've written - a guided revision

This is the time when students are gathered in a helping circle, equipped with their green editing pen and their writing, to reflect on their efforts.

So, how did you get on?
What helped you today?
Who managed to include the sentence that we practised beforehand?
Let's hear some …
Who's still working on that? How can we help?

There is an expectation here that all students are going to succeed.

Who managed a sentence with a semi-colon? Read it out.
Yes, two separate statements there - closely connected.

It has been my experience that a class of students gathered in a helping circle regularly will be keen to share parts of their writing and innovations on text, sometimes surprising themselves with their success. They will begin to use the sentence patterns, structures and punctuation that we have discovered and explored together,

making choices and decisions that create meaning. Over time they will develop their own style.

What does this piece of text offer my students?

> The tyres have a tread of small, pyramid-shaped blocks. These give good grip on soft ground and they also let soil or mud slip off so it does not get stuck in the tread.

Taken from a mountain bike poster, this piece was chosen to launch a group of Year 2 writers into transactional text. They were very competent with their memoir writing and the teacher wished to extend their purposes for writing. It was decided that a simple factual description would be a good place to start. The text was found on a mountain bike poster on the classroom wall. The learning is that factual description has a particular purpose and a particular structure. For these very young students the learning is around not only ordering their writing, but the skill of looking closely and describing exactly what they see – using precise language.

As with any model, the first job for the teacher is to identify the features of the piece and to consider the possibilities for the learning. It is important for us to know how the text is constructed in order for us to lead students to create similar texts themselves.

- Structure – two sentences, one describing the appearance of the bike part, one telling what it does.

- Hyphenated adjective (compound adjective) – can be tighter than a simile and more suited to the purpose.

- Adverbial clause – the why? ... *so it does not get stuck in the mud.*

- Prepositional phrase – the where? ... *on soft ground* ...

- Subject specific vocabulary.

- Precise economical language.

- Continuous present tense.

- Complex sentence showing cause and effect.

Now to design a lesson that will lead these students to the learning. I have found it relatively easy to access a real mountain bike, with permission, from a school bike stand. So with an actual bike in the classroom, the first task for students is to look very closely. The lesson begins with a discussion about the parts of the bike, what they look like and what they do. To support students to look very closely for detail, they were given time to sketch the bike (observational drawing). It was explained that we would be choosing a part and describing what our part looks like and what our part does.

The model was read and discussed, drawing particular attention to the structure – what it looks like and what it does. We needed to go back to the actual bike to determine the language that we would need to describe the chosen bike-part in specific language. It was necessary to point, elicit and share, so the expectation was modelled. For example:

Teacher: *The pedal – what does it look like?*

Student: *It's kind of shaped like a block. They're spiky.*
They have little orange reflectors.

Teacher: *The poster talks of shape – it says the treads were*
'pyramid-shaped'.

Student: *You could say 'block-shaped'.*

Teacher: *How might we put that together, starting with 'The pedals …?'*

Student: *The pedals are block-shaped with little orange reflectors.*

Teacher: *Where?*

Student: *Right around it.*

Teacher: *So how could you include that?*

Student: *The pedals are block-shaped with little orange reflectors around it.*

For older students you could work towards a more sophisticated construction using the passive voice.

Teacher: *If we were to use the word 'surrounded' in there, where would*
that fit? How might the sentence read then? (Students asked to
collaborate with partner.)

Student: *The pedals are block-shaped, surrounded by little orange reflectors.*

Teacher: *What do the pedals do?*

Student: *They're to put your feet on.*

Teacher: *So what do they actually do?* (This elicits the specific verbs.)
Make the wheels turn. Move the chain.

Teacher: *And what do they do for feet?*

Student: *Support them.*

Teacher: *Okay – what do we have now?*

Student: *The pedals are block-shaped, surrounded by little orange reflectors.*
The pedals support the rider's feet to make the wheels turn.

This seems a simple piece of writing, but students need tight support and a carefully framed discussion to achieve an effective result, suited to the purpose: a factual description. This illustrates again that every kind of writing has description, but how it is put together is dependent on the purpose (see appendix, pages 277–278).

In the helping circle it was clear that it was an issue for students to take out the 'you'. For example, several students wrote 'You steer the bike with the handlebars …'. Instead, we may want to lead them to record their observations in the third person, or at least have them be aware of the choice that they make.

Teacher: *How could we write that sentence without a 'you'?*
Who rides the bike?
Student: *The biker.*
Teacher: *Or?*
Student: *The rider.*
Teacher: *Yes … or the cyclist.* (extending vocabulary)
So, we now have: The rider steers the bike with the handlebars …

The teacher must be responsive to contributions from students, yet skilled in steering the students towards the required learning with carefully framed comments and questions. The teacher's aim is to have students make new links with what they

already know. The students should feel confident to apply their new learning in their own writing attempts.

Teacher knowledge around sentences

Many teachers protest that their own schooling never addressed a working knowledge of the mechanics of writing – particularly of sentence structure – knowledge they now realise they need in order to lead their students to confident authorship. Now it is common to see groups of teachers huddled over texts as they learn to notice, explore and analyse what gives a text its effect and power.

So what is a sentence?

Teachers have often complained that their students find it difficult to elaborate their ideas. What is more to the point, teachers often seem unsure about how to address this difficulty. A lesson in adjectives may be planned, followed by further disappointment when students liberally pepper their work with unnecessary descriptors.

I want students to walk out of my classroom with deep structures and patterns etched in their minds – building pathways, making connections, discovering a way of 'thinking' about mechanics' meaning.

Jeff Anderson (2007)

Experience has shown that, as teachers, we need to deepen our own understanding of how language works, and how effective writing is constructed, in order to be able to teach some of the essential skills our student writers need. Even if the students in our care are at the very beginning of their formal schooling, a teacher of writing will need to know basic sentence structures, and how the deliberate choice of these has an impact on the created text.

The question *What is a sentence?* is more difficult than it might appear, and there are many definitions. For our purpose as teachers, it might be useful to remember that the sentence is the basic building block of written language, and a simple definition is:

a word or group of words which makes complete sense on its own.

Sentences can have different purposes. In their basic form, they can be structured as statements, commands, questions or exclamations.

Statements	Questions
Sentences that convey information	Sentences that require an answer
e.g. *This is a book about ladybirds.*	e.g. *Have you read this book?*
Commands	**Exclamations**
Sentences that give orders or requests	Sentences that express strong feelings
e.g. *Read this book.*	e.g. *This is the best book I have ever read!*

The anatomy of a sentence

A *simple sentence* consists of one *clause*, which is a group of words containing a subject and a verb.

The boy	rode	his bike.
subject	verb	object

You can add any number of descriptors to this sentence, but it is still a simple sentence:

The	*small, curly-haired*	**boy**	*enthusiastically*	**rode**
	adjectives	noun	*adverb*	verb

his	*shiny new*	**bike**	*on the footpath*	*after breakfast.*
	adjectives	noun	*adverbial phrase*	*adverbial phrase*

Despite all the added description the sentence still has only *one subject and one verb*. It is still a simple sentence.

We can join two or more simple sentences with *coordinating conjunctions*, to make a **compound sentence:**

Jack was a chef.		He made a cake.		
Jack was a chef	*and*	he made a cake.		

Jack was a chef.		He specialised in baking.		He made a cake.
Jack was a chef	*and*	he specialised in baking	*and*	he made a cake.

Each part of the compound sentence is a ***main clause***. We can say that each clause has equal weight and can stand alone. When we join clauses of equal weight, the conjunctions we use are coordinating conjunctions.

The first sign of complexity in children's writing is seen with the development of compound sentences. When young children begin to write, they often begin with a series of separate statements:

I went to the pools. I swim at the pools.

One development that we notice is when they begin to use 'and'.

I went to the pools and I swim at the pools.

The sequence of events in a narrative is also conveyed by 'and then', often with little, if any, punctuation.

Yesterday I went to Nana's house and I had chicken and then I had pudding and then I watched TV and we went home and then I went to bed.

As they get older, children use fewer compound sentences and more complex sentences, but some children need help to move to this stage.

In **complex sentences**, there is one main clause, and one or more *subordinate clauses*:

Jack made cakes	because he was a chef	who had specialised in baking.
main clause	subordinate clause (adverbial clause)	subordinate clause (adjectival clause)

- An adverbial clause answers the questions How? When? Where? or Why?

- An adjectival clause often begins with who, which, that or whom, and tells us more about the noun.

- Each clause contains a verb.

- The subordinate clause depends on the main clause – it cannot stand alone.

When we join a main clause to a subordinate clause, we use a subordinating conjunction:

> ***after, although, as, when, while, until, because, before, if, since,***
> **(AAAWWUBBIS)**

or a relative pronoun:

> *whom, who, which, that, whose, whomever, whichever, whatever*

Simple sentences:

Fred lived near the harbour.   He was probably aware of the marina plans.

Written like this, the connection between living near the harbour and the marina plans is not made clear. If you link the sentences to make a compound sentence, the logical connection is still not clear:

Fred lived near the harbour   *and*   was probably aware of the marina plans.

A **complex sentence**, with a main clause and subordinate clause, makes the link clear:

Because he lived near the harbour, Fred was probably aware of the marina plans.

A **phrase** is a group of related words that does not stand on its own and does not contain a verb. It is not a complete sentence. We can use phrases instead of nouns, adjectives and adverbs.

The chef baked a cake	as quickly as possible.	
	adverbial phrase	
The chef	with the tall hat	baked a cake.
	adjectival phrase	
All the chefs in the hotel	baked a cake.	
noun phrase		

The impact that a sentence has does not depend on whether it is simple, compound or complex. Effective writers combine the use of all types and forms of sentences, deliberately, for different purposes and with different effects.

Reminders:

- A simple sentence can be powerful, when a strong verb is used:
  He *struggled* up the mountain.

- A strong verb often has more impact than adding adverbs:
  The bull *charged* across the field.
  The bull *ran very quickly* across the field.

- A sentence is not necessarily improved by adding lots of descriptors:
  The small, curly-haired boy enthusiastically rode his shiny new bike on the footpath after breakfast.

- Specific nouns in a sentence often add more impact than a list of adjectives:
  The *tall, lovely, old, gracious tree* was shedding its leaves.
  The *oak* was shedding its leaves.

- A variety of sentence length, sentence structure and sentence beginnings will make for more effective writing.

- There is little evidence to support the notion that isolated lessons in 'grammar' improve student writing. Grammatical points that teachers feel need to be addressed, will best be absorbed by students when they are explained in context. For example, during a close reading lesson, where students are unpacking the meaning of a text, a teacher can direct them to identify word classifications or types of sentence – and, most importantly, discuss the effect that the writer's deliberate choice has on the reader (see Chapter 8: *'The Old Alley'*).

- As teachers of writing, we need to have a basic understanding of how language is structured; how much of the grammatical terminology we share with students will need professional judgement. Students can develop an understanding of why some sentences are effective without being able to label such techniques as 'adverbial phrases' or 'subordinate clauses'.

- When we are teaching, we often want students to 'make their writing more interesting by adding detail'. Teaching adjectives or adverbs, and encouraging students to include many of these descriptors is not going to do it (similarly with similes and metaphors).

- We can often encourage additional effective detail by considered questioning, for example, *'Tell me more about ... Tell me how ..., where ..., when ..., why ..., how ...'* (which may prompt the addition of a prepositional phrase, adverbial or adjectival clause). In time, children will internalise this questioning.

- Some students will develop sophistication and variety of sentence structure as they mature; others find it more difficult. These students need scaffolding as they learn to recognise why some words, and some structures, are more effective than others.

- Students need to be immersed in quality texts, written and spoken, to support their development in the control of language.

Exploring a sentence

The short story *Norton's Hut*, by John Marsden and Peter Gouldthorpe (1998), has rich language use as well as strong illustrations. One sentence from the story has been a useful model for learning about the structure of sentences and the impact of deliberately chosen words.

> *Outside, mist, cold and cloud flooded over the peak and the wind pushed and pulled and groaned around the hut.*

Teachers, and students, who have been asked to respond to this sentence taken out of context have been quick to agree that it does indeed have impact. They recognise that its purpose is to describe, and that it provides us with a strong image of the scene. If we break it up to analyse it, we can see that it has two main parts:

> *Outside, mist, cold and cloud flooded over the peak*

and

> *the wind pushed and pulled and groaned around the hut.*

The writer chooses to use a group of three nouns in the first part (mist, cold, cloud) which are activated with one verb (flooded) to describe the action of all three nouns. In the second part the author chooses to use three verbs (pushed, pulled, groaned), all describing the action of the one noun (wind).

The technique which helps create the image so strongly is the careful selection of words: specific nouns, powerful verbs and adverbials. We are placed in the setting with the adverb of place (outside), we are able to 'see' the *what* (nouns), the *action* (verbs) and the *where* the action is taking place (prepositional phrases):

Outside	**mist, cold and cloud**	flooded	*over the peak.*
Adverb of place	**subject (3 nouns)**	verb	*adverbial phrase*
			- where?
			prepositional phrase -
			a group of words with
			an adverbial function
and			
conjunction			

the wind	pushed and pulled and groaned *around the hut.*		
subject	verb	verb	verb
(1 noun)			*prepositional phrase -*
			a group of words with an
			adverbial function

adverbial phrase - where?

The sentence is effectively descriptive - the strength of the description comes from the choice of verbs and simple prepositional phrases. This writer did not rely on adjectives to enhance the image he wanted.

Groups of teachers have been led through this unpacking of Marsden's carefully constructed sentence, and are always quick to acknowledge that there is some basic grammatical learning for themselves in the session. It is learning that they can see will guide them to a more secure starting place as they lead the learning in their classrooms.

They have been eager to consolidate their learning by trying out the structure for themselves. I cannot transport them to a mountain hut for this exercise, so to make the learning relevant, I ask teachers to notice what is around them. The guidelines are simple:

- look out of the window and select three nouns, depicting what you observe
  sun, shadows, stillness

- select one verb that will serve to activate the three nouns
  settle

- locate the 'action' with a prepositional phrase
  over the elm

- select a further noun
  sparrows

- choose three verbs that describe what this noun does
  flit, dart, chatter

- position that action with another prepositional phrase
  among the leaves

The results are always pleasing:

Outside, sun, shadows and stillness settle over the elm and the sparrows flit and dart and chatter among the leaves.

Outside, timber, leaves and rubbish lay around the playground and the sun drifted and sank and died below the horizon.

Outside, elm, willow and silver birch reign over the school and the moon rises and shines and splays over the roofs.

Outside, sparrows, starlings and mynahs squabble beside the seats and the seagull spies, glides and steals from under their beaks.

To find sentences worthy of zooming in on, simply look at the books you love. They are packed with examples. You don't need certain books; you only need to develop your eye for finding such sentences in any book – or any text, for that matter.

Jeff Anderson (2007)

Grammar and mechanics are the business of shaping our writing, shaping our meaning, and creating effects that dazzle ... I intend for students and teachers to view grammar and mechanics as a creational facility rather than a correctional one. The teaching of conventions is about what punctuation can do to enhance the writer's message. Wouldn't it be cool if students thought of grammar and mechanics as play? If they had a 'let's see what this does' attitude?

Jeff Anderson (2005)

Editing sentences

In his books *Mechanically Inclined* (2005) and *Everyday Editing* (2007), Jeff Anderson inspires us with his approach to grammar and punctuation. He believes the learning needs to be embedded in all of our explorations of how texts work. Our experiments and play with *Piano Rock* (Bishop 2008) have borne this out. Students have successfully integrated and transferred their learning to their own writing.

Anderson asks us to think about editing as a creational facility rather than a correctional one. He says that we may not be able to mirror exactly how professional writers edit, but we can discover how they learned to shape their writing and how they learned to craft sentences and meaning.

Like him, I know that editing needs to be taught, and that it is a process that starts with the sentence.

> *'Powerful sentences, sentences that teach, sentences that marinate our students in powerful models of what writing can be, not what it shouldn't be.'*

Writing under the influence

I began tinkering with the idea of making editing more invitational, of taking an approach that invites kids in and shows them how other authors did it. My students were writing under the influence - of literature, of powerful, effective, beautiful writing. Editing instruction starts with students observing how powerful texts work. What are the writers doing? What can we learn from their effectiveness - and, more often than not, their correctness? This way of editing is inquiry based, open-ended, and bound by meaning:

What do you notice?
What else?
How does it sound when we read it?
What would change if we removed this or that?
Which do you prefer?
Why?

These questions put students in the driver's seat. The instruction actually comes from the students. They see what effect the sentence has on them as readers.
Anderson (2007)

Summary - *Using Models*

- Appreciating and recognising what is good in writing.

- Indicators of good writing.

- Finding models.

- Links between reading and writing.

- Identifying deeper features.

- Leading students to the point of understanding.

- Classroom conversations.

- Sentences - what we need to know.

- Editing.

Appendix - Using Models

Guided Writing Plan
Memoir: swimming lessons – getting into cold water

Model text: excerpt from 'Piano Rock' by Gavin Bishop

Purpose for the lesson	• We are focusing on ideas for writing – finding out what makes a connection for us. • We are writing to record a moment in our own lives as a description or 'vignette'. • Some of us have been dependent on others for topic ideas and selection and so our writing lacks 'voice'. We need to tap into the wealth of experiences that we all have, find the significances in them and bring our stories to life for our readers.
Learning focus	• We are learning to use literature to make connections with our own lives and to gather possible topics for writing. • We are learning to look closely at the choices authors make in order to involve us in their stories. • We are learning to notice how punctuation is used in a text and the effect it has on the meaning. • We are learning to use punctuation to enhance the meaning in our own texts.

How will I lead the learning?
Reading, thinking and talking

What tasks will I need to design?
- Read the first two paragraphs of 'Swimming Lessons'
  - Discuss the topic of getting into cold water and having swimming lessons in a lake.
  - Connect student and teacher experiences.
  - Teacher tells own story of getting into cold water – detail of how it affects the body: breathing, posture, face, thoughts, speech.

- Students have a copy of the passage and a highlighter and, as aspects of language are discussed, students are directed to mark and highlight.
- Discuss and annotate
  - How has the writer made it sound like a child talking?
  - Which part stands out for you?
  - Do you get a picture of the character/scene?
  - What do we know about the boy?
  - What tells us how he is feeling?
  - What senses does the writer include?
- Discuss the language use - what has the writer done to make his writing effective? Possibilities include:
  - **strong verbs**: *dreaded, rose, snatched*
  - **phrases of 'when'**: *now and then, but not often,*
  - **adverbial clauses**: *when the day was warm enough; As you slid in*
  - **contrast**: *no matter how hot the day was, the water was always cold*
  - **adjectival phrase, information between commas**: *prickly with goosebumps* (telling more about the noun)
  - **personification**: *icy water snatched your breath away; stones would take you*
  - **semi-colon**: *If you tried to get in slowly you couldn't; the stones would take you …*
- Ask students to bring up a memory of a time when they were getting into very cold water.
- Lead a visualisation.
- Share with a partner.
- Share one or two individual student images with the whole class.
- Co-construct a sentence which uses an adjectival phrase - innovate on Gavin Bishop's sentence - *So with wriggly macaroni legs, prickly with goose bumps, I would stagger back onto the beach.*
- Prepare for writing by co-construction of criteria for success (what needs to be included).
- Write.
- Peer respond in groups for effectiveness, checking in with success criteria.
- Lead a guided revision in The Helping Circle.

Success criteria *How will we know we have been successful?* Co-construct with the students	• I have described a time when I entered cold water.
	 • I **will** have included
	   - a phrase telling when
	   - extra information about a noun *between comma*s (an adjectival phrase)
	 • I **may** have used
	   - an adverbial clause
	   - a semi colon to join two clauses with similar ideas

Challenges for writers	• to make decisions about what to include and what to leave out • to be conscious of parts of the sentences as they write • to think about the cohesion of the piece: linking ideas effectively with appropriate sentence structure
Transfer to other writing	Apply the sentence structures and punctuation used to a wide range of texts and purposes.

Swimming Lessons

Now and then, but not often, when the day was warm enough, Mr McLeod took us swimming in the lake. I dreaded swimming lessons and always tried to come up with a sniffle or a sore leg that might excuse me from going.

It didn't matter how hot the day was, the water was always cold. If you tried to get in slowly, you couldn't; the stones would take you before you were ready. As you slid in, the icy water rose quickly to your chest and snatched your breath away. I would try to float a bit, but it was hopeless and all I wanted to do was get out again. So with wriggly macaroni legs, prickly with goose bumps, I would stagger back onto the beach. My soggy woollen togs would be sagging almost to my knees. A driftwood fire and a melting moment from my lunch tin were the only things that could help a little to warm me up.

(from *Piano Rock* by Gavin Bishop 2008)

Guided Writing Plan
Factual description: The Bike

Model text: excerpt from a mountain bike poster

Purpose for the lesson	To write transactional text (curriculum and student need). To write a factual description. What do I want them to learn? • that factual description has a structure • precision in choice of vocabulary
Learning focus	We are learning to • order our writing (simple structure) • look closely and describe exactly what we see • be precise in our choice of vocabulary
Resources	The subject will be a mountain bike that has been brought into the classroom. The model text: *The tyres have a tread of small, pyramid-shaped blocks.* *These give good grip on soft ground and they also let soil* *or mud slip off so it does not get stuck in the tread.*

Leading the learning

Reading, thinking and talking

- Discuss prior learning about (memoir) writing.
- Introduce the new learning and discuss the purpose for doing this.
- Gather children around a mountain bike.
- Lead a discussion about the parts of the bike.
- Observe closely to describe
  - what the part looks like and
  - what the part does.
- Record the bike part names *(nouns)* as discussed.
- Sketch the bike (restate learning to observe, to look closely).

- Invite students to choose a bike part that they would like to describe.
- Ask them to circle it lightly on their drawing.
- Analyse the written model from the class poster, drawing attention to the two part structure – what it *looks like* and what it *does*.
- Outline the writing task: to describe your bike part.
- Form criteria for success – what do I need to include?
- Students write.
- Gather students in helping circle for a guided revision:
  - invite some students to share their writing
  - respond by eliciting or providing precise language
- Help reframe student language where necessary - instead of **you** steer the bike, try the specific noun, ***the rider*** steers the bike.
- Check on individual student needs and goals as you proceed.
- Students revise and complete.

Success criteria *How will I know I have been successful?* Co-construct with the students	I have • a sentence telling what *a part looks like;* • a sentence telling what it *does;* • used the present tense; • extended the sentences to include extra information (where, how, why etc); • used precise words. I *may* have used a hyphenated adjective (compound adjective).
Challenges for writers	Keeping the language tight and subject-specific
Transfer to other writing	The use of precise language in all writing

12 Nurturing our Teaching
Fostering our own literacy

The message that is threaded throughout the preceding pages is that we support our students so that all know they have the potential to be independent writers. Further, it is we who give them the skills to become independent writers. While it is only a small percentage of the population who will earn their living by writing alone, who will become Writers with a capital W, it would be a tragedy if our students left our care without realising that they are able to articulate 'the real stuff of their lives' through words.

> *The first requisite for any writer is to know just what meaning he wants to convey, and it is only by clothing his thoughts in words that he can think at all.*
> (Ernest Gowers 1954)

It seems clear to me that regardless of whether it is the function of writing, or the aesthetics of writing that we are concerned with, it is never going to be OK to allow our students to miss the opportunity of enjoying their authorship. My experience has shown me, and continues to show me, that when teachers are enthusiastic learners, enthusiastic readers and enthusiastic writers in the classroom, the students will want to share in the satisfaction that comes with the enjoyment of words and how they are put together.

Our job as teachers entails nurturing groups of young people through many learning areas. It is unlikely that any of us will be 'expert in everything', yet each of us has our own particular strengths and interests to bring to our classrooms. Your students will be quick to pick up on whether you have a special interest, whether it be techno music, classical music, team sports, organic gardening, or literature.

Each of us can recall the teachers who inspired us, and we remain aware of what their interests and strengths were. What shone through in those teachers was love: their love of calculus, of Shakespeare, of history, of drama ...

Equally, it is your love that will inspire your students: your love of insects, of fishing, of stories, or your love of words and the magic they make when they are mixed, combined and baked together in different recipes.

Putting students in the driver's seat

When I ask teachers participating in workshops what it is they would like most for themselves and their students in relation to writing, the answer is always that they would like their students to be independent writers. Teachers know intuitively that if their writers were independent, their jobs would be much more pleasurable. When these same teachers sit down and work out together what constitutes an independent writer they come up with a list that looks like this:

An independent learner-writer would

- love words, and stories, and talking, and patterns of sound;

- know they have something to say;

- experience writing as an important part of their lives;

- be enthusiastic and gain deep satisfaction from their writing;

- jot in a notebook regularly and use their jottings as springboards for writing;

- be able to talk about their writing knowledgeably;

- practise proofreading and editing as an integral part of their writing;

- seek responses to their writings from their peers and from the teacher;

- understand that the purpose of their writing demands a particular form, or combination of forms, or language features;

- experiment with ideas that have been explored in mini lessons, crafting and recrafting for better effect;

- be constantly aware of possibilities for writing in their world and beyond;

- use author mentors from a range of literature, for inspiration, guidance and modelling;

- write for the love of it.

This is a far cry from the frightening images that pop up for some at the mention of independent writers: images of everyone doing their own thing in a chaotic fashion, with students choosing light-weight or inappropriate topics, or writing 'free choice' in personal diaries – which no one ever sees. This scenario is of no help to our young writers and constitutes the sin of 'busy work', marking time until the bell goes.

Writing is living work

rather than deskwork.

Lucy Calkins (1991)

While teachers do have an innate 'knowing' of the profile of the independent writer, it has not always been so clear to them how they would set up their classrooms and routines to build a community of confident, competent learner-writers who are writing for genuine purposes across the curriculum, all with differing levels of competence.

In the earlier chapters of this book I described some considerations for the classroom set-up which teachers have employed to create the ideal climate to 'grow' independent learner-writers. In the later chapters are some of the acts of teaching and the content that will provide the stimulation and the rigour to inspire independent learner-writers. The final ingredient is the list that teachers compiled with the characteristics of the independent learner-writer. That checklist is not for students alone, it is for teachers, because in the end, we teach who we are. Read the list again and notice where you are on your journey, all the while remembering that the best place to start – and the only place to start – is where you are now. Just as your students learn to work out the next step on their journey for themselves, you will work out the next step for you.

In his foreword to this book, my friend Stan spoke about something wonderful that happened to him when he was a young, bored twelve year old, something that changed the course of his life. Miss Salmon, an elderly middle school teacher, opened his eyes and ears to the world about him, and engendered a love of life, a passion for learning, and an interest in people that has never left him.

Unless you were extremely unlucky at school with your teachers, you too will be able to recall with affection and appreciation your own 'Miss Salmon', the teacher who inspired you in a way that will always be with you.

These teachers generously shared their 'loves' with us, and in doing so they gave us a love for those parts of life which might otherwise have remained a mystery.

And in the end the love you take is equal to the love you make.

Paul McCartney

We nurture our teaching by watching a cicada bug shed its skin and by curling up in a window seat with a novel and our notebooks, letting the sound of the screen door evoke a world of memories. All of us have these moments, but we don't always draw on them when we teach.

Lucy Calkins (1991)

In our hands

You and I can be that teacher for our students. When we embark on the journey of 'joyful literacy' ourselves, taking time to read, to write and to reflect, we increase our knowledge and skill with the code that is written language. Nurturing our own literacy sets us up perfectly to lead our students to authorship.

Summary - *Nurturing our Teaching*

- The role of a teacher.

- The profile of the independent learner-writer.

- You teach who you are.

- The journey in becoming 'joyfully literate'.

References

Abbs, P. & Richardson, J. (1990a). *The forms of narrative*. Cambridge, UK: Cambridge University Press.
Abbs, P. & Richardson, J. (1990b). *The forms of poetry*. Cambridge, UK: Cambridge University Press.
Anderson, J. (2005). *Mechanically inclined*. Portland, ME: Stenhouse.
Anderson, J. (2007). *Everyday editing*. Portland, ME: Stenhouse.
Atwell, N. (2002). *Lessons that change writers*. Portsmouth, NH: Heinemann.
Boyle, S. (1986). Personal communication. Hamilton, NZ.
Britton, J., Burgess, T., Martin, N., McLeod, A. & Rosen, H. (1975). *The development of writing abilities*. London: Macmillan Education.
Brownlee, P. (2010). Step outside the classroom... Personal communication. Thames, NZ.
Buckner, A. (2005). *Notebook know-how*. Portland, ME: Stenhouse .
Calkins, L. (1991). *Living between the lines*. Portsmouth, NH: Heinemann.
Calkins, L. (1994). *The art of teaching writing*. Portsmouth, NH: Heinemann.
Connolly, C. (2008 [1938]). *Enemies of promise* (Revised edition). Chicago, IL: University of Chicago Press.
Dyson, A.H. & Freedman, S.W. (2003). *The handbook of research on teaching the English language arts* (2nd edition). Philadelphia, PA: Taylor & Francis.
Frost, R. (c. 1960). Interview. In *The Saturday Evening Post* (USA).
Goodwyn, J. & Goodwyn, A. (1992). *Descriptions*. Cambridge, UK: Cambridge University Press.
Gowers, E. (1954). *The complete plain words*. London: HMSO.
Graves, D. (1982). *Writing: Teachers and children at work*. Exeter, NH: Heinemann.
Harbage, M. (source unknown).
Harwayne, S. (1992). *Lasting Impressions*. Portsmouth, NH: Heinemann.
Johnston, P. (2004). *Choice words*. Portland, ME: Stenhouse.
Kirby, D. & Liner, T. with Vinz, R. (1988). *Inside out: Developmental strategies for teaching writing*. Portsmouth, NH: Heinemann.
Little, J. (1987). *Little by little*. Toronto, Canada: Penguin.
Macrorie, K. (1984). *Writing to be read*. Portsmouth, NH: Heinemann.
Ministry of Education. (2003). *New Zealand curriculum exemplars*. Wellington, NZ: Learning Media, with The Learning Trust of NZ.
Ministry of Education. (2003a). *Effective literacy practice years 1-4*. Wellington, NZ: Learning Media.
Murray, D. (1982). *Learning by teaching*. Portsmouth, NH: Heinemann.
Murray, D. (1984). *Write to learn*. New York: Holt, Reinhart & Winston.
Pearce, J.C. (1977). *Magical child*. New York: Bantam.
Postman, N. & Weingartner, C. (1969). *Teaching as a subversive activity*. Harmondsworth, UK: Penguin.
Reader's Digest. (1985). *Complete book of New Zealand birds*. Sydney, Australia: Reed Methuen.
Richardson, E. (1964). *In the early world*. New York: Pantheon Books.
Vygotsky, L.S. (1978). *Mind in society*. Cambridge, MA: Harvard University Press.
Wilbur, R. (1988 [1921]). *New and collected poems*. New York: Harcourt Brace.

Works Cited

Amis, M. (2000). *Experience*. London: Jonathan Cape.
Angelou, M. (1984). *I know why the caged bird sings*. London: Virago.
Applegate, M. (c. 1950). *Be Specific* (source unknown, USA).

Baars, M. (2000). From the back corner. In *Waikato Times* (issue unknown).

Baxter, J. (2013). *Selected poems*. Auckland, NZ: Auckland University Press.

Bennett, J. (2005). *A land of two halves*. Auckland, NZ: Harper Collins.

Bernen, R. (1978). *Tales from the blue stacks*. New York: Scribner.

Betjeman, J. (1958). *John Betjeman's collected poems*. Boston, MA: John Murray.

Bishop, G. (2008). *Piano Rock: A 1950's childhood*. Auckland, NZ: Random House.

Bradley, J. (1992). *Jewels in the grass*. Thames, NZ: Get Ahead Publishing.

Brooke, R. (1914). *The collected poems of Rupert Brooke*. London: Sidgwick & Jackson.

Browne, A. (1992). *ZOO*. London: Random House.

Bryan, L. (c. 1998). Travel footnotes. *NZ Listener*.

Clarkson, W. (1992). *Observations at the outset: The role of drawing in the process of inquiry*. New Plymouth, NZ: Curriculum Concepts.

Copeman, C. & Barrett, G. (1975). *Feelings into words: A creative English course*. London: Ward Lock Educational.

Creech, S. (2001). *Love that dog*. London: Bloomsbury.

Crowley, E. (1992). *The petunia-coloured coat*. London: Penguin.

Dahl, R. (1975). *Danny champion of the world*. London: Puffin.

Dahl, R. (1983). *The witches*. London: Jonathan Cape.

Daish, L. (c. 1996) Food. In *The Listener* (NZ).

Dickens, C. (2008 [1852]). *Bleak house*. Oxford: Oxford University Press.

Frost, R. (c. 1960). Interview. In *The Saturday Evening Post* (USA).

Gabolinscy, J. (1991 [1981]). The Blue Humber 80. In Gwen Gawith (ed.), *Falling off the edge of the world*. Auckland, NZ: Penguin.

Gee, M. (1987). *The fire raiser*. Auckland, NZ: Penguin.

Gibbons, S. (2006 [1932]). *Cold comfort farm*. London: Penguin.

Grace, P. (1980). *The dream sleepers and other stories*. Auckland, NZ: Longman Paul.

Grace, P. (1986). *Potiki*. Auckland, NZ: Penguin.

Grace, P. (1991). A special stone. In Gwen Gawith (ed.), *Falling off the edge of the world*. Auckland, NZ: Penguin.

Jordan, S. (1993). *Winter of fire*. Auckland, NZ: Scholastic.

Kendon, F. (1976). *Feelings into words: A creative English course*. London: Ward Lock Educational.

McCourt, F. (1996). *Angela's ashes*. London: Flamingo.

Mahy, M. (1998). *A summery Saturday morning*. Auckland, NZ: Scholastic.

Mansfield, K. (1974). *The complete stories of Katherine Mansfield*. Auckland, NZ: Golden Press.

Marsden, J. & Gouldthorpe, P. (1998). *Norton's hut*. Port Melbourne: Lothian.

May, S. (1990). *Pakeha girl*. Personal communication. Thames, NZ.

Maybury, B. (1970). *Wordscapes*. Oxford: Oxford University Press.

Milne, A. (1928). *The house at Pooh Corner*. London: Methuen.

Muir, S. (2003). *Autumn mist*. Personal communication. Thames, NZ.

Naughton, W. (1988). *The goalkeeper's revenge*. Harmondsworth, UK: Puffin.

Orwell, G. (2001 [1939]). *Coming up for air*. London: Penguin Modern Classics.

Owen, W. (1914). From my diary, July 1914. In (1977) *The collected poems of Wilfred Owen*. Edited by Cecil Day Lewis. London: Chatto & Windus.

Partridge, R. (1981). *Wordspinners*. Oxford: Oxford University Press.

Piercy, M. (1978). Sentimental poem. In *Bits 8* (periodical, USA).

Potter B. (1995 [1908]) *The tale of Jemima Puddle-Duck*. London: Penguin.

Ranger, L. (1995). *Laura's poems*. Auckland, NZ: Godwit (with the author's permission).

Ridlon, M. (1969). *That was summer*. Chicago, IL: Follett.

Rose, J. & Young, P. (1975). *Passwords*. Edinburgh: Oliver & Boyd.

Ross, A. (1976 [1967]). *Feelings into words: A creative English course*. London: Ward Lock Educational.

Russell, W. (2000). *The wrong boy*. London: Black Swan.

Scannell, V. (1996). *The new Oxford book of children's verse*. Oxford: Oxford University Press.

Scott Fitzgerald, F. (1979 [1925]). *The great Gatsby*. Harmondsworth, UK: Penguin.

Strachan, I. (1983). *Moses Beech*. Harmondsworth, UK: Puffin.

Thiele, C. & Haldane, R. (1979). *Magpie Island*. Adelaide, Australia: Rigby.

Thomas, D. (2000 [1944]). *Dylan Thomas - collected stories*. Edited by Walford Davies. London: Phoenix.

Tolkien, J. (1975). *The hobbit*. London: Unwin.

Tombleson, R. (1999). *Wockagilla, journal of young people's writing*. Wellington, NZ: Learning Media (with the author's permission).

Wagner, J. (1980). *John Brown, Rose and the midnight cat*. Ringwood, Victoria, Australia: Puffin.

Wane, J. (1995). The lakes of Rakaihautu. In *Pacific Way* (issue unknown).

Waterhouse, K. (1964). *There is a happy land*. London: Penguin.

Whipple, D. (1950). *Feelings into words*. London: Ward Lock Educational.

Williams, W. (1923). *Spring and all*. New York: Contact Publishing Company.

Winterson, J. (1993). *Written on the body*. London: Vintage.

Woolf, V. (1992). *Virginia Woolf, paper darts*. London: Collins & Brown.

Woolf, V. (2004 [1927]). *To the lighthouse*. London: Vintage.

Zander, B. (c. 2000). Cargo pants. In *NZ Listener* (issue unknown).

Index

Taylor & Francis eBooks

Helping you to choose the right eBooks for your Library

Add Routledge titles to your library's digital collection today. Taylor and Francis ebooks contains over 50,000 titles in the Humanities, Social Sciences, Behavioural Sciences, Built Environment and Law.

Choose from a range of subject packages or create your own!

Benefits for you

» Free MARC records
» COUNTER-compliant usage statistics
» Flexible purchase and pricing options
» All titles DRM-free.

Benefits for your user

» Off-site, anytime access via Athens or referring URL
» Print or copy pages or chapters
» Full content search
» Bookmark, highlight and annotate text
» Access to thousands of pages of quality research at the click of a button.

REQUEST YOUR
FREE
INSTITUTIONAL
TRIAL TODAY

Free Trials Available
We offer free trials to qualifying academic, corporate and government customers.

eCollections – Choose from over 30 subject eCollections, including:

Archaeology	Language Learning
Architecture	Law
Asian Studies	Literature
Business & Management	Media & Communication
Classical Studies	Middle East Studies
Construction	Music
Creative & Media Arts	Philosophy
Criminology & Criminal Justice	Planning
Economics	Politics
Education	Psychology & Mental Health
Energy	Religion
Engineering	Security
English Language & Linguistics	Social Work
Environment & Sustainability	Sociology
Geography	Sport
Health Studies	Theatre & Performance
History	Tourism, Hospitality & Events

For more information, pricing enquiries or to order a free trial, please contact your local sales team:
www.tandfebooks.com/page/sales

Routledge
Taylor & Francis Group

The home of
Routledge books

www.tandfebooks.com